Soul of the
Dark Knight

Soul of the Dark Knight

Batman as Mythic Figure in Comics and Film

ALEX M. WAINER

McFarland & Company, Inc., Publishers

Jefferson, North Carolina

LIBRARY OF CONGRESS CATALOGUING-IN-PUBLICATION DATA

Wainer, Alex, 1954–
    Soul of the Dark Knight : Batman as Mythic Figure in Comics and
Film / Alex Wainer.
        p.   cm.
    Includes bibliographical references and index.

    ISBN 978-0-7864-7128-7 (softcover : acid free paper) ∞
    ISBN 978-1-4766-1505-9 (ebook)

    1. Batman (Fictitious character) 2. Comic books, strips, etc.—
Language.   3. Comic books, strips, etc.—History and criticism.
4. Film adaptations—History and criticism.   5. Literature—Adaptations—History and criticism.   I. Title.
    PN6728.B36W356 2014
    741.5'973—dc23   2014015156

BRITISH LIBRARY CATALOGUING DATA ARE AVAILABLE

On the cover: moon (Thinkstock); city skyline (Paulo Barcellos, Jr.)

Printed in the United States of America

McFarland & Company, Inc., Publishers
    Box 611, Jefferson, North Carolina 28640
        www.mcfarlandpub.com

Dedicated to Judith,
whose X-Men expertise
God used to draw us together

Table of Contents

Acknowledgments

This work allowed me to channel the thoughts, feelings, and ideas on the subject of myth, comics and popular narratives that had been simmering in my mind since childhood. Yet it took the help of others to see these concepts developed into the form presented here. My dissertation committee chair, Dennis Bounds, came along just in time to bring his interest in comics (and his comics collection) to bear on my preliminary investigations, and his professionalism helped keep the project properly focused and executed. Committee member Michael Graves' suggestions were invaluable for sharpening my scholarship. Committee member Robert Schihl had, during a class several years earlier, explained that the appeal of comics lay in their use of closure. That little seed sprouted as my research continued. Kathy Merlock Jackson gave me my first real teaching opportunity at Virginia Wesleyan College. My gratitude extends to the Regent University College of Communication and the Arts for being a place where one is encouraged to pursue the things stirring in one's mind and heart. Similarly, this manuscript preparation was made possible by Palm Beach Atlantic University's gracious granting of release time (and by my colleagues in the School of Communication & Media) while I was teaching classes over the past year and half.

Thomas Parham's shared interest in comics and his generosity with his collection made it possible for me to obtain a much better first-hand sense of the comics, particularly those featuring Batman. A rare friend indeed, he also went out of his way to interview four comics professionals at the 1995 San Diego Comicon: Dennis O'Neil, Mark Waid, Paul Deni, and Bruce Timm. The information gleaned from these insightful interviews found its way into this text.

Pamela Robles was crucially influential in bringing this whole study to a healthy, successful fruition. From our first conversation when I barely glimpsed where I wanted to take my research, Pam, though unfamiliar with the comics medium, selflessly served as a parabolic reflector of my thinking, bouncing my thoughts back more focused than before, making me see the implications of the ideas I was working through. She also freely did yeoman's work proofreading my chapters, catching a myriad of grammatical and stylistic mistakes. *Muchísimas gracias, amiga.*

Thanks are also due to my friend, artist Thom Marrion, who, while we were co-workers, shared his comics and gave me my first fateful look at Scott McCloud's *Understanding Comics.* This introduction to comics theory sparked my belief in the validity of comics as an art form, making the conception of this study possible. Thanks to Randy Richards for his generous advice on preparing my manuscript. Also, thanks to Joshua Richards for his many suggestions on the crucial Introduction, and to Salvatore Ciano for helping me develop ideas in my analysis of the Christopher Nolan films. My late mother, Rachael Wainer, through her amazing generosity, made possible my educational experience from its inception to academic teaching and research.

Most importantly, my wife, Judith, worked tirelessly during the years of my research and writing, believing in me, encouraging me and just loving me as I stumbled through this work. It is not possible to imagine a better life partner.

Finally, I am grateful to God for seeing us through the valleys and the peaks of this time. I am thankful, too, for having been given a topic that is always exciting and fulfilling in so many ways.

Preface

This book on comics and Batman started with a question I was asking in the 1990s as a doctoral student in communication at Regent University. My studies stressed cinema but I was actually more taken with explaining the appeal of Batman as an enduring comic book superhero and periodic popular culture phenomenon. In 1993 I had read a new book on the nature of the comics medium, Scott McCloud's *Understanding Comics*, and felt it explained far more about this medium than many film theories elucidating cinema. Applying McCloud's theories to Batman was probably the analytical beginning of what would become a thesis that opened up into my doctoral dissertation, "Mythic Expression in Comic Book Technique: Mythopoeic Aspects of Batman." I found that I needed to define what I meant by "mythic," and in what way Batman could be called mythic. That opened up a world of discovery as I found authors who reflected my thinking and brought some degree of coherency to my argument. It also elevated the comics medium, particularly the superhero genre, as I began to see how well the character of Batman fit into literary analysis, particularly in the writings of Northrop Frye and C. S. Lewis. By the time I completed and defended the dissertation in 1996, I had reached the point at which I could explain why Batman's natural home was comics and how the medium was best able to express his mythic nature, and why efforts at adaptation so often fell short or felt incomplete. As a film scholar, I felt I could explain why the Batman films were flawed to varying degrees, but as a Batman fan who had seen mature treatments of the character in such graphic novels as Frank Miller's *The Dark Knight Returns* and *Batman: Year One,* I still hoped someone could succeed in adapting Batman into a great film.

When Christopher Nolan's *Batman Begins* premiered in 2005, I was struck by how its premise aligned with the thesis of my dissertation. By fore-grounding Bruce Wayne's conscious strategy of constructing a mythic persona to scare criminals and offer hope to Gotham City, Nolan and his collaborators had arrived at the same conclusion as I had as to what constituted Batman's core appeal, and had done so in cinematic terms. In updating and considerably expanding my original scope, this project has become not just an analysis of Batman's mythic nature as realized by the comics medium but also a study in successful adaptation from comics to film. The chapters that follow will distinguish my intentions from other valid approaches to understanding Batman in various media. His potential for mythic narrative continually reveals new levels of meaning and entertainment.

Introduction

Seeing Through a Knight Darkly

———————

Scene 1: 1939. Vincent Sullivan, an editor at National Periodical Publications, the publisher of *Action* comics, asked one of his young artists, Bob Kane, then 22, to come up with another costumed character to cash in on the popularity of Superman. In his autobiography, Kane recounts how he set to work immediately, tracing various costume designs over a generic superhero figure. Then he remembered having once seen a Leonardo da Vinci drawing of a flying machine with bat-like wings. Only 13 years old at the time, Kane had sketched figures with batwings, including one that prefigured Batman. He reworked these juvenile sketches, and soon settled on a name for his new hero: "The Bat-man."

Kane had long been a fan of silent movie swashbuckler Douglas Fairbanks, Sr., whose acrobatic heroics had been featured in his 1920 film *The Mark of Zorro*. As a teenager Kane had belonged to a neighborhood gang called the Zorros, who wore black masks and engaged in Fairbanksian athleticism. From the Zorro character, Kane borrowed the dual-identity device: unmasked, Zorro was, in fact, his alter ego, the foppish Don Diego.

An old high school friend of Kane's, Bill Finger, looked at Kane's preliminary sketches of his "bat-man." In his autobiography, Kane described Finger's suggestions for changes:

> At the time, I only had a small domino mask, like the one Robin later wore, on Batman's face. Bill said, "Why not make him look more like a bat and put a hood on him, and take the eyeballs out and just put slits for eyes to make him look more mysterious?" [Kane 41].

Finger's inspiration ran parallel to Kane's: "My idea was to have Batman be a combination of Douglas Fairbanks, Sherlock Holmes, The Shadow and Doc Savage as well," he said (quoted in Steranko 44).

3

Scene 2: 2008. July 18, the opening weekend of *The Dark Knight* drew long lines of fans dressed as the Joker and Batman. Long anticipated, the film had received a singular jolt of publicity months before when Heath Ledger, who had essayed the role of the Joker, died of a drug overdose. A viral marketing campaign keying off of the villain's signature line, "Why so serious?" fueled excitement for director Christopher Nolan's sequel to *Batman Begins*. The opening domestic weekend box-office take of $158,411,483 was the first of the film's record-breaking milestones; it would eventually gross more than a billion dollars. Critics were, for the most part, enthusiastic about the film. The *New York Times* critic Manohla Dargis's noted:

> This is a darker Batman, less obviously human, more strangely other. When he perches over Gotham on the edge of a skyscraper roof, he looks more like a gargoyle than a savior. There's a touch of demon in his stealthy menace. During a crucial scene, one of the film's saner characters asserts that this isn't a time for heroes, the implication being that the moment belongs to villains and madmen. Which is why, when Batman takes flight in this film, his wings stretching across the sky like webbed hands, it's as if he were trying to possess the world as much as save it ["Showdown"].

Why the Dark Knight Keeps Rising

Comic book scholar Richard Reynolds, in his book *Super Heroes: A Modern Mythology*, writes that contemporary superheroes constitute a modern pantheon of mythical beings. Writer Elizabeth Danna concurs: "The influence of Greco-Roman mythology and Jewish tradition found in the Old Testament has left its insignia on the contemporary comic book world as well as pop culture" (67). And indeed much of the appeal of many superheroes is derived from the manner in which they exhibit abilities, traits, and motivations evocative of the gods and heroes of ancient times. Critical to this is the comics medium with its unique properties that enable levels of mythic evocation unattainable in other media.

Though Superman was invulnerable to everything but kryptonite, his narrative viability in recent decades has faded while Batman's has only grown. Though a character like Ian Fleming's superspy James Bond found his true calling not in print but on screen, Batman's source of strength has always been the manner in which the comics form allowed him to become a powerful presence in the reader's imagination. This presence takes on mythic qualities. Therefore, successful adaptations must, to some degree, locate the equivalent of those qualities in whatever medium attempts to adapt the character.

Chapter 1 examines various meanings of "myth," and "mythic" in relation to the superhero. Chapter 2 is an in-depth historical profile of Batman as he has changed with the times without totally surrendering the unique mythic qualities that are explored in Chapter 3. Chapter 4 examines how Batman's mythic essence is expressed uniquely in the comics medium. Chapter 5, conversely, discusses the challenges inherent to capturing these mythic elements in live-action film. Chapter 6 further explores such challenges to adapt Batman in other media. Chapter 7 focuses on the Christopher Nolan–directed trilogy. And finally, Chapter 8 considers how the mythic content in other comics might be profitably examined.

To demonstrate Batman's durability, herewith is a brief overview of his history. Following Superman's success, the publisher, National Periodical Publications (later known as DC Comics), hoped to build on the popularity of the colorfully costumed character and sought the creation of a similar superhero. The assignment was given to a young artist, Bob Kane, who virtually created Batman during one weekend. Batman debuted a year after Superman, in 1939, and also met with success. Batman was depicted as a lone avenger in the first year of his existence, but soon his publisher found that he needed someone to talk to as he pursued criminals and solved mysteries. Enter Robin, the Boy Wonder, which began the tradition of superhero sidekicks. With Robin's arrival, Batman's character softened into that of a father figure. The Golden Age of Comics, as it has come to be called, peaked during World War II, when its heroes were enlisted in the war against Axis powers. During the forties, Columbia Pictures produced two serials featuring the Dynamic Duo, *Batman* (1943) and *Batman and Robin* (1949).

The postwar years saw the decline of comic book titles as various factors, including censorship concerns and the coming of television, resulted in a decline in readership. The ranks of superheroes markedly thinned, although both Superman and Batman survived in the 1950s by catering to the science fiction craze. Any traces of Batman's original dark mystique all but disappeared as he and Robin battled space aliens and traveled through time and other dimensions. Other DC superhero characters staged a comeback in the late 1950s and early 1960s "Silver Age." Further innovation was led by Marvel Comics' push toward more realistic characterizations, a development that affected the entire industry. Since the 1960s, comics' fortunes waxed and waned through periods of creative surges and slumps. At crucial points along the way, DC sought to keep Batman relevant to readers. In the 1960s the company moved Batman to a realistic "new look" art style that marked a departure from Kane's stiff and more cartoony figures. This tactic was turned into a genuine popular mania in 1966 when the characters were brought to television in the campy *Batman* series. Bob Kane once said, "Maybe every ten years Batman has to go through an evolution to keep up with the times" (quoted in Daniels and Kidd, p. 17). By the end of the 1960s, however, DC editors again perceived a need to revise Batman's image. A return to his original grim vigilante roots began, sparked by artist Neal Adam's strikingly evocative renderings, writer Dennis O'Neil's renewed focus on "realistic" crime stories, and a new stress on Batman's obsessive quest for justice. In the 1980s, direct marketing made a profound impact as publishers began shipping not only to drug stores and supermarkets but to comic shops aimed at discriminating fans.

Though in the years that followed Batman comics were intermittent in their quality of execution, Batman has stayed firmly fixed in his "dark" persona, realized to its fullest extent in Frank Miller's 1985 graphic novel, *The Dark Knight Returns. The Dark Knight*'s bold narrative innovations once more revived interest in the character, contributing to the momentum that led to the highly successful Warner Bros. film, *Batman,* in 1989. Writing was now aimed less at the preadolescent demographic and more at adult males who had grown up with comics but who had developed a taste for more mature treatments of their heroes. Today the comic book medium is no longer seen only as entertainment for a relatively small reading audience but as a source for adaptations into other media. Since the late 1980s, Batman has been one of Time Warner's most lucrative properties. The comic book industry is thriving as well, with combined sales amounting to just over $400 million, much of that revenue generated by superhero titles. And of all the characters from the Golden Age of Comics, none has survived and flourished in print and on the big screen as Batman. While retaining his core identity, he has demonstrated the ability to change with the times for more than half a century.

The success of the film franchise led to the production of *Batman: The Animated Series*, which aired weekday afternoons on the Fox network beginning in 1992. Since then, there has usually been an animated Batman series either on the air or in the works. *Batman Beyond*, which ran from 1999 to 2001, had an elderly Bruce Wayne mentoring a teenage replacement wearing a futuristic Batsuit to fight high-tech criminals. *The Batman,* focusing on Bruce Wayne's early days as the superhero, ran from 2004 to 2008, followed by *Batman: The Brave and the Bold* from 2008 to 2011, and *Beware the Batman,* which debuted in 2013.

Since 1939, the Batman story has been elaborated in many ways, as its creators and corporate owners have sought to develop the full narrative, artistic, and commercial potential of the character. There are a number of reasons for this longevity. For example, Mary K. Leigh applies Aristotle's Nicomachean Ethics to the Batman of the film, *The Dark Knight,* arguing that, while he is on the road to a virtuous character, he still struggles to grasp the right moral choice. C. K. Robertson applies the theories of another philosopher, Nietzsche, to Batman, arguing that, as a self-made *Übermensch,* he transcends human morality. All great figures of myth and popular culture are distinguished by their capacity for diverse plausible interpretations. It is this writer's contention that the mythic appeal, as set forth here, is one of the chief reasons for Batman's endurance.

Comics and Myth

Besides offering escapism through their fantastic adventure stories, comics' formulaic plots function mythically, as do other examples of popular narratives. Harold Schechter refers to a 1953 article by British psychotherapist Alan McGlashan which asserted that "certain comic-strip characters were modern-day incarnations of primordial figures" (Schechter 264). Commenting on the compelling power of these characters, McGlashan believed them to be "the echo of something unimaginably archaic: the adventure cycle of the early gods" (quoted in Schechter 265). Though humankind may consciously disavow religion, McGlashan argues, our inherently religious nature has continuing ties to mythic forms which reappear in the unlikely setting of the comic strip:

> And "there all smothered up in shade" they sit, radiating that strange compelling power which is Man's unconscious tribute to the Unknowable. In the comic strip may lie concealed the indestructible germ of natural religion [quoted in Schechter 265].

In an article, "Me Tarzan. You, Odysseus: Classical Myth in Popular Culture," Jeff Lehr describes research on how the heroic patterns in many myths find new expression in the heroes of modern popular culture. Although there is little agreement on what constitutes the mythological, or the mythic, or on how scholarship should determine what are mythic artifacts, even so, there is a sizable body of literature that refers to comic superheroes as mythic. In "Survivals and Camouflages of Myth," for example, Mircea Eliade discusses the persistence of myth in this, the supposedly demythologized, modern era. He points to the mythic nature of heroes in comic strips and, in particular, to how Superman simply updates older heroic themes.

"Realistic" Superheroes

To clarify what is meant in this study by "mythic content" in comics, perhaps a brief discussion of what is *not* meant specifically in the superhero genre would be helpful. Ties to earlier myths tend to characterize DC comics super-heroes in particular. When DC Comics launched the superhero genre in the late 1930s, it established a paradigm of the superhero whose stories had roots in classical mythology: Superman was an industrial-age Hercules; Batman, a type of Dionysus, and so on. Other DC characters hinted at the mythic. Elements of Flash's costume, for instance, were derived from depictions of the Greek god Hermes. The helmet worn by the Golden Age version of the Flash and the winged boots worn by his successor in the Silver Age, both recalled the god Mercury, known for his speed. Green Lantern's ring was reminiscent of the powerful gifts bestowed on heroes by the gods. When Marvel comics began innovations that moved its superhero characters' personalities closer to psychological realism, the nature of many of its characters reflected that change. For example, one of Marvel's best-known characters, Spiderman, was known as much for the personal problems of his alter ego, Peter Parker, as for his superpowers. There is very little mythic resonance in this character, whose arachnidan powers give him a spider's proportionate strength, allowing him to climb walls. Similarly Iron Man, who wears a high-tech suit of armor, owes more to science fiction than to any clearly mythical precedent. Marvel's most popular titles, those connected with the mutant X-Men characters, have been typically characterized more by its theme of social discrimination than by mythic associations. This is not to say that no mythic evocation occurs in these stories. According to Northrop Frye, in *Anatomy of Criticism,* any time heroism is a central component of a story, one is in the realm of romance, approaching the mythic (*Anatomy* 186–187). The difference between Marvel's and DC's approach is one of emphasis. Historically, Marvel chose to emphasize the psychological complexity of its characters and found that many readers related to the realism of its problem-ridden superheroes. Since the 1960s, the success of Marvel's psychological characterizations has led other comics publishers, including DC, to attempt similar realizations, with varying success.

The Mythic Nature of Batman

Although the particular attraction Batman holds may be understood and explained from diverse critical approaches, this book maintains that Batman's essential attraction is based on the appeal of the mythopoeic, that he is something more than a flamboyantly costumed vigilante engaged in thrilling adventures and hairbreadth escapes. This quality involves the perception of his being not solely human but, rather, a man who transforms himself into a liminal creature. Neither human nor animal, in the pursuit of wrongdoers within the fictional world of the comics, Batman exhibits dual qualities: a keen human ratiocination and a relentless predatory instinctiveness. The appearance of the "bat/man" is calculated to inspire fear and dread in criminals. This "mythical effect," so to speak, arises out of Batman's incarnation as an avenging spirit of justice, which has tremendous appeal to an audience disturbed by the fear of crime and chaos. Mythically, Batman functions as a figure onto which such fears are displaced and who, by taking on aspects of darkness himself, is able to attack the evil that inspires such fears. Writing on the ancient uses of masks, Mircea Eliade has noted, such a being created through the use of a fearsome mask operates in patterns similar to some cultures' ritualistic practices (Eliade, "Masks" 64–71). In Chapter 3, the ancient use of masks to evoke fear in one's enemies, or to invoke the qualities of the animal represented by the mask, is discussed in greater detail.

The Mythic Batman and Comic Book Style

If the comic book style is what best enables the mythic depiction of Batman, then the question arises: what is it about this humble medium that enables it to communicate the mythopoeic? This question is central to this book, which explores mythic evocation through the medium of the comic book, comparing and contrasting comics' success in this realm with attempts by other media to do the same.

Although this study compares and contrasts the comic book version of Batman with its translation into film serials, feature films, animated and live-action television, this is not primarily a study of the adaptations per se. Although published scholarship in this area may be referred to at times for relevant insights, the purpose of this examination is to substantiate arguments about the distinctive qualities of sequential art and not to discuss what strategies were used in the adaptation process except insofar as it relates to adapting mythic content from comics to film. Discussions of genre and formula, therefore, though helpful in explaining what happened in the adaptation process, will be subordinate to the aesthetic concerns of the study.

Definitions

At various times the terms "comic book" or "comics" will be used interchangeably. These terms refer, of course, to the well-known medium composed of pictures and printed text on inexpensive paper with four-color art. "Comic book style" or "art" refers to the narrative and aesthetic codes or overall grammar used to present the comic book stories. In many minds, the terms "comics" or "comic book" connote cheap and disposable juvenile literature. Comics writer and artist Will Eisner's term "sequential art," will therefore be used alternately with the term "comics" because it avoids the narrow associations attached to comic books and recognizes the broad and age-old variations on the basic presentational style. The term "comics," as used here, will follow the application as defined by comic book writer, artist and theorist Scott McCloud. It will be a collective noun, "plural in form, used with a singular verb," so that it may be used like other terms for a medium or art form: "film is a medium," and "comics is a medium," and so forth (McCloud 9).

There are, as mentioned above, many views on what is "mythic" and it may be the difference between calling something "mythic" and calling it "a myth." From the outset, this study will distinguish between myth and mythic. In his negative analysis of broad approaches to mythic criticism, communication scholar Robert C. Rowland attacks them for not adhering to the functional/formal criteria he believes to be characteristic of myth and mythologies (101). By doing so, he fails to perceive that critics using a broader approach do not necessarily equate the mythic with myths, i.e., one can distinguish between what in a narrative is myth-like and what is a formal or "classic" myth. Calling Batman a mythic figure is not saying that the Batman story is a myth, like Greek myths, but that it has qualities that are like them.

But what is meant by calling Batman mythic? In what way is he myth-like? Chapter 3 contains a discussion on how the character of Batman, as well as the actions and setting of his stories, partake of qualities, incidents, and representations that suggest patterns drawn from earlier mythological situations. For instance, the dualistic character of Bruce Wayne/Batman can be said to resemble the Greek god Dionysus's two-sided nature, both jubilant and savage. Just as Dionysus descended into the underworld to rescue his mother, so Bruce Wayne nightly descends from his manor home down into the Batcave and, transforming into the Batman, continues his descent into Gotham City's "underworld," where he battles the forces of chaos to save crime's victims— surrogates for his murdered mother and father.

Batman stories are also myth-like because of their literary genre. Northrop Frye's theory of myths would place comic book adventures, in general, under the "mythos of summer: romance" (*Anatomy* 186). At one end of the narrative spectrum in Frye's scheme are "actions near or at the conceivable limits of desire," featuring exalted, ideal figures, or myth. On the other end of the spectrum is "naturalism" (136). In between the two lies the broad realm of "romance," where there is the "tendency ... to displace myth in a human direction and yet, in contrast to 'realism,' to conventionalize content in an idealized direction" (137). Thus, in the romance, mythic ingredients such as thrilling heroics, figures of superior ability, the quest, and the battle between good and evil, find representation in circumstances that appear realistic, to varying degrees, but admit the presence and actions of such figures. Frye goes on to assert that "the essential element of plot in romance is adventure" (186). His description continues:

> At its most naïve [the romance] is an endless form in which a central character who never develops or ages goes through one adventure after another until the author himself collapses. We see this form in comic strips, where the central characters persist for years in a state of refrigerated deathlessness [186].

Batman certainly falls into the broad category of romance, and I place him in the upper reaches of the romance, and argue this area can be termed mythic, being the nearest to myth itself.

This study stands in contradistinction to anthropological approaches such as those of Levi-Strauss, Propp, and others, who attempt to codify mythological patterns by a scientific methodology. This study, rather, associates itself with the large body of historical, literary, and rhetorical studies on myth and the mythic. Like these, this book take a humanistic approach that attempts to understand what the mythic aspects of a given story are and how they are expressed in a certain medium.

Methodology

Using Batman as an exemplar, the main thrust of this book is to develop an understanding of how the comic book is successful at evoking the mythic, by comparing and contrasting its technique with depictions of Batman in other media. In devising a method for comparing the comic book text and other media's versions of Batman, theories from both comics theorist Scott McCloud and literary critic Northrop Frye will be employed. In his book *Understanding Comics,* McCloud discusses how artistic representation falls along a continuum with photographic realism at one end and moves toward increasingly more abstract depiction at the other end until it reaches pure symbolic representation, i.e., the word. In terms of artistic depiction, he maintains that increasing the simplicity and abstraction of a representation draws the reader in by requiring greater use of the imagination in order to provide closure and achieve meaning. Ultimately, it is because of the increased participation of the reader's imagination in comics art that the mythic aspects of a story can be so well realized. McCloud's scale of abstraction can be correlated with Frye's aforementioned narrative continuum in which myth is at one end, naturalism at the other, and romance in between. The following, somewhat oversimplified formulae, demonstrates how McCloud's and Frye's schemes may be correlated:

McCloud:

PHOTOGRAPHIC REALISM>——>SEQUENTIAL ART——>THE WORD
                    Toward greater simplicity and abstraction——>

Frye:

NATURALISM>——>Broad Area of ROMANCE——>Realm of Pure MYTH
            Toward more idealized characters, settings, and narratives

A schema adapted from McCloud's and Frye's scales is developed throughout the book, with the aid of other works discussing the use of words and images in various media. From this I develop a model for approximating where respective media can be located relative to their capacity to express the mythic (see Appendix). Thus, the results of the study are two-fold: it establishes how comic book art expresses the mythic, using the Batman story as the case study, and it establishes criteria for comparing attempts at mythic expression among various media.

Comics into Film

As both Will Eisner and Scott McCloud have shown, there is nothing new about sequential art. Comic strips and comic books are the popular modern incarnations of an age-old medium. Of the two, it is the comic book that has generally been consigned to the margins of mainstream scholarship. This study is not necessarily intended to valorize the comic book, but it does intend to recognize the way in which the mythopoeic impulse has been expressed through a medium that continues to capture the imagination of a faithful, multi-generational audience. Comics' influence belies its status.

Comics has long been the interest of the purveyors of entertainment in film and television and from the late–1970s' beginning of the Superman films up to the present day has seen increasing focus on adapting comic book characters into film, with varying levels of success. These films have been among the biggest blockbusters for Hollywood studios, which are always on the lookout for a sure thing. According to the Box Office Mojo movie website, the 100 top-grossing films, seven comic book adaptations are in the top 50 tier ("All Time Worldwide Box-Office Grosses").

Building on this investigation of Batman's mythic qualities, I will examine how the comics medium works, particularly in its rendering of Batman, and how those qualities have been translated into live-action productions. This would place the book alongside studies in literary and transmedia adaptations. This rich area of scholarship, found in such journals such as *Literature/Film Quarterly*, is valuable in that it can increase our understanding of what strategies are involved in adapting the print medium into a cinematic one. As comics have grown as an object of scholarly attention, so this book seeks to elucidate the transition Batman has experienced from the comics panel to the big screen.

Much of the research in the comics field tends to focus either on historical aspects of a given title, character or genre, or are critical studies seeking to interpret comics as an expression of the culture. Although in places I will touch on certain larger cultural implications of Batman stories, this is not an examination of Batman's larger cultural meaning. Others may take a literary approach by exploring themes, symbols, and formulas employed by the texts. Still others seek to use a discussion of Batman to express their views of philosophy or religion. These may all be valuable approaches that have yielded valuable insights, and examples of this type of criticism is discussed in Chapter 1, but the focus of this book differs from much of the research on comics in its exploration of Batman's mythic character and how it is evoked by comics technique. The book examines how a deceptively simple art form created a character whose appeal has made it a cultural force and a hugely profitable one for a giant media conglomerate. I then explore the challenges to translating Batman into other media, particularly film, and investigate how various adaptive strategies have fared. As such, it examines the formal elements of two media and how they work on either end of the adaptation process.

The success of films drawn from comic book continues to hold Hollywood's attention as potential tentpole pictures upon which studios invest enormous sums. The knowledge a study of a comic book hero's journey from three-color panels to film frames yields a greater understanding of how each medium functions, each in its own sphere and how each is related to the other.

• 1 •

Myth and the Mythic

It has been frequently remarked upon how superhero stories carry an echo of ancient mythologies. Elizabeth Danna remarks that "the ancient world did not have comic books, but they did tell stories about their own 'super' heroes," such as Herakles and Samson (67). Peter Coogan's history of the superhero genre devotes a chapter to "The Prehistory of the Superhero: The Roots in Myth, Epic, and Legend." He notes that there are certain parallels between heroes of mythology and spandex, such as a comic company's cast of characters resembling a mythology's pantheon of gods and heroes, or the way that the appearance of gods in each other's stories is like the way Batman might appear in a Superman comic book. "Another surface similarity is the use of various characters by succeeding authors who retell stories and add to the mythos' continuity: Virgil's retelling of the Trojan War in the *Aeneid,* or Frank Miller's retelling of Batman's early career in *Year One*" (117). However much these and other elements seem to mirror each other in mythology and comics, the deeper religious significance that an ancient mythology held for its followers will always set it apart from the four-color adventures of comic book superheroes. This chapter will, therefore, focus on the pertinent qualities of myth that inform this thesis of Batman's mythic, rather than mythological, nature.

Myth

The history of the study of myth over the last several hundred years has often focused on the function that myths served in societies. The word "myth" itself is derived from the Greek word *mythos,* which can mean "word," "saying," "story," or "fiction." It refers to something of unquestioned validity, according to Jonathan Z. Smith, writing in the *Encyclopædia Britannica* (715). This assumption of the inherent truthfulness of myth, of course, contrasts sharply with the modern popular meaning of something false or fanciful. Mircea Eliade, a prominent historian of religion, discussed myth in the light of how it had come to mean, in the 19th century, something opposed to reality (*Myths* 23). In archaic times, i.e., in times of "primitive" religion

> myth [was] thought to express the absolute truth, because it narrates a sacred history; that is, a transhuman revelation which took place at the dawn of the Great Time, in the holy time of the beginnings (in illo tempore) [*Myths* 23].

As such, the myth is "exemplary," i.e., it offers a pattern for action and is therefore repeatable (through ritual and retelling) by human agents who follow it as a "true history" of time's beginnings. Eliade continues:

> In imitating the exemplary acts of a god or of a mythic hero, or simply by recounting their adventures, the man of an archaic society detaches himself from profane time and magically re-enters the Great Time, the sacred time [Ibid.].

Thus the meaning and function of myths in ancient times differs radically from the usual contemporary sense we have of it in our age, which is of something that is untrue and patently false, although possibly believed by the uneducated. The archaic sense of myth certainly involved a religious component, since it provided the sense of meaning and comprehension of the universe. Through myth, archaic man understood whence he came, who he was, and where he would end.

Myth is generally understood as a set of related stories (mythologies), both imaginative and explanatory, of a civilization's founding and of its relationship to its gods. For a time, cults formed around the gods and mythologies functioned in a religious manner. Even after the cults died out, the myths remained, retaining a compelling narrative power that ensured their survival in the civilization's cultural legacy. Anthropologists have studied and organized world mythologies, comparing and contrasting them, seeking to understand their persistence and universality. It is these systems, i.e., myths proper, around which are formed mythologies. Here the term "myth" will be used to refer only to the stories and characters of classical mythology and not to subsequent beliefs and stories formed around events, characters, or historical persons that may derive characters, events, or other patterns from them.

Robert C. Rowland, a communication scholar, discussed various views explaining the functions of myths and concluded that, despite contrasting views, it is generally found that myth serves a "larger function, answering human problems which cannot be answered discursively. The key point is that through myth we define the good society and solve problems, *not subject to rational solution*" (102, his emphasis). Myth is a mode of thinking, distinct from the philosophical, that is considered true by its adherents, even if the events of the myth are not historical. Myth's universality makes it "a basic constituent of human society" (Jonathan Z. Smith 715).

Views of Myth

The attempt to understand the function of myth in modern times has led to several schools of thought. To facilitate a general understanding of these schools, several groups into which much of the thinking on myth falls will be sketched. This is not an attempt to create formal or rigid categories but simply to orient the reader into a rough organizational layout. The four groups are the scientific/sociological, the psychological, the literary/classical, and the philosophical.

The Scientific/Sociological Group

Claude Levi-Strauss, perhaps the foremost anthropologist to study myth, sought to understand the structures of myths by which "primitive" peoples expressed relationships. By studying all the versions of a myth, he sought to make them yield knowledge about the customs and beliefs of a given society. Philosopher Alisdair MacIntyre describes how one of Levi-Strauss's major findings was the manner in which a culture's myths

> incorporate and exhibit binary oppositions, which are present in the structure of the society in which the myth was born. In the myth these oppositions are reconciled and overcome. The function of the myth is to render intellectually and socially tolerable what would otherwise be experienced as incoherence. The myth is a form in which society both understands and misunderstands its own structure [MacIntyre 437].

As a scientist, Levi-Strauss was not at all interested in the qualitative aspects of myth. The formal literary qualities and meaning were inconsequential. Characterizing him as a sort of physicist of myth, Dudley Andrew asserts that Levi-Strauss "finds the values of various mythical elements and measures the overall energy level of the relationships between particles" (78–79). This empirical approach to myth, Andrew believes, sees myths as valuable only for what the analysis of their structures yields, not as things interesting in themselves.

This stress upon the general structures of myth is echoed somewhat by Vladimir Propp's study of the Russian folktale. By a structural analysis of the

100 tales he examined, he found them limited to 31 functions, or kinds of action (Andrew 83). Such propositions as "an interdiction is addressed to the hero"; "the interdiction is violated"; "the false hero or villain is exposed"; and "the hero is married and ascends the throne" are always arranged in fixed sequences (Propp 26–64). A strict adherence to this formula produced what could be drawn as a flow chart of narrative options. Both Levi-Strauss's and Propp's stress upon the empirical qualities of mythical narratives limits their usefulness in a study such as this, although, as will be seen later, Levi-Strauss's concept of myth as a means of reconciling opposites will bear upon the analysis of Batman's mythical function.

The Psychological Group

Another branch of science has sought to discover how myths function to explain psychological phenomena. Psychological theories seek to interpret behavioral phenomena using a mythological framework. The general assumption is that myths began as psychic insights that captured common human experience in narrative form. The Freudian approach posits the familiar Oedipal notion of a son's rebellion against his father because of the son's desire for his mother and is projected into the many variations on the Oedipus story, all being more or less disguised elaborations of this conflict. Otto Rank sought to comprehensively grasp myths' symbolic language as an explanation for such Oedipal conflicts (MacIntyre 436). Though now less in vogue as an explanatory view of myth, Freud's theories have retained a niche in scholarly thinking about myth and culture (Jonathan Z. Smith 720).

More pervasive are Carl Jung's theories of archetypes and the collective unconscious. Similar stories and characters reappear in all cultures around the world and throughout history, according to Jung, because all humanity shares a common psychic source of mythic symbolism, which is the archetype in the collective unconscious (MacIntyre 436). MacIntyre points out that the difficulties with Jung's thesis lie in its unprovability. Nevertheless, it has fueled such studies as those of Joseph Campbell's who sees the heroic pattern universally recurring, as demonstrated in the title of his best-known book, *The Hero with a Thousand Faces*. More recent Jungian scholarship, such as that of Rushing and Frentz, demonstrates the continuing attraction of his theories which seems to offer insight into certain narratives. Terrill's "Put on a Happy Face: *Batman* as Schizophrenic Savior," for instance, is an exercise in applying Jung's theories to Tim Burton's film. The 1989 *Batman* movie, he avers, is a neat illustration of a Gotham City whose psychic disintegration is preserved by Batman, an insane hero who represses the Joker's attempts to make the city face its obsession with its persona, i.e., the solely conscious aspects of reality. Batman's success at preventing the city from getting in touch with its unconscious is a cinematic dream projection of "the unbalanced American psyche"— a projection which the American audience could safely enjoy and endorse, making it the hit of the summer of 1989 (321).

Psychological approaches tend to attribute certain psychological conditions to audiences in a wholesale manner. Theories intended for the clinical treatment of individuals by trained professionals can too easily be reductionistically applied to mass audiences as an explanation of the appeal of fictional characters and stories. While this study does discuss the nature of Batman's appeal to his audience, it will do so through a less clinical inference, based on the linking of Batman's quest for justice with his audience's concern with crime and public order.

The Literary/Classical Group

In the literary/classical group, myth is seen as a cultural object to be understood and appreciated as a bearer of symbolic meaning that has formal genealogies and thematic structures. Literary critics seek to understand the way stories weave human concerns and values into artful creations in ways that are both traditional and innovative. Critics studying the mythical in stories seek to detect patterns and forms and trace them as far back as the primeval mythologies, thus establishing the connections between them. They are concerned with how symbols, motifs, and figures may change or sustain their meaning over time as they are traced through a succession of works. C. S. Lewis and J. R. R. Tolkien also detected the mythical qualities in literature, yet placed greater weight on the spiritual significance of such content, believing it to be a signpost of the transcendent, produced by creatures created in the image of God. This study will most closely follow the principles of the literary/classical approach.

The Philosophical Group

Scholarship in the philosophical group seeks to detect and explicate mythic content in works of popular culture in order to identify the work's underlying philosophical implications. This may be done in order to argue for a certain interpretation that the critic believes to be valid, but it may also function as a critique of what the given work reveals about societal practices and beliefs. Thus, the critic is concerned with the social and political implications of the work being examined. In the works of this group, it is often the case that the writer may be approaching the object from his or her own philosophical position in order to demonstrate the presence or absence of that philosophy in the work.

Geoffrey Hall has sought to elucidate modern films by analyzing the mythic content and patterns contained therein. For example, all the characters in *It's a Wonderful Life* (1946) are analyzed in terms of their names' historical and mythical antecedents: George Bailey as both St. George and Christ figure; Mary as the Virgin Mary; the fall into the gym pool as a symbolic baptism, etc.

Such an approach yields numerous connections of film content to earlier archetypal precedents. Like Joseph Campbell, Hall sees these films as mythic signposts on the road to better living. Further, his belief in actual cosmic forces being expressed through such cultural artifacts indicate that, for him, this approach is not just a method of interpretation, it is a means of divining what immanent forces (such as a patriarchal monstrous masculinity or the feminine principle, a manifestation of the Goddess) are expressing in terms of social conflict. This is mythic interpretation taken to the level of religion.

Another scholar who has dealt with many popular culture artifacts from a mythic perspective is Janice Hocker Rushing. In "*E.T.* as Rhetorical Transcendence," Rushing analyzes the Spielberg film as an expression of "the perennial philosophy," a mythic narrative that is about the search for wholeness using age-old symbolism.

Similar to this is a strain of scholarly critical writing which draws on such sources as Jung, and seeks to discern deeply rooted societal beliefs as they are expressed in mass media examples. These beliefs are held to be the (current) "myths" of society and may be analyzed for their philosophical content in order to understand a society's often hidden motivations as well as to offer criticism and alternative philosophical prescriptions. For example, Rushing and Thomas S. Frentz examine "The Frankenstein Myth in Contemporary Cinema." The films *Rocky IV* (1985), *Blade Runner* (1982), and *The Terminator* (1984), they assert, are stories which present dystopian shadow myths that express fears society has repressed concerning technology. Being expressions of a patriarchal myth of progress which fears that technology will overtake its creators, these films teach us, the authors argue, that "culture must reintegrate feminine values into its consciousness, thereby activating an oppositional entelechial motive to reidentify agent [i.e., humanity] with agency [technology]" (61). This is an example of an approach to mythic criticism that advocates social change through cultural analysis. The operating rationale of this approach holds that by deconstructing the deeply held myths of a society, one may discursively diagnose ills and recommend therapeutic philosophical correctives. This is a response to perceived myths that seeks to operate simultaneously on two levels, the mythical and the philosophical in a consciously (and problematically) utilitarian manner. If Rowland is correct in holding that myth deals with matters that cannot be addressed discursively, such an approach discounts the power myths hold in a culture or else believes them vulnerable to a redressing countermythology.

It should be stressed that the preceding categorization is an informal orientation of the field of mythic criticism and is in no way intended to be definitive. Concepts and influences may be shared by writers in different groups yet still remain distinct enough in their motivation and goals to merit placement in that group. What these and other writers (who will be discussed herein) share is the conviction that mythic content is recognizable in certain works and that to explicate this content is the best way to understand these works.

From Myth to the Mythic

Such understandings of myth as ongoing human expressions, not limited to some ancient era, see myth expressed in human activity as diverse as political speech, feature films, and television series. Rowland's concern is that a too broad conception of myth leads to an overgeneralized application of it to explain all sorts of cultural phenomena, thus debasing the term. Much writing on myths and myth-making in various works does not draw a fine distinction between classic myths and myths found in later cultural expressions. One cannot assume whether these writers are equating these so-called myths with classic myths (although it can be assumed they would make distinctions if asked), but are simply asserting that something like the great myths are discernible in later works. The possibility of being misunderstood as to the distinction leads to this study's differentiation of "myth" from "mythic." The mythic is myth-like in that it draws on figures, motifs, narrative patterns, and symbols which have their origin in myths proper. Much of the literature that offers what is generally known as mythic criticism (or which discusses such perspectives) tends to use such terms as "myth," "mythic," "mythical," "myth-making," as well as others, almost interchangeably and does not recognize Rowland's more formal, narrow view of myth. These writers see an impulse in human society to create cultural objects that can transcend a positivistic view of story, plot, and character to attain a resonance with much earlier forms of story found in myths.

To make it clear that this study's subject matter is not considered a myth proper, i.e., a classical myth, it will distinguish between myths proper, which arise out of civilizations over long periods of time, and mythic expressions which occur within various cultures and which do not necessarily span a civilization. Rollin observes that the myths of popular culture, being tied to the trends of the age and because of their easily imaged forms and simplistic discourse, tend to, in fact, overwhelm the sacred myths of religion, which usually require greater contemplation (35). He defines popular culture heroes as "gestalts of the popular mind, symbolic figures whose totality is greater than the sum of their parts" (44). Such mythic expressions may wax and wane in popularity and influence, even going through dramatic changes in meaning and representation. For example, the myth of the Wild West in Hollywood films of the last 60 years has seen a procession through various expressions over a relatively brief time. What was in the 1930s a relatively primitive genre grew into its classic stage by the 1940s. This phase continued into the 1950s, but began showing signs of wear as the audience grew overly familiar with the generic conventions. By the 1960s, it was common to see parodies of westerns as straight treatments grew rarer. Thus, though it was possible to treat westerns for their "mythic" content concerning certain themes, motifs, and characters, the meaning of these objects changed rather quickly over time, in response to societal changes. Richard D. McGhee's discussion of John Wayne's evolving screen persona illustrates these changes. McGhee discusses how the Hollywood star's persona takes on mythical qualities, calling John Wayne, after Campbell, the "hero with a thousand faces." McGhee finds both Campbell and Northrop Frye useful in describing how Wayne's screen persona "becomes the hero of comedy, romance, irony and tragedy" after Northrop Frye's schemata (10). This illustrates the protean quality of popular culture figures whose stories, while partaking of mythic qualities, are too mutable to be proper myths.

Another typical example of how scholarship seeks to explain certain popular culture phenomena in terms of the mythic is found in several articles on *Star Trek*. Looking at the literature on the television and film versions, one soon finds that writers see it as a "modern myth" because it functions in ways that renew certain cultural values by projecting them into a completely realized future setting. William Blake Tyrell argues this regarding the displacement of United States history, in the original *Star Trek* series, into the final frontier of space exploration. "In effect," he says, "*Star Trek* takes our roots and disguises them as branches for some of us to cling to" (712). Lane Roth examines how the narrative of *Star Trek II: The Wrath of Khan* follows the classic conventions in heroic myths noted by Joseph Campbell. Roth examines the death-rebirth cycle, the doppelgänger, and other mythic concepts as they apply to the film's components.

The wide use of such terms as "myth" and "myth-making" among scholars of diverse backgrounds indicates a general belief that some sort of ongoing human cultural activity continues to draw on earlier mythologies, symbolism, and narratives in order to express rich and complex meanings. It is possible to recognize types of characters that arguably have their first appearances in some mythology. Of course, among these various archaic societies myths frequently displayed patterns and types that resembled each other. Creation myths, heroic exploits and quests all seem to repeat themselves with some variation across the mythologies. For example, the figure of the Trickster has been identified as a type who recurs in many mythologies as well as in folk tales. The Trickster can have several widely ranging permutations, from culture hero to antagonist (Biallas 88). In his culture-hero manifestation, the Trickster stands between men and the gods and brings something of the gods to men, such as Prometheus's stealing of fire to give to mankind. This creator of culture is known by his benevolent actions. In his degenerate form, the Trickster is one who seeks to bring the world into disorder and chaos like the Norse god Loki. An updated recurrence of the Loki myth is found in the film *The Mask* (1994), wherein Loki's mask causes the powerful eruption of a person's innermost character.

While seemingly detached from this mythological mode, modern societies still display manifestations of such figures in their cultural expressions. Hero and villain figures in fictional narratives continue to contain the essence of these types. Whether consciously intended by an author or not, patterns of earlier myths regularly recur in modern culture. Whether the source of recurring mythic patterns is the aforementioned mechanisms or some other, it is undeniable that they do recur in countless forms globally. Several schools, such as the psychological schools mentioned above, offered explanations for such recurrences of the mythic, but literary scholars recognize that regardless of the psychological sources, mythopoeic works are a constant in human culture. It is these mythic dimensions of popular culture that this study examines in the Batman story.

Numerous writers study stories and characters in various media to analyze the mythic patterns contained therein. In several places Eliade discusses the survival of myths into modern times. Even a society with an apparently secular mindset finds itself attracted to stories with strong mythic patterns, such as the detective story (*Myths* 35). Eliade develops this concept of the extension of myth into modern times by noting how the experience of time has changed as our experience of myth has changed. As referred to at the start of the chapter, Eliade recounts the manner in which archaic man, by recounting the myths of the Great Time, moved out of his own time into Sacred Time. In fact, he viewed the environment as imbued with the sacred so that his mundane actions echoed those exemplary ones of gods and heroes of the Great Time, and attained mythical significance (*Myths* 36–37). Modern man, lacking this mythic worldview, still experiences the mythic as it recurs in cultural manifestations. In the detachment from the sense of mundane time experienced in reading a story, for instance, we are "taken out of our own duration to move in other rhythms, to live in a different history," thus experiencing, in a diminished, secularized sense, the same "escape" into sacred time as archaic man.

As mentioned in the Introduction, Eliade noted a specific example of a surviving mythic archetype in popular culture, the comic book character Superman. The character draws his strength, so to speak, from earlier mythological sources. The mighty Superman disguises himself as a meek, ineffectual human, Clark Kent.

> This humiliating camouflage of a Hero whose powers are literally unlimited revives a well-known mythical theme. In the last analysis, the myth of Superman satisfies the secret longings of modern man who, though he knows he is a fallen, limited creature, dreams of one day proving himself an "exceptional person," a "Hero" ["Survivals" 45].

Whether or not the creators of stories like Superman or their audiences are conscious of its mythological predecessors, such tales become embedded in a given culture because they evoke the mythic. A mythic approach to Superman, in terms of the so-called American monomyth, is an example of scholarship in this mode (Lang and Trimble). Identifying the classical monomyth of the hero described by Campbell and its more specific version of the American monomyth, the authors demonstrate how Superman fits this American mythic archetype for the 20th century. As an "immigrant" from another world, he comes to this country and absorbs its deepest values during his upbringing in the heartland. Following the classic pattern, his true identity remains cloaked until the need arises and his power is revealed. When the danger is passed he recedes back into his humble guise as an ordinary American.

Such recurring stories or plots are often perpetuated as fairy tales. A good example would be the story we know as "Beauty and the Beast," repeated in many forms in different places (Bettelhiem 282–283). An unlovable man, cursed into a trapped state through enchantment, must be freely loved for himself by a woman before he can escape the enchantment. Even today, a film such as *Groundhog Day* (1993) retains the same core concept while varying the particulars. Set in a contemporary locale, an obnoxious television weatherman finds himself stuck in the repetition of the same day until he learns to love unselfishly. This purgatorial transformation results in the love of a woman, which ends his temporal recycling. This variation on a theme is, of course, the pattern of all recurring mythic expressions. Like film genres such as the detective mystery or the western, recurring mythic expressions perpetuate their central motif over time, but adapt character and setting specifics to a particular time and place. The Greek myth of Pygmalion, wherein a sculptor brings his work of art to life as a beautiful woman, is perpetuated by George Bernard Shaw in his play of that name, later adapted into the musical *My Fair Lady*, and transmogrified yet again in the film *Pretty Woman* (1990).

The concerns carried in the themes and plots of such perpetuated myths are similar to, or at least not unlike, those of the original myths, which offered explanatory stories about the meaning and purpose of the cosmos as well as exemplary models of behavior. More than moralizing fables, they seek to address complex questions of existence in the form of story that speaks more deeply than other, discursive forms. Just as scholars view myth as an historically earlier mode of thought (as opposed to philosophy) about the world, so mythic expressions today cloak their meaning in story forms rich in motifs and symbols (MacIntyre 434).[1]

Some approach mythic themes and patterns as irruptions of Jung's collective unconscious. Campbell sees myth as the persistent font of wisdom slaking the world's thirst.

> It would not be too much to say that myth is the secret opening through which the inexhaustible energies of the cosmos pour into human cultural manifestations. Religions, philosophies, arts, the social forms of primitive and historic man, prime discoveries in science and technology, the very dreams that blister sleep, boil up from the basic, magic ring of myth [Campbell 3].

In Campbell's view, myth is the vital ongoing force of human consciousness, an all-encompassing principle from which we draw our meaning in the world. All religions and philosophies are only manifestations of and conveyors for myth. Campbell seems to locate divinity in the immanent, with myth serving as a divine spirit sent from the collective unconscious to comfort us and to guide us into all truth. Building on Jung, Campbell might fall into the psychological camp or philosophical for his focus on interpretation of myth as a therapeutic or corrective means to human thriving.

This study takes a more conservative and tentative approach to the study of myth and the mythic. Much can be gained toward understanding cultural objects by discerning intrinsic mythic patterns without vesting such objects with seemingly gnostic significance or oracular powers. The perspective of this study is closer to Tolkien's belief that as creatures made in the creator God's image, humans are therefore sub-creators and makers of culture. As we inherit the vast legacy of culture from the past, we, having mythopathic potential, in turn become mythopoeic. We make myths; that is, we create stories and characters like those we have received. We do not necessarily think that we are consciously creating a highly meaningful set of symbols in our narratives

("X corresponds to this myth"); rather, we have an innate capacity both to think and create mythically and to respond to the mythic content we encounter. So, when it is asserted that Batman is a mythic figure, it is being said that his creators called on, consciously and unconsciously, the vast source of mythic inspiration contained in our cultural legacy. From da Vinci's batwing to the Shadow's pulp fiction; and from ancient folklore of bats to the film of Mary Roberts Rinehart's novel *The Bat Whispers* (1930), Batman's creators filtered various sources through their human creativity to produce something new, made of older ingredients.

This book's discussion is influenced to some degree by all four approaches to myth that have been named. It is difficult to completely discount psychological insights offered by those who espouse that approach. Their analysis of various works offer seemingly compelling interpretations, but the specific mechanics behind psychological theories, i.e., repression, complexes, the collective unconscious are, strangely, less intellectually compelling than the interpretations themselves. The philosophical grouping ties theory to action, yet such an approach is often hampered by its conflation of myth, philosophy, and, sometimes, frankly, political/ideological concerns, in scholarly work. In contrast, this study fits mostly in the literary/classical grouping. It allows for both a comprehension and appreciation of the many ways myth has come down to us, such as Frye exhibits, as well as allowing for the transcendent function of the mythic, such as that demonstrated by such scholars as C. S. Lewis.

Romance and the Hero's Quest

All these types of stories featuring adventure as the chief attraction come under the literary category of the romance. Northrop Frye remarks that the "romance is nearest of all literary forms to the wish-fulfillment dream" and notes its persistence through much social and cultural change (*Anatomy* 186). Frye remarked that various and diverse ideologies find their expression through the romance, from aristocracy to Marxism. It should not be surprising to find this essential form in many popular narratives, though many would be considered "sub-literary." As a "wish-fulfillment dream," a given romance follows its inherent form "where the virtuous heroes and beautiful heroines represent the ideals and the villains the threats to their ascendancy," according to Frye (*Anatomy* 186). As such, all popular story forms share these characteristics generally while varying according to their respective styles and formats.

Frye discerned clear patterns of heroic action in the romance. He situated romance in the broad area between realism and myth (*Anatomy* 136). In order for myth to be expressed through the form of the romance, Frye maintains, the device of displacement must be used. "In a myth," he writes, "we can have a sun-god or a tree-god; in a romance we may have a person who is significantly associated with the sun or trees" (137). (Thus the romance may evoke the mythic without itself being a myth.) As for plot, typically this mythic hero is sent on or undertakes a quest. Noting that adventure is the "essential element of plot in romance" and that the quest is the literary form of the romance, Frye proceeds to describe the three-stage structure of the successful quest (186–7):

> The stage of the perilous journey and the preliminary minor adventures; the crucial struggle, usually some kind of battle in which either the hero or his foe, or both, must die; and the exaltation of the hero. We may call these three stages respectively, using Greek terms, the *agon* or conflict, the *pathos* or death-struggle, and the *anagnorisis* or discovery, the recognition of the hero [187].

Such a quest includes not only the requisite hero but of course his antagonist.

> The enemy may be an ordinary human being, but the nearer the romance is to myth, the more attributes of divinity will cling to the hero and the more the enemy will take on demonic mythical qualities. The central form of romance is dialectical: everything is focused on a conflict between the hero and his enemy, and *all the reader's values are bound up with the hero* [my emphasis]. Hence the hero of romance is analogous to the mythical Messiah or deliverer who comes from an upper world, and his enemy is analogous to the demonic powers of a lower world. The conflict however takes place in, or at any rate primarily concerns, *our* world [Ibid.].

Such a scenario fits the comic book superhero genre as well as other romance narratives. Frye concludes that "myth and romance both belong in the general category of mythopoeic literature" and this is how these terms will be used in this study as well (188).

The Mythic Plane in Popular Narrative

It is in the romance that we may detect an audience's deepest longings, fears, and values, these being the core elements upon which the romance writers construct their high adventures. These tales are not myths proper but rather share some relations to myth in that they displace some of life's deepest concerns into another, fictional place and time, into what Tolkien called a "sub-creation" or the mythic plane. These other worlds, whether urban streets or distant planets, are the author's own creation. Not intended to be realistic, they serve as the environment wherein romance will occur, with its own format of expectations, types of incidents, and other parameters outside of which the story will not go. The reader soon understands what the "rules" of this world are and is happy as long as the story is internally consistent. This, of course, is typical of many genres, all coming under the aegis of the romance. It is the meaning derived from the experiencing of the story (often repeated many times, whether the same story or others like it) that is one of its chief attractions.

In writing about the enjoyment of story, C. S. Lewis observed that there may be very little difference between the pleasure derived by a cultivated reader of great literature and the "unliterary" reader of sensational fare. Such fare, low-brow material to the literary reader, may be a source of the mythopoeic to the unliterary. Lewis argued that the unliterary reader "may also, I believe, be receiving certain profound experiences which are, for him, not acceptable in any other form" and that "something which the educated receive from poetry can reach the masses through stories of adventure, and in almost no other way" (*Stories* 16).

For Lewis, the quality of a story lies in its ability to suggest meanings that transcend mere plot and incident. A story can create a sense of some quality that transcends its particulars, such as when a science fiction story about isolation on a barren planet suggests not merely being marooned but a cosmic sense of alienation. Certain stories (such as Oedipus and others, which show how efforts to prevent a prophesy may in fact bring it about) have the power to instill awe, wonder, and meaning far more powerfully than a mere theoretical account of a concept.

> We have just had set before our imagination something that has always baffled the intellect: we have seen how destiny and free will can be combined, even how free will is the modus operandi of destiny. The story does what no theorem can quite do. It may not be "like real life" in the superficial sense: but it sets before us an image of what reality may well be like at some more central region [*Stories* 15].

It is this effect that Lewis posits which may be experienced in stories of varying levels of quality by readers of varying sophistication and maturity. The type of story may differ but it is often the romance that treats issues such as these.

Elsewhere, Lewis describes the type of writing that may successfully evoke what he calls the mythopoeic and what I am calling the mythic. In describing the work of adventure writer H. Rider Haggard, Lewis is unsparing in acknowledging the writer's stylistic faults, but maintains that despite these literary shortcomings, Haggard survived other writers because of his "mythopoeic gift" ("Haggard" 97). This ability to cast his story in mythic terms transcended his mediocre writing talent.

> What keeps us reading in spite of all these defects is of course the story itself, the myth. Haggard is a text-book case of the mythopoeic gift pure and simple—isolated, as if for inspection, from nearly all those more specifically literary powers with which it so

fortunately co-exists in, say, [*Rime of the*] *Ancient Mariner, Dr. Jekyll and Mr. Hyde,* or *The Lord of the Rings* ["Haggard" 99].

Lewis suggests that, in addition to the more conventional reasons many critics have disliked Haggard, there is the fact that some readers simply hate the mythopoeic.

> This hatred comes in part from a reluctance to meet Archetypes; it is an involuntary witness to their disquieting vitality. Partly it springs from an uneasy awareness that the most "popular" fiction, if only it embodies a real myth, is so very much more serious than what is generally called "serious" literature. For it deals with the permanent and inevitable, whereas an hour's shelling, or perhaps a ten-mile walk, or even a dose of salts, might annihilate many of the problems in which the characters of a refined and subtle novel are entangled [100].

Once again, Lewis observes that the mythic can come to us in stories less refined and "literary" than that which is greatly esteemed by cultural arbiters.

It is particularly with what might be called the "subliterary" that this study of mythic expression is concerned. Just as in film history, the dramatic film has received more esteem than the genre film; so the novel is considered literary where the dime novel, pulp magazine and comic book are thought to be low-brow entertainments. Yet it is in these works by prolific authors seeking to meet mass tastes that one may find at times the echoes of the mythic in the contemporary adventure romance. As stated earlier, the creators of Batman drew on the accumulated wealth of diverse sources to produce a compelling figure as a new attraction to the nascent comic book medium. They did this with their target audience in mind. In his book *Virgin Land,* cultural historian Henry Nash Smith observes that comic book producers followed the tradition of pulp writers who in turn had inherited the legacy of their 19th century predecessors, the dime novelists. These astonishingly prolific writers, able to produce enormous quantities of fictional text, did not write literature in the usual sense (H. Smith 100). As Smith demonstrated, their writing efforts were directed not toward new works of the imagination but toward the prodigious production of formula stories tied to the fantasies, desires, and values of their audience.

> Such work tends to become an objectified mass dream, like the moving pictures, the soap operas, or the comic books that are the present day equivalents of the [publisher] Beadle stories. The individual writer abandons his own personality and identifies himself with the reveries of his readers. It is the presumably close fidelity of the Beadle stories to the dream life of a vast inarticulate public that renders them valuable to the social historian and the historian of ideas [Smith 101].

As the dime novelists mediated between their readership and its "reveries," so pulp novelists in the early 20th century, and comic book writers now, turn out vast quantities of a certain style and formula to an audience looking for a dependable, known product. Smith's concept of these works as reflections of their readers' interests, concerns, and imaginative preoccupations highlight how their evocation of the mythic seems to occur. What all these popular media, dime novels, pulp magazines, and comics share is their emphasis on colorful larger-than-life heroics or what could commonly be called myth-making. This tapping into the fantasies of a mass-audience and perpetuating what is responded to by that audience is indeed a fecund source for the study of the popular mythic imagination. This is not to say that, perforce, this technique always produces expressions of the mythic; rather, that it sometimes produces a form of the romance, that has, in Frye's terms, a mythic structure in which mythic "ingredients" may be cultivated. It is worth noting that comic books foster audience feedback through their popular letter columns or "lettercols," as they are known. Here avid readers give their responses to the latest stories, offering detailed lay critiques to the book editors, who often respond to letters with explanations, corrections, and defenses of story elements. In this exchange, comic book producers may grasp readers' likes and dislikes of current or recent storylines, learning more precisely what their audiences want.

Since their inception, comic books have been despised by many elitists, seeing them at best as juvenilia, at worst as dangerous to young minds. Frederic Wertham's *Seduction of the Innocent*, is only the most well known of the many attacks on comics as a threat to the public order by youth driven to crime by imitation of what they read in the pulpy pages of their favorite comics. This tradition of condemning cheap story magazines goes back to the 19th century and is refuted by G. K. Chesterton in his 1901 essay, "A Defense of Penny-Dreadfuls." Distinguishing, as Lewis would later would, between adventure fiction and literature, Chesterton remarked,

> Literature is a luxury; fiction is a necessity. A work of art can hardly be too short, for its climax is its merit. A story can never be too long, for its conclusion is merely to be deplored, like the last halfpenny or the last pipelight. And so, while the increase of the artistic conscience tends in more ambitious works to brevity and impressionism, voluminous industry still marks the producer of the true romantic trash. There was no end to the ballads of Robin Hood; there is no end to the volumes about Dick Deadshot and the Avenging Nine. These two heroes are deliberately conceived as immortal ["Defense"].

Chesterton goes on to assert that such stories provide essential reaffirmations of "sanguine and heroic truisms on which civilization is built; for it is clear that unless civilization is built on truisms, it is not built at all" (Ibid.). His remarks could easily describe that nature and function of comic book superheroes from the birth of Superman in 1938 to today. Narratively open-ended, profuse, and obsessed with good versus evil, noble heroes and evil foes, though now more sophisticated in structure and technique, the genre retains its essential thematic core.

Tarzan as Mythic Exemplar

Just as the comic book and its predecessors have been considered low art, so has the work of Edgar Rice Burroughs. Nevertheless, his famous creation, Tarzan of the Apes, is a good illustration of how a figure in popular culture may draw upon classical sources. Classics scholar Erling B. Holtsmark devoted a volume, *Tarzan and Tradition,* to discerning how Burroughs, in fact, stands in the tradition of classical prototypes, particularly Homer's *Iliad* and *Odyssey.* Holtsmark substantiates Burroughs's mythopoeic achievement by an in-depth analysis of how the writer drew on his knowledge of classical languages and heroic themes. In discussing Burroughs's critics, who dismissed him for his lack of literary artistry and syntactical correctness, Holtsmark demonstrated that Burroughs's "use of repetition and his reliance on formulaic language" was in fact built upon his knowledge of the similar patterns found in Homer's epics (Holtsmark 7). His use of the jungle setting as a metaphor for Tarzan's internal emotional states indicated a subtle use of symbolism such as is found in Homer, Virgil, and Ovid (9). Tarzan's oft-mentioned shrewdness is reminiscent of Odysseus's cleverness in his adventures. Tarzan's journey down into the lost city in the Valley of Opar mirrors those journeys of classical heroes like Heracles and Aenas, who made descents into Hell. Holtsmark's linking of these characters' and Tarzan's shared experience of a *katabasis* (journey down) indicates the influence of epic narratives on Burroughs (97–99).

Tarzan's character itself is often a source of mythic appeal, in that he embodies opposing qualities: superb human rationality, and "superhuman sensitivities of smell, hearing and sight," as well as extraordinary physical strength like that of a jungle beast (92). He is no mere man, yet he is no jungle savage either. He inhabits two worlds: as Lord of the Apes he has, through strength and cunning, conquered all challengers, while his ancestral title of Lord Greystoke makes him part of civilized aristocracy as well. By being of two worlds, Tarzan transcends the ordinary experience of his audience, becoming a true fantasy figure that reconciles opposites. His appeal is further based on his power to cut through "due process" in his pursuit of wrongdoers, being less bound by a civilized bureaucracy (116). Holtsmark also notes that one of Tarzan's chief attributes, his "self-assured control at critical moments," is perhaps his most coveted characteristic (119). Holtsmark describes how Tarzan's cleverness is expressed in one story as he operates in both aspects of the Trickster archetype (122). Acting as a culture hero, Tarzan institutes a sentry system among his tribe of apes to protect them from attacks. Later, as much out of mischief as to teach a lesson, he tests the tribe's vigilance by donning a lion skin and pretending to approach their territory. Though not meeting all characteristics of the Trickster, Tarzan here exemplifies both the beneficial and underhanded expressions of that mythic type.

Holtsmark's study shows how a fictional character in modern popular culture can draw narrative, thematic, and characteristic patterns from classical sources. Burroughs's youthful exposure to these sources led to their influence on his writing, which arguably accounts for the stories' mythic resonance and enduring appeal. This study of the Batman story will also seek to explicate the classical roots and influences that contribute to its mythic stature. The Batman stories are myriad and written by many authors who may not have had the same exposure to classical influences as did Burroughs. But as mentioned above, mythic patterns in a culture are diffuse and pervasive and often arise unconsciously as well as deliberately, as the writer draws on his or her cultural memory.

Discussion

As the preceding indicates, discerning the mythic in stories can be approached in different ways. Writers may seek to interpret a popular culture artifact's meaning using psychological theories. Or they can, as Rushing illustrates, argue for a particular philosophical and symbolic interpretation of a work of art to demonstrate how it may embody certain concepts and beliefs. McGhee uses Frye's concept of myth to show how a Hollywood star's changing persona may display attributes of different heroic phases. These and others noted here, as well as many other scholars who could be noted, may use different methodologies but all believe that cultural artifacts may be better understood through discerning their mythic structures and patterns. Lewis posits that the mythopoeic is evident in a work whatever its literary quality, through recognition of the presence of archetypes and the rendering of themes. Frye maintains that some form of myth underlies all literary works and that, in the romance, the mythic manifests itself through displacement. Henry Nash Smith describes how popular fiction operating through deliberate reflection of its audiences' values, hopes, and fears, perpetuates mythic patterns, forms, and figures in myriad stories.

With this background on theories of myth in place, this study next turns to an examination of the comic book character Batman, seeking to discern the mythic traits that distinguish him and to discover how this mythic rendering occurs in the comic book medium. In the next chapter, a concise history of the Batman comics will be offered along with a profile of Batman as a character. This will be the raw material necessary to analyze what it is about the Batman saga that transcends mere comic book content to attain mythic stature, the subject of Chapter 3.

"I shall become a *bat*!"

Batman's History, Personality and Legend

Begun as a means of exploiting the success of Superman, Batman was an early arrival to the nascent superhero genre and would eventually emerge as the prototype of the successful masked vigilante. Although the character was a synthesis of numerous influences and earlier fictional characters, Batman proved to be difficult to improve upon in later attempts because of the remarkable set of ingredients that constitute the character's mythos. The first section of this chapter examines the history of the Batman comic book titles, showing how the magazines developed from their 1939 beginnings to the present. In the second section, the personality (or, perhaps, persona) of Batman is examined in order to better understand his unique appeal and other ingredients of his mythos.

A Brief History of Batman Comics

An examination of the history of Batman comics indicates that, though one man is generally credited with the creation of Batman, the character had many "fathers," i.e., collaborators who shared in his inception and development. This development continued over decades, maintaining the viability of the Batman comic books while demonstrating the character's adaptability.

Kane's Influences

In *Batman & Me,* Bob Kane gives a detailed account of how the Dark Knight came into existence. The Batman character is a combination of more than a few sources from history and popular culture. Perhaps the chief characteristic of Batman's ethos is the darkly clad figure of the night who carries out his own vigilante justice. This tradition, as noted by Mark Cotta Vaz in his history of Batman, appeared in popular periodicals at least as far back as the late 19th-century with the character, the "Man in Black" (16–18). Appearing in *The Boys of New York: A Paper for Young Americans* in December of 1882, the character wore a black overcoat, cape, and slouch hat, an appearance highly suggestive of the later 1930s pulp character, the Shadow. Another popular nocturnal hero of the early 20th century was Zorro, who battled oppression in old California by night and played the rich dandy by day.

The aforementioned Shadow, created in 1931, was the apotheosis of the mysterious, relentless pulp heroes who had appeared in magazines, novels, and films for years, according to comic book artist, writer, and historian Jim Steranko (17). The pulps, which were magazines named for the cheap paper they used, featured countless thrilling tales of fantastic adventures with lurid villains. Distinguished by sensational cover art, their titles offered clues to their content: *Thrilling Wonder Stories, Adventure, Weird Tales, The Mysterious Wu Fang, Black Book Detective,* and perhaps the most prominent, *The Shadow.* Playing the dashing socialite Lamont Cranston by day, the Shadow stalked criminals by night, using a variety of devices, disguises, and operatives. Dispensing justice with two flashing .45 automatics, the Shadow's reign of terror over the underworld lasted until the 1950s. Appearing in his own magazine and on the famous radio show, the pulp figure was one of the most well-known fictional characters of the era.

The year 1938 saw the advent of Superman, an innovation in the young field of comic books. Distinct from the pulps, comic books had developed in the 1930s as a new medium growing out of the popularity of the comic strips. The modern comic book began in 1933 when comic strips from Sunday supplements were repackaged to fit magazine form; the first original stories appeared in 1935, according to comic book historian Paul Sassienie (14, 15). The comic books featured various tales of high adventure showcasing the comedy, heroism, and villainy of its many characters in such titles as *Adventure* and *Detective* comics. Superman first appeared in *Action Comics* in June 1938, and it was soon apparent that the public was fascinated by this super-powered modern Hercules in the gaudy red, blue, and yellow costume.

Vincent Sullivan, an editor at National Periodical Publications, the publisher of *Action* comics, asked one of his young artists, Bob Kane, then 22, to come up with another costumed character to exploit the popularity of Superman. In his autobiography, Kane recounts how he set to work immediately, tracing various costume designs over a generic heroic figure. Then he remembered that, at 13 years of age, he saw a Leonardo da Vinci drawing of a flying machine with bat-like wings. At the time he had sketched figures with batwings including one that prefigured Batman. Kane reworked these juvenile sketches, and soon settled on a name for his new hero: "Bat-man" (Kane 35–37).

Kane had long been a fan of silent movie swashbuckler Douglas Fairbanks, Sr., whose acrobatic heroics had been featured in his film *The Mark of Zorro* (1920). As a teenager, Kane had belonged to a neighborhood gang called the Zorros, who wore black masks and engaged in Fairbanksian athleticism. From the Zorro character Kane borrowed the dual identity device of the masked hero who pretends to be a wealthy fop. Another film that had influenced Kane's imagination was *The Bat Whispers* (1930), a mystery thriller based on Mary Roberts Rinehart's novel *The Bat*. In the film, a mysterious killer resembling a great bat stalks his victims in an old house and announces his next murder by throwing a beam of light on the wall with a bat's silhouette in the center. The killer's frightening bat-disguise and the "Batsignal" both became staples of the later Batman stories (Kane 38). With the change from a domino mask to a horned hood with piercing white eye slits described in the Introduction, the basic design of Batman, which has never significantly changed, was complete.

Bat-man's alter-ego, Bruce Wayne, was a playboy socialite who used his wealth to finance his crime-fighting career. In an interview, Finger explained to James Steranko the sources of Wayne's name:

> Bruce Wayne's first name came from Robert Bruce, the Scottish patriot. Wayne, being a playboy, was a man of gentry. I searched for a name that would suggest colonialism. I tried Adams, Hancock ... then I thought of Mad Anthony Wayne [quoted In Steranko 45].

This essential characterization, drawn from many sources, became Batman's established alter ego, the carefree wealthy socialite, often seen in the early years with a pipe and smoking jacket. Wayne's depiction changed little from then on, remaining a generically rendered, blandly handsome brunette with a very square jaw and tiny black dots for eyes. It is almost as though Wayne himself is a cipher—a transparent, empty vessel that is filled with the dark Batman persona.

Creating a Legend

The first Batman story ran in *Detective Comics* #27 in May of 1939. Written by Bill Finger and called "The Case of the Chemical Syndicate," the story's success led to continuous appearances by the new hero in *Detective*. The next year a new magazine, *Batman,* appeared. The demand for Batman stories led to Kane's assembling a team of artists, writers, and other talents who would, through a system of divided labor, create the Batman stories in assembly-line fashion. Kane oversaw the production of the stories and freely acknowledges the contributions of others in developing Batman. Working against tight deadlines, the young men labored to create, in essence, a new story form with its own ethos and style. Kane oversaw the artwork, and his style set the basic approach that would distinguish the stories for decades to come. "His Caligarieseque landscapes," Steranko commented, "delineated a world of large moons and long shadows, weird perspectives and weirder people. Batman flitted silently across a nocturnal chiaroscuro with the aid of grappling hook and rope" (Ibid.). Artist Jerry Robinson credited Batman's visual style to his, Kane's, and Finger's love of movies: "We went to see *Citizen Kane* a dozen times" (quoted In Steranko 47). Kane's primitive artistic style also distinguished the stories, as Jules Feiffer's analysis of Kane's art points out:

> Kane's strength ... lay not in his draftsmanship (which was never quite believable) but in his total involvement in what he was doing (which made everything believable). However badly drawn and crudely written, Batman's world took control of the reader.... [I]f Kane said so heads were not egg shaped, but rectangular; chins occupied not the bottom sixth of the face but the bottom half—because Kane's was an authentic fantasy, a genuine vision, so that however one might nit-pick the components, the end product remained an impregnable whole: gripping and original.... Kane, more than any other comic book man ... set and made believable the terms offered to the reader [Feiffer 28].

DC's new character was an immediate success; young readers sensed something both familiar and new and that there was a distinct difference between Superman and the Bat-Man: "Superman was of the day; Batman was of the night and the shadows. Superman was rational, Apollonian; Batman was Dionysian" writes Grant Morrison in *Supergods.* "This fascinating new hero was horned like the Devil, and most at home in darkness; a terrifying, demonic presence who worked on the side of the angels," Morrison continues. "Whatever the reasons, these carefully calculated tensions and contradictions ensured Batman's cyclically renewed popularity" (26). The muscular yet graceful figure in a cowl, with long, horn-like bat ears, grimly waging a solitary and sometimes merciless war on crime, would last only about a year before adjustments were made. This included adding Robin, thereby softening the Batman character for the next generation. In the early 1940s, Robinson contributed an artistic rendering of the figures that was anatomically better than Kane's. Where Kane's heroic figures were stiff and mannered, Robinson's renderings depicted bodies in fluid athletic motion.

Development in the Golden Age and Beyond

All of Batman's important characteristics, as described above, were set by the early 1940s. Several artists and writers contributed to the prodigious output of the two magazines featuring Batman—*Detective Comics* and *Batman* (and, later, a third, *World's Finest*) and also to a daily newspaper strip, which lasted for several years. The demand for Batman stories led to the diversification of types of adventures and to the creation of new villains to offer fresh challenges to the Dynamic Duo. For comic book superheroes in general, these middle years of the 1940s were the halcyon days, the height of the Golden Age of comics. World War II had given these now-myriad costumed characters a focus against which to pit their efforts. The Axis forces seemed like a terrifying real-life ful-fillment of the worst pulp villainy. Batman's efforts, however, were devoted mainly to the homefront, because, in concept, he was less dependent on an international threat for his livelihood. By war's end, many costumed heroes' *raison d'etre* faded with the Allied victory. The next few years saw a dying off of most comic superhero titles, leaving Superman, Batman, and Wonder Woman among the few remaining. After the war, new talent was brought in to assist or relieve the veterans who had developed and maintained the Batman mythos through the 1940s. Although Bob Kane's name was routinely on the title page of each story, he has since made no secret that others ghosted the art, basing their work on his but adding their personal touches and refinements. Dick Sprang in the 1940s and Sheldon Moldoff beginning in 1954 both made significant contributions to perpetuating the distinctive Batman look.

The 1950s was a time of resorting to various devices to maintain reader interest in the Batman stories. Forced by Frederic Wertham's attack on supposed subversive comic book elements, the Comics Code narrowed the range of content available to creators, including lurid crime stories. The Batman "family" was gradually expanded, first with the coming of Bat-woman, then with Bat-girl, and soon regular appearances were made by Bat-hound and the mischievous Bat-mite. Attempting to catch the popular wave of interest in science fiction stories, Batman and Robin were thrust into bizarre and fantastic space adventures and time travels. Such preoccupations further distanced the Dark Knight from his original mystique. Even as early as 1942, it had been common to see him giving television interviews and signing autographs afterwards such as in "The Secret of Bruce Wayne," reprinted in Kane, *Batman* 72–73. In a 1952 story he guest-lectured on criminology at State University ("The Man Behind the Red Hood" in *Batman: From the 30s to the 70s,* 100–112). By such civic activities the camp 1960s television series was inspired.

Though strange science fiction adventures were a mainstay of Batman stories in the latter 1950s and into the 1960s, these have been considered lean years (*Greatest Batman Stories*, "Endnotes" 347). By the mid–1960s, DC Comics was concerned about the vitality of the Batman series. Jack Schiff, who had edited the stories for over two decades and had managed to weather the silly science fiction era, had begun bringing back the classic villains. He was replaced by Julius Schwartz in 1964, who set out to revive the Batman ethos. The "new look" he soon ushered in was most immediately distinguished by a more realistic drawing style, the most distinctive version being Carmine Infantino's more limber figures in larger panels. It was at this time that the first significant change in Batman's costume was made: the bat symbol on his chest was enclosed in a yellow oval to mimic the Batsignal. The stories also returned to an emphasis on crime and detection. After years of service, the 1950s Batmobile was exchanged for a lower, sleeker model and all the additional members of the Batman family from the 1950s were dropped. At this time, interest in popular mass-mediated art or "pop art" was growing, and comics were included in the new appreciation of the movies and other popular culture artifacts.

ABC's adaptation of Batman into a television series exploited this interest in popular art by creating a camp version of the Dynamic Duo that, for differing reasons, appealed to both children and adults. In turn the Batman comics benefited from television's huge exposure of the characters to a mass audience. The television series had adapted the Batman stories and given them a parodic twist. Although the comics never went strongly in that direction, the success of the series encouraged the comic to become lighter in tone (Vaz 95). It also led to the creation, in the comic books, of a new Batgirl, at the behest of the *Batman* series producer William Dozier, because of the perceived need in the show for a female interest. Her introduction in the comic books was made to coincide with the appearance of the character on the series in 1967.

The end of the television series also signaled the beginning of another new approach to the Batman stories. Since the "new look" era had begun, a more realistic art style and a reemphasis on detective work had characterized the Batman comics. The character was now to be moved back further to the style of his first year of publication, when Batman was a solitary figure who sought to avenge his parents' murders by "warring on all criminals" (*Archives* 67). Robin was moved off to college and Bruce Wayne changed his residence to a downtown penthouse. More importantly, in the late 1960s and early 1970s, writer Dennis O'Neil and artist Neal Adams collaborated on renovating the depiction of Batman. The realistic "new look" was moved stylistically further toward a darker mood and setting. "The Batman" according to O'Neil and Adams was grimmer and less concerned with law enforcement and more with rough justice. Adams brought an illustrator's skill with anatomy to Batman's physical form. Artistically, his cowl's ears were lengthened; his cape grew longer and billowed out dramatically, as if part of him. He now had a more intimidating attitude and a scarier presence. Gone was the "ebullient scoutmaster" as O'Neil referred to the Caped Crusader of the 1950s (quoted in Pearson and Uricchio 19). It is this general depiction that has continued until now. Fan response was very positive and soon other artists and writers assigned to Batman stories were emulating the style.

Comics historians Will Jacobs and Gerard Jones indicate that, though this new style became the accepted depiction of Batman, the artists and writers doing the stories were not always as good as the innovators had been (172). Whereas the previous eras were characterized by a team staying on a comic book title for years, offering a consistency of story and art, the new artists and writers served brief tenures (a practice begun by Adams) that resulted in inconsistent quality in the Batman titles. According to O'Neil, by 1986, the series "was in a curious kind of doldrums" (*Hero* 34). Within the next year, however, the character would once more be revitalized by the work of Frank Miller, who would write two multi-part stories: *Batman: The Dark Knight Returns*, which he also drew, and *Batman: Year One*. *The Dark Knight Returns* is set in Batman's near future, when, ten years after he has been forced to retire by the federal government, the extreme levels of crime and corruption in Gotham City force the reemergence of Bruce Wayne's alter ego. As a middle-aged Batman fights many of his old foes for the last time, the story grows increasingly dystopian and apocalyptic. In contrast, *Batman: Year One* retold Batman's origin from the parallel perspectives of Bruce Wayne and James Gordon, the police commissioner-to-be, then a lieutenant on the force. Miller's device of substituting running internal monologues in boxes over the panels instead of thought balloons added a novelistic, psychological point of view that allowed for greater fleshing out of the characters as well as a greater degree of realism. Both stories pushed the traditional ethos of the Batman stories to violent extremes and were plotted with much more complexity than before; they also explored more sophisticated themes than the usual comics tale. Both stories were printed on high quality paper with artwork colored in subtle, muted tones to match the story's mood. Their popularity and positive critical response resulted in the Batman titles (as well as other comic book characters) turning to darker stories. It also fueled enthusiasm for the Warner Bros. film *Batman*, released in 1989.

Since then, the success of graphic novels has produced a proliferation of other works, printed in the so-called "prestige format" by various writers with varying artistic styles. The creative expansions ventured in different directions, allowing a multitude of different interpretations of the Batman character. *The Killing Joke*, written by Alan Moore, takes the Batman-Joker relationship to new psychological depths as Batman's foremost foe performs unspeakable acts to taunt Batman and draw him into a confrontation. *Gotham by Gaslight* sets the Batman mythos in the late 19th century, where Batman hunts for Jack the Ripper. *Batman and Dracula: Red Rain* pits the fictional characters against each other in a horrific battle that results in Dracula's demise but at the cost of Batman's becoming a vampire, albeit a "good" one. These two stories were part of the DC Comics "Elseworlds" series, which feature "imaginary" tales of familiar characters in alternative realities, allowing writers greater freedom with storylines. Both in a wider range of narratives and artistic renderings, this era, Les Daniels remarks, introduced "an editorial policy of accommodation to artistic vision." Striking in its diversity, this new look contrasted with the decades of the Kane-modeled depiction, followed by years of the Adams-based model. Les Daniels quotes Batman editor Denny O'Neill as saying, "We now say that Batman has two hundred suits hanging in the Batcave so they don't have to look the same" (Daniels and Kidd 159).

The flood of new perspectives also brought about the creation of three new ongoing Batman titles. *Legends of the Dark Knight* began shortly after the 1989 movie and typically featured a multi-part story set in the earliest days of Batman's career (pre–Robin). A different writer and artist handled each story. *Shadow of the Bat,* which began a few years later, was printed in the "prestige format" and drawn in a less traditional style. When Warner Bros.' *Batman: The Animated Series* debuted, so did the comic title *The Batman Adventures,* drawn in the style used in the series. Intended for a generally younger audience, it is set in a separate continuity (or history) from the established one on *Batman* and *Detective Comics.* No other character in the comic book industry has inspired so many different visions, all extrapolating from the same basic story to explore new narrative directions.

The images on page 42 demonstrate how the character's depiction has developed over the decades. In each era, artists seem to find a version of Batman to which his audience finds a renewed response. The explanation for such fecundity lies in the character's origin and personality as it has been developed over the years.

Comics scholar Paul Crutcher asserts that many of the Batman narratives, such as those described above, can "provide unique complexity not found in prose-based novels and traditional films" (53). Grounding his discussion in McCloud's and others' theoretical analyses of the comics medium, comics'

Four eras of Batman.
A (top left): Batman as he first appeared in 1939 (from Mark Cotta Vaz, *Tales of the Dark Knight*). B (top right): The Golden Age look from 1950 (from *Detective Comics* #235, September 1956). C (bottom left): Neal Adams's grim vigilante from 1970 (from Cary Bates and Bob Haney, *Batman by Neal Adams*). D (bottom right): Synthesis—The early 1990s animated style from *Batman: The Animated Series* (from http://www.digitalspy.com/tv/tubetalk/a443472/batman-the-animated-series-tube-talk-gold.html).

visual and verbal ability to control the reader's perception of many elements including atmosphere, story time, multiple parallel psychological perspectives, Crutcher argues that even one graphic novel, *Arkham Asylum,* a psychodrama pitting Batman against the Joker and other denizens of the sanitarium, is "evidence enough to validate comics and graphic novels as something at least as worthy of critical attention as literature and film" (63). Since the 1980s, Batman has, more than any other superhero, inspired artistically complex narratives from multiple creators. As writers and artists have mined the inherent duality and depth of character of the Dark Knight, Batman's narratives have been able to progress, from the initially primitive, then Golden Age classic story mode, to a mature art form.

Profile of Batman

For several months after his debut in 1939, readers followed the Batman's adventures, wondering what it was that drove this character to pursue this dangerous mission. They had their questions answered five issues after Batman's debut when, in *Detective Comics* #33, a two-page origin tale began the story. A model of conciseness at less than a page-and-a-half of actual panels, the action begins in the first panel as Bruce Wayne's parents are accosted by a gunman demanding their valuables. In the next panel Bruce's father is shot, as is his mother in the third panel. The next two panels depict the tearful young Bruce in shock, gazing at his dead parents crying, "Father ... Mother! ... Dead! They're D. . Dead!" (reprinted in Daniels and Kidd 34–35). The next panel depicts young Bruce Wayne kneeling by his bedside making a vow: "And I swear by the spirits of my parents to avenge their deaths by spending the rest of my life warring on all criminals." The following two panels show a grown Bruce, first in a laboratory becoming a "master scientist," and then dressed only in trunks, lifting a great barbell overhead as he "trains his body to physical perfection until he is able to perform amazing athletic feats." Over the next three panels we see Wayne sitting in the great room of his family's manor home (indicative of his wealth), as he broods on how to accomplish his mission. Recognizing the need for a disguise, he muses: "Criminals are a superstitious cowardly lot. So my disguise must be able to strike terror into their hearts. I must be a creature of the night, black, terrible...." Then a huge bat flies through the window into the room. "A bat! That's it!" Wayne exclaims, "It's an omen. I shall become a *bat* !" The last panel shows Batman on a rooftop, crouched to leap, silhouetted with three bats against the large full moon, with the caption, "And thus is born this weird figure of the dark ... this avenger of evil, '*the Batman*'" (67).

This origin story has been recounted innumerable times but has never been essentially altered. Batman editor Dennis O'Neil, discussing why this is so, when other superhero characters' origin stories have been changed and sometimes radically updated, stated that Batman's story has never changed because of its being, in his words, "perfect. When the question of changing it came up, I said, 'How are you going to improve on this?' It simply in one incident explains everything that anybody will ever need to know about the character" (quoted in Pearson and Uricchio 24). Thus vengeance for his parents' murders is directed at the criminal community at large in a quest that can never be fulfilled, only pursued in installments. The quest is a search for justice beyond that of mere law enforcement. Batman must operate outside of legal methods to seek justice. Rather than wearing the uniform of sanctioned officialdom, he wears a strange costume designed to instill fear in the criminal heart. As Arthur Asa Berger puts it in his essay on Batman, "When he takes on his disguise he becomes a grotesque, a macabre figure whose sacred mission is to battle other grotesques" (163).

The singular qualities of the Batman character are seen even more clearly when contrasted with another Golden Age superhero, the Flash. Begun in the 1940s, the original character was Jay Garrick, a college student who gained his powers in a laboratory accident. Soon, clad in lightning-streaked blue tights and red jersey, with winged boots and a helmet like the Greek god Mercury, he sped about, fighting crime. After the war he, like so many other superheroes, sped from the comic shelves. In the 1950s, DC sought to revive some of its Golden Age heroes by reinventing them with new characters. Thus the Flash was now Barry Allen, a police scientist and fan of the old *Flash* comic book character that gained his powers in another lab accident when lightning struck some chemicals. The Flash's rebirth sparked what became known as the Silver Age of comics, characterized in DC's case by more revivals of Golden Age characters that recall their predecessors but were more up to date with the then-current popular interest in science fiction. Later in the Silver Age, DC's main competitor, Marvel Comics, made radical innovations by creating characters with recognizable human problems and conflicts.

This moving of characterization toward realism eventually revolutionized the comic industry. Years later, Marvel would outsell DC in books, partly because DC's stable of characters were conceived as less psychologically complex. The Barry Allen/Flash adventures continued for decades until DC, by now overwhelmed with a myriad of superpowered characters, decided to clean house in a one-year series of stories entitled *Crisis on Infinite Earths.* Certain characters were no longer viable. In the story, Flash, to save the world, sacrifices himself and is killed. Soon, his boy sidekick, Wally West/Speedy, now a young man, takes on the Flash identity. The new incarnation featured livelier characterization and stronger youth appeal, including West's sleeping with his girlfriend. This need to make major changes in a character to maintain its viability can be explained in part by the essential one-dimensionality of a character like the Flash, whose chief characteristic is his speed. Such simplicity inspires and is inspired by no great themes, and such a character symbolizes no larger concerns other than the fantasy of super speed. To keep him interesting, his creators must, over the succeeding generations, keep the superpower the same, but update the person with the power. Indeed, in 2008, DC brought Barry Allen back as the Flash in another comic book resurrection.

Batman/Bruce Wayne escaped this predicament through containing in his origin, as Dennis O'Neil said, all that one needed to know about the character. There is such richness in the original concept that, though Batman goes through periodic adjustments to meet the perceived audience desires of the times, he maintains, nonetheless, his mythic core, an appeal that transcends the colorful traits and trappings of the genre.

Personality Characteristics

As stated earlier, Batman's persona can be divided into two main aspects: a highly rational mind committed to the scientific detection of crime and an animal instinctiveness, relentlessly focused on the pursuit of criminals. This expression of divergent qualities creates the dichotomy that makes the Batman character so compelling. The rational/scientific aspect is expressed in Batman's meticulous examination of forensic evidence. Scott Bukatman observes, "Batman inherits from the urban pulp tradition of The Shadow and The Spider, and there is more than a little Holmes and Dupin in his ratiocentrism"(203). In fact, Batman has credited Sherlock Holmes as one of his inspirations and in one story, the two great detectives met in *Detective Comics,* vol. 1, #572. The Batcave contains a modern laboratory and a huge crime computer, where clues can be examined and files accessed to enable correct deductions.

Batman's animal instinctiveness, a relentless, predatory drive, allows him the full expression of his grim determination to track down wrongdoers. Trained in all manner of martial arts and equipped with an arsenal of nonlethal devices for attacking the enemy, he brings a superhuman will to his war on crime. With a character this grimly determined to bring criminals to justice, the tendency for his creators to make him judge, jury, and executioner was strong. In his seminal issues, Batman was known to use a gun when necessary, or, when wrestling with thugs on a rooftop, to toss one or two to their likely demise. In a Bill Finger story in *Batman* #1, the crimefighter pursues two men driving a truck carrying a giant, created by Prof. Hugo Strange, to wreak havoc. Swooping down in the Batplane, he cuts loose with his mounted machine guns on the truck. *"Much as I hate to take human life, I'm afraid this time it's neces-*

sary!" (*Greatest Batman Stories* 45). Surviving the attack, the giant is then lassoed around the neck by Batman from his plane and lifted up until he hangs to death. "He's probably better off this way," Batman remarks (46). The last giant climbs the top of a great skyscraper à la *King Kong* and, dislodged by Batman's gas pellets, falls to his death.

Steranko reports that readers were appalled by Batman's use of a gun. Finger admitted: "I goofed. I had Batman use a gun to shoot a villain and I was called on the carpet by [executive editor] Whit Ellsworth. He said, 'Never let us have Batman carry a gun again.' He was right" (47). The fictional shooting resulted in the company creating an editorial code to govern the behavior of its heroes. Thus, Batman's personal code arose out of the moral climate of his audience. Contemporary editorial policy remains the same. Former editor and writer Dennis O'Neil comments that he must edit stories that have Batman kill someone. "I think this is not something he does. The trauma that made him Batman had to do with a wanton waste of life. That same trauma that makes him go catch criminals will forbid his ever taking a life" (quoted in Pearson and Uricchio 19).

It is Batman's relentlessness, expressed in his grim demeanor, that fuels his ability to instill fear in criminals by his very appearance. In the story "Batman for a Night," in *Detective* 417, Jan Paxton, a reporter who engages in occupations, à la George Plimpton, in order to write about them firsthand, asks Batman to let him fill his boots for a night." Confronting some truck hijackers, Paxton grabs one of their guns and orders them to surrender. The gunman instinctively scoffs at Paxton, sensing he is a phony. At that moment the real Batman swings down and the gunman knows something is different. "Why is m-my hand sh-shaking s-so?" he wonders (11). Dispatching the gunman, Batman rebukes Paxton for "dirtying your hands with a—gun! And smearing my name in front of the human filth I fight! The Batman never uses a gun! He uses only the decent weapons of outrage and indignation to bring criminals to justice! Put that in your article!" (12).[1] It is Batman's ferocious obsession with the eradication of crime that fuels his mission. The tenuous balance between his coolly rational side and his obsessive quest for justice is one of the chief reasons that Batman remains an intriguing character.

Components of the Batman Mythos

Over the span of more than 70 years that the Batman stories have been produced, certain constants have remained in place almost without interruption. These have withstood trends and vicissitudes to become the enduring ingredients of the Batman "legend." The following are not listed in any order of importance.

Acrobatic Adventures and Hairbreadth Escapes

As his origin story related, Bruce Wayne trained his body to perfection, and the typical depiction of the Caped Crusader shows him swinging through a cityscape (his Bat-rope having no visible means of support). More at home above the ground, he patrols Gotham City as much from its heights as from street level. The vantage from this elevation has often enabled him to spot a situation requiring his services, whereupon he swoops down like his namesake to take action. From his first adventure in *Detective Comics* #27, when he is trapped in a gas-filled glass dome, up until the present, Batman stories have featured the Dark Knight in elaborate deathtrap predicaments, requiring all of his wits and skill to escape.

Alfred

Bruce Wayne's loyal butler, the family servant since Bruce's childhood, is one of the few persons to know Wayne is Batman. Introduced in the 1940s as a mystery-loving armchair sleuth, Alfred has served double-duty, maintaining order both in the Wayne Estate as well as in the Batcave. Especially since the early 1970s, when Dick Grayson went off to Hudson University, Alfred has served Robin's functions as a sounding board for Batman's musings and as a convenient victim for villains to snatch in order to be rescued by Batman. As Dennis O'Neil has pointed out, when he has had to write stories without Robin, he must make Alfred a little wittier to supply the needed levity that the Boy Wonder would have otherwise provided (quoted in Pearson and Uricchio 20). Alfred is often called upon to be the voice of caution and sanity to the driven personality of Batman. He is the one "ordinary" person in the Batcave and, thus, helps to maintain a degree of normalcy in Batman's world.

Commissioner Gordon

In the first story panel of the first Batman story in Detective #27 we see Bruce Wayne chatting with his friend, Police Commissioner Gordon. Wayne finds Gordon a useful source of information on the activities of the underworld. Gordon finds the "Bat-man" a meddling interference and orders him captured. Eventually, Gordon comes to trust Batman and sets up the Batsignal as a way of calling for his help. The meetings of the crusty Gordon and the aloof Batman next to the Batsignal on the rooftop of police headquarters are one of the constants of the Batman stories. Gordon's quasi-official working relationship with Batman (who has never revealed his true identity to him) legitimates the vigilante activities that would otherwise render him marginalized and unable to coordinate his efforts with the police. In a city steeped in crime and corruption, Gordon is the incorruptible lawman who recognizes Batman's value.

Detection

The ratiocinative aspect of Batman's persona is devoted to the meticulous investigation of crime, the influence of the aforementioned Sherlock Holmes in his character's DNA. His birth in *Detective Comics* has continually shaped his approach to crime solving, although his investigative style frequently slips from the cool, stoic, classic British mode to the fierce, violent, hard-boiled American approach that uses fear and coercion to obtain information. Writer Mark Cotta Vaz notes the way Batman (often referred to as the Darknight Detective) has achieved such a level of artistry in his detection skill that he operates as much by intuition as by logical deduction (104–106).

Gotham City

The first setting for Batman's urban adventures was New York City, but by the fourth issue of *Batman,* the venue was known as Gotham City, when Bill Finger, searching for an alternative to New York City, spotted the name "Gotham Jewelers" in the phone book (Kane, *Batman* 44). Although the dark and moody style established by Bob Kane and other artists was part of the Batman comics depiction, it contrasted sharply with the rather jovial turn Batman had taken following the introduction of Robin. Randy Duncan asserts that it took Gotham's development for Batman to become "a fully intellectualized icon, because he operated in a void ... Batman became more fully defined only as Gotham City became more fully defined" (*Rolling the Boulder* 153). Jimmy Stamp, a blogger on architecture, describes the relationship of Batman to Gotham thusly: "Perhaps more than any other person—real or fictional— Batman is integrally linked to his city, the city he has sworn to protect. In every sense of the word, he is a true avatar of Gotham. And Gotham City itself is an avatar, not only of the dreams of its fictional architects, but of our collective urban paranoia."

Dennis O'Neil describes the specific qualities of New York City that characterize Batman's Gotham: "'My standard definition of Gotham City is, it's New York below Fourteenth Street after eleven o'clock at night. Recognizably New York, but with emphasis on the grimmer aspects of the city'" (quoted in Vaz 66). As Batman was born of an urban crime, so his natural habitat is the urban setting of the corrupt, somewhat seedy environs of Gotham City. The writers of Batman stories have not missed the relation of "Gotham" to "gothic," with its associations of the darkly romantic, melodramatic, and grotesque. Scott Bukatman writes, "Gotham is a city defined more by its underworld. It's a concatenation of hidden spaces, corners and traps. This city needs to be read, deciphered, made legible, and the one to do it lives among the bats in his own subterranean hideout" (203). Gotham City is often depicted as a city arrested in its progress, overbuilt not with the smooth, gleaming glass towers of modernism, but rather with the often gargoyle-ornamented towers of stone and iron of an earlier age. Such anachronistic characteristics underline the tortured romantic nature of the city's hero, who crouches on a ledge, like one more watching gargoyle. Even though Gotham is his chief environment, Batman writers occasionally take him out of town, into the countryside, and even overseas for adventures.

Robin

The first year of his career in comics, Batman waged a solitary war on crime. Bob Kane felt that, for a number of reasons, Batman should have a partner in crimefighting. He believed that young readers would identify with a character their age who could assist Batman in his adventures.

> I thought that every young boy would like to be like Robin; instead of having to wait to grow up to be a superhero, they wanted to be one now. A laughing daredevil ... living in a mansion over the Bat Cave, riding in the Batmobile—he appealed to the imagination of every kid in the world [*Batman* 46].

There was also the practical consideration of narration, which was described by Finger: "The thing that bothered me was that Batman didn't have anyone to talk to, and it got a little tiresome always having him thinking. I found as I went along Batman needed a Watson to talk to. That's how Robin came to be" (quoted in Steranko 47).

Robin's real name is Dick Grayson. His parents were killed in a circus acrobatics disaster, their trapeze sabotaged by a protection gang. Bruce Wayne, essentially, took on the role of Dick's surrogate father (or perhaps that of an older brother). Bob Kane named this "Boy Wonder" Robin after Robin Hood, another famous role essayed by Douglas Fairbanks. In a way, this youthful figure was patterned after Kane himself. In his autobiography, Kane recalled one of his adolescent fantasies:

> I visualized myself as a young boy fighting alongside my idol, Douglas Fairbanks, Sr. I imagined that young boys reading about Batman's exploits would project their own images into the story and daydream about fighting alongside the Caped Crusader as junior Batmen [*Batman* 46].

Not everyone approved of Batman's new assistant. As cartoonist Jules Feiffer stated,

> I couldn't stand boy companions. If the theory behind Robin the Boy Wonder [and others] was to give young readers a character with whom to identify it failed dismally in my case. The super grown-ups were the ones I identified with. They were versions of me in the future [42–43].

Nevertheless, the Boy Wonder evidently did connect with the youthful readership, because in his tryout debut in *Detective* #38, twice as many issues sold, according to Kane's account (46). Robin was there to stay—for decades. His presence even precipitated a change in Batman's demeanor. This, apparently, was no accident. Robinson has been quoted as saying that Robin was added "in an effort to humanize Batman" (quoted in Steranko 47). Indeed, from the time of his first adventure with Robin, Batman registered much more than the occasional smile and soon even his appearance had changed from the sleek, eerie, slightly demonic-looking night creature to the smiling, short-eared, barrel-chested big-brother. The chemistry worked. As Batman editor and writer Dennis O'Neil noted, Robin's youthful enthusiasm helped to lighten the stories' dark tone. This "counterbalance" to Batman's grimness was a useful source of comic relief (Pearson and Uricchio 20). Kicking a criminal during one of their heroic adventures, Robin chirps, "A heel for a heel!" After a successful 30-year stretch as crime-solving partners, Batman and Robin went their separate ways. Dick Grayson left for college, allowing Batman to once again become a grim solo adventurer.

Strange Villains in Strange Crimes

Just as Kane and company had borrowed ideas and devices from other sources to create Batman, so they looked elsewhere for ideas for creating new villains. The pulps, of course, offered ready-made models of flamboyantly exotic types to emulate in the Batman stories. Mad scientists were some of the first to appear, such as Prof. Hugo Strange. The first major classic villain was the Joker, appearing in the first issue of *Batman*. The character was inspired by the playing card character, as well as by stills of the title character from the 1928 silent film *The Man Who Laughs*, an adaptation of Victor Hugo's novel *L'homme Qui Rit*. Viewed today, the pictures of Conrad Veidt as the character Gwynplaine, a man cursed with a permanent hideous grin, present a creepy real-life incarnation of Batman's greatest foe. Representing all that is chaotic and amoral in the world, the Joker kills for the thrill of it; he has been known to kill even his own henchmen on a whim. His role as bringer-of-chaos has often been expressed in his ability to easily take over radio and television air-waves in order to broadcast his threats to the city and his taunts to Batman. The Joker is an almost elemental force which, more than any other antagonist, represents all that Batman opposes.

Chester Gould's Dick Tracy has been credited as an inspiration for the "rogues' gallery" of bizarre villains, such as Pruneface and Flattop, that distinguished the Batman stories. However, Max Allen Collins, who has written for both the Dick Tracy comic strip and Batman comic books, points out that the Joker appeared prior to most of Tracy's weird villains (quoted in Vaz 155). Villains usually had a device or "hook," a concept or motif that defined them. Two-Face was Harvey Dent, a zealous district attorney whose life was ruined when a criminal tossed acid in his face, destroying half of his handsome countenance. The physical scarring created a psychological one and, sliding into insanity, Dent split into a dual persona. By the flip of his scarred coin he would decide at a given point whether to do good or evil, to keep stolen goods or give them to charity, to kill or to spare. Everything was viewed in terms of two. Batman has sought, through the years, to save Dent and help restore his old friend to wholeness, with little lasting success.

Two-Face and the Joker represent the truly crazed side of the rogue's gallery, which includes others who are no longer in their right minds. It is their mono-mania that produces their criminal identity, often because of some trauma that pushed them over the edge of sanity. When captured by Batman, they are returned to Gotham's mental health facilities, typically Arkham Asylum, rather than prison. These and many others follow the pattern of a soul subjected to a traumatic event, followed by a descent into an obsessive commitment to terrible, elaborate crimes. Despite their insanity, these villains seem lucid enough to plot and appreciate the chaos they create. As their counterpart, Batman is equally traumatized but has turned his obsessions to the pursuit of justice, tinged with vengeance. Other villains, lacking the psychosis to qualify them for commitment, are still obsessive enough to organize their criminal efforts around their personal fetish or theme. The Scarecrow is fascinated with the study of the effects of fear and uses chemicals to reduce his "subjects" to states of abject terror. The Penguin is a frustrated social climber whose crimes have bird themes. The Riddler cannot resist leaving riddles as clues to his crimes, just for the challenge it gives to Batman. The never-ending merry-go-round of Batman's tracking, fighting, and capture of his antagonists, until their next escapade, is the narrative continuum of the Batman legend.

Technological Devices

Batman's war on criminals is often facilitated by some device Batman has brought with him, either on his yellow utility belt, or somewhere else on his costume. The well-known gadgets with the "Bat" prefix (batarang, Bat-rope, etc.) are all crafted to be compact (they never show until needed) and efficacious in giving Batman the edge he needs against heavily armed and fortified opponents. Bruce Wayne's vast fortune is directed at the invention and construction of an ingenious fleet of vehicles, all featuring the bat motif, to transport Batman and Robin to their adventures. The finned Batmobile is the most well known and most used but it is accompanied by the Batplane, Batboat, Whirligigs (small, personal helicopters), and others, as the need requires. In this shrewd and unquestioning use of technology, Batman was a true 20th- (and now 21st-) century hero, using his devices as extensions of himself. This modern hero has the financial means to compensate for what he lacks in superpowers by creating devices that empower him, a logical development of the origin story's self-improvement motif, whereby Bruce Wayne transforms himself into an unbeatable foe of crime.

Batman's Adaptability to Changing Times

An examination of Batman's ability to change with the times while retaining his mythic core is aided by looking briefly at movie genres. Louis Giannetti describes the four stages of cycles movie genres tend to run in over their development and history (348). For a film genre like the western, it's possible to trace its development through decades of development. The primitive stage, when the story form is new, novel, and naïve, sets up the basic formula, conventions, and function of a genre. Here, foundational films like *The Great Train Robbery* (1903) established a crude structure that would survive through the silent era and up to the present time. The western grew in length as narrative films grew in running time, pacing the progress of film technology.

It's generally agreed that the primitive phase of westerns ended in 1939 when John Ford's *Stagecoach* brought the genre to its classic stage and narratives took on a more adult sensibility. Giannetti attributes to this stage "such classical ideals as balance, richness and poise. The genre's values are assured and widely shared by the audience" (Ibid.). As the audience shared the western's ideology of westward expansion in growing and completing the American nation, so the western prospered in valorizing this vision of Manifest Destiny. However, no genre is static, and each genre film adds to the sum of the total genre's meanings and interacts with the audience's sense of time and history. By the 1950s, some westerns manifested a revisionist take on the genre, becoming "more symbolic, ambiguous, less certain of its values," and increasing in stylistic complexity (Ibid.). The audience becomes more aware of the conventions that it had earlier unconsciously enjoyed, now quite accustomed to the tropes and themes, but open to new interpretations of the western myth, even a demythologized one. Films like John Ford's *The Man Who Shot Liberty Valance* (1962) reexamined the vision of this most mythmaking of western directors, questioning the notion of the western hero as he had presented it in many classic films. Once a film genre has become overly familiar to the audience, it may be only a short time before the last stage, the parodic, arrives, as it did with such comedies as *Cat Ballou* (1965) and *Blazing Saddles* (1974). Humor in these films arises usually because we, the audience, understand the source of the jokes taken from the older films whose golden tropes are long since played out creatively.

Though a genre has run through all four stages, this doesn't necessarily signal its creative exhaustion. Giannetti asserts that the western saw examples of returns to classical form such as Clint Eastwood's *Pale Rider* (1985), although it's clear Eastwood took his western gunman persona in the revisionist direction with *Unforgiven* (1992). Similarly, the comics' depiction of Batman found renewal after its parodic stage by O'Neil and Adams returning the character to his primitive depiction of a nocturnal avenger but with stronger ideals of balance, richness, and poise. In that sense, this "neo-classical" phase took note of its contemporary audience—not just young boys, but older readers who appreciated the superhero's original qualities.

Finding the presentational style appropriate to its time has kept Batman in a state of continuing popularity. The history of the Batman comic books demonstrates the ingenuity of its creators and editors in retaining the core elements of the story while remaining flexible enough to allow changes— sometimes subtle, sometimes not—in order to keep the character fresh and appealing. As was seen in the comparison of Batman's history with the Flash's, there is a compelling essence to the Dark Knight that keeps him as viable as he is. Rather than being subjected to radical changes in personality or identity, as has happened to other superheroes, Batman contains within himself an inherent flexibility without great risk of compromise. In an extended story arc, "Knightfall," Bruce Wayne is badly injured and replaced as Batman by a vicious and unstable man, partly to test whether his audience would accept a meaner, grittier version of the hero more in keeping with current (1990s) comic characters. To the editors' relief, readers rejected this new "interpretation" as a complete violation of the Batman character. Batman is a known quantity which will not stand fundamental changes. Batman, as he has been known for over 70 years, contains a complex of mythic traits that readers have come to know and expect. In the next chapter I will seek to elaborate the ways in which Batman is mythic and how this contributes to his enduring popularity.

• 3 •

Mythic Characteristics in Batman

In real life, criminals have a penchant for assigning nicknames to each other (like Vincent "Mad Dog" Coll or John Gotti, the "Dapper Don") and in comics, sometimes, gangsters refer to Batman as "the Bat." This moniker seems to capture his essential quality. They know he must be a man, but their naming emphasizes the guise Bruce Wayne chose to scare—or at least unsettle—the criminal class. By choosing the bat motif, and assuming the creature's appearance, he begins the process of transformation into a mythic being. These mythic qualities fall into two basic categories: his duality and his symbolic appeal as a hero figure. Aspects of duality include his liminality or his interstitiality, i.e., the ways Batman partakes of categorically different qualities in one being. These and other distinct qualities are essential to the maintaining of Batman's intriguing mystique. It is through this ability to encapsulate the wish-fulfillment of societal concerns about crime and chaos that he becomes a mythically cloaked reflection of readers' hopes, fears, and values.

Batman's Duality

Dual identity is one of the more common traits shared by classic superheroes. An established convention well before Batman's creation, it was a device used by Zorro, the Green Hornet, and the Shadow, among others. When Superman was created, the use of a dual identity reached its most explicit expression up to that time. The ordinary male reader identifying with mild-mannered Clark Kent could vicariously enjoy Kent's secret identity as Superman. The dual identify as a mythical pattern, noted by Eliade, has already been mentioned. When Batman was created by Bob Kane, the secret identity device was retained, patterned this time after the familiar rich man/masked hero motif (e.g., Don Diego/Zorro and Lamont Cranston/The Shadow). Like these nocturnal adventurers, Batman fit the type of the hero who must go outside the legal system to seek justice. Wayne's wealth functioned, in a sense, as a partial substitute for the superpowers he lacked, since it enabled him to fund his "bat-technology," all the vehicles and equipment needed to assist him in his battle against crime.

In "The Superhero's Two Worlds," Robert Inchausti examines the nature of the comic book hero's secret identity and suggests that the concept functions as a sort of audience fantasy of perfectly harmonized competing inner selves: the one which is publicly known and the secret, powerful self only we know. His analysis of Batman's duality can offer helpful insights into his mythos.

> The two poles of the superhero are the two poles of human experience. On the one hand there is the world of power and pure possibility depicted by the surrealistic iconography of bizarre villains, time warps, interpenetrating dimensions, invisible forces, magic allies and sacred objects such as Kryptonite. It is a mythological world whose imagery inspires our spiritual aspirations and desires [68].

On the other hand, Inchausti notes, the everyday world is prosaic and literal and it is this world the superhero protects from the forces of the mythic one. By doing so, the delicate balance of his dualistic life is maintained. According to this view, Batman is actually in perfect psychological harmony as he actively and consciously negotiates between the two worlds. This view contrasts with that of Batman as a character who is somewhere between neurotic and insane, as he has, at times, been characterized. Inchausti notes how the cosmos of Batman's adventures are on a mythic plane, where values and characteristics are overt and "exteriorized," i.e., internalized qualities are plainly revealed. The mythic self of Batman that Bruce Wayne has chosen to become is fiercely guarded to enable him to stave off the "killing literalism" of being merely the prosaic Bruce Wayne (Inchausti 71).

This interpretation of the superhero's dual identity as applied to Batman is interesting less for its psychological focus than for the way Inchausti describes a type of fiction in which values, characteristics, and morality may be overtly expressed. Through the device of the dual identity, the character is allowed to enter an existence that is larger than the mundane life. This new plane allows for the existence of the character as someone purely devoted to justice and vengeance in a way the mundane world will not allow. Here, Wayne can become a being capable of feats he could never accomplish as his literal self. This "exteriorization" of internal characteristics and desires is a chief characteristic of superhero comics (as well as of many fantasy stories) and it characterizes mythical beings as well. As a narrative device, the secret identity—the mask, if you will—is the door to a mythic world. Like Tarzan, much of Batman's appeal lies in his dual citizenship in both the mundane and the mythic realms. Being the human Bruce Wayne, the character shares our mortality. As Batman, the character transcends his ordinary humanity to rise to a mythic plane and we, the audience, rise with him.

"Why bats, Master Wayne?"

Alfred's query to Bruce Wayne in *Batman Begins* is the key to the character's mythic core. Bats are liminal creatures, flying mammals that have long carried loaded meanings in various cultures. Being nocturnal hunters who sleep upside down in caves by day, with their webbed wings, fangs, that associate them with vampires, they spark the mythic imagination. Writing in *The Continuum Encyclopedia of Animal Symbolism in Art*, Hope V. Werness notes, "Bats are nocturnal and thus they are linked with the dark underworld of the earth's interior and the realm of death." From the beginning of Batman's run in comics, his adventures were often associated with morbid elements, such as ancient castles, fiendish villains, and vampires. In the previous chapter, Grant Morrison's discussion of Batman and Superman highlights the contrast between the sunlit and modern urban settings of the Man of Steel's adventures and the moonlit and shadowed world of Batman. Werness continues: "For Romantic poets and artists, the bat evoked night, mystery, haunted ruins and lonely places" (32). The urban setting of Gotham City, of course, is an alternate name for New York City, but also lends itself to "gothic," with its links to mystery, ancient curses, horror, and other lurid elements. Finally, Werness notes that "like Durer, Goya linked the bat to melancholy." In the traumatic events of Bruce Wayne's childhood, to his brooding discovery and adopting of the bat motif, to his unending struggle against the warped psyches of his rogue's gallery, the symbol of the bat unites Batman in an iconicity of related themes.

Liminality

Considering the depiction of the Wayne/Batman character, a question arises. Has Bruce Wayne *chosen* to take on the guise of a great bat to pursue his war on crime? Or, as some stories such as *The Dark Knight Returns* suggest, was Wayne himself *chosen* the night the bat flew into his study? He remains haunted by visions of a great bat that defined him, marked him out to become something more than a masked vigilante. Taking on the guise of a bat and preying on criminals, Batman becomes a creature of the night, yet remains a man.

The concept of liminality becomes useful, if applied here, to understand Batman's dual nature. The state of being liminal has to do with being on a threshold, in a doorway between two places. Liminality therefore is the condition of being between spheres or states.[1] Another word, "interstitiality," is akin to it, being a state of conflicting categories, or of possessing traits of more than one nature or form. A bat is itself a liminal creature, being a mammal that flies, seemingly defying the natural division of creation that divides birds from nursing animals. Throughout his book on horror, Noël Carroll discusses the concept of interstitiality as characteristic of the horror monster, which usually combines two distinct traits not found in nature. The Creature from the Black Lagoon was a being which, though human-shaped, had gills and fins like a fish, a sort of fish-man.[2] It is this sort of combination that horrifies and disgusts, yet fascinates audiences (Carroll 185). Borrowing from the work of Mary Douglas on interstitiality, Noël Carroll discusses horror in terms of purity and impurity: monsters, having traits from diverse categories, are impure and therefore both revolting and fascinating. Carroll's discussion is directed to the nature of horror in narrative forms, yet this concept can apply to a heroic figure, such as Batman, as well. Though the physical traits of Batman are not grotesque enough to make him monstrous, they do diverge enough to make him eerie and fearsome. Human in form, he possesses characteristics that suggest something other than the human. His horned head and pale white slits for eyes immediately suggest the demonic or creaturely. It is, in this sense, that Carroll's notion of a fascinating impurity applies. It is this quality of liminality or interstitiality that accounts, in part, for Batman's intriguing nature, for it is a complex duality that encompasses numerous symbolic meanings. This is a character devoted to both justice and vengeance. He fights for light with darkness. He is both human and animal. It is this complexity that conveys mythic qualities to readers, since much of what we know as mythical contains such dualities.

Related to Batman's liminal nature is his *ambiguity,* the manner in which it is not always clear what motivates his mission. Is it vengeance or justice? Does he sometimes use more than the requisite force to subdue and capture criminals, or is he meting out (non-lethal) punishment, too? Does he distinguish between taking revenge; that is, attacking criminals based on his personal hatred of all wrongdoers in which he ritually punishes proxies for the murderer of his parents, or is he, rather, avenging society's victims, warring on criminals on their behalf? No matter what a particular story may claim, a large part of Batman's appeal is the intriguing lack of certainty, the mystery that obscures his deepest drives. In that sense, Batman remains open to various interpretations both by his writers and by those seeking to determine his enduring appeal. Hence, the variety of scholarly analyses in the previous chapter which alternately argue for either Batman as Nietzschean superman or Aristotle's virtuous hero. It is the very complexity of this character's levels of dualistic, or even multiple, aspects that continues to fascinate readers and is an expression of his mythic nature.

Mythical Creatures and Masks

Mythologies contain many creatures that share the physical traits of more than one creature. Centaurs have the body of a horse, atop which sit the trunk, arms, and head of a man, and are usually characterized by cruelty, savagery, and drunkenness (Guirand 185). Satyrs have human faces and trunks but with ape-like facial features and the legs of a goat. They are known for their lechery and maliciousness. Characteristically, in such mythical beings, their inner nature is exteriorized in their appearance. In his appearance, also, Batman suggests dual qualities of being both human and animal. His mask covers only half his face. The top half of his head is covered by the bat-like horned cowl with only mysterious white slits where eyes should be. The bottom half of the face features the human mouth and jaw. The dualistic symbolism of Batman's head could not be plainer. His costume of gray bodysuit, black trunks, and boots display his human physical prowess, but this is contrasted by the creaturely quality of the wing-like billowing black cape with its serrated edge.

In his dissertation, Ralph Randolph Duncan refers to the recurrence of animal symbols in ancient cultures, where warriors wore the skin and horns of slain beasts, and in contemporary comics, where many characters are named after and bear the motifs of certain animals. Such characters, he says, are "a melding of man and beast; these characters actually possess the abilities of the creatures whose names they take. They are humankind's subconscious urges personified" (46). Batman, he says, is one of the purer examples of such a character. "In the symbol of the bat both primitive animalistic urges and primitive fear of what waits in the shadows just beyond the glow of the fire or the glare of the street light combine in a frightful manifestation" (47). More than a costume, Batman's attire is also the outward expression of his mythic persona.

Mircea Eliade's description of the universal ritual use of masks is useful in a discussion of the mythic aspects of Batman's disguise. One of the several types of ritualistic uses of masks is the war mask: "War masks are fashioned to frighten and paralyze the enemy; they represent terrifying monstrous faces" (*Masks* 64). Such was Bruce Wayne's intention in designing the Bat-mask. "My disguise must be able to strike terror into their hearts," he says in Batman's origin story. "I must be a creature of the night, black, terrible ... a bat!" (*Archives* 67). This he accomplishes: criminals are often startled by the sudden appearance of this great bat creature plunging down upon them. This criminal-specific nature of this frightening effect is exemplified in a Batman story in which Bruce Wayne takes three "ghetto-hardened kids" on a camping trip (*Greatest* 208–213). Sitting around a campfire, the three boys describe their respective perceptions of Batman's prowess, each offering a different version of a great mythical night creature with uncanny powers, performing incredible exploits. Wayne is amazed at how his adventures have become so exaggerated through the imagination of these boys. As the three boys argue over what Batman is *really* like, Wayne steps out of the firelight into the darkness, saying, "Let me tell you what *I* think, fellas." Then, as Batman, he leaps into their circle of light, proclaiming, "The Batman looks like this!" At this, the boys scoff at him for his weak impersonation of their hero and roll over and go to sleep. In the last panel, Batman is left standing sheepishly by the fire, thinking, "Hmm, what ever else it proves—the Batman's frightening image scares the guilty ... not the innocent!" (213). This demonstration of the differing effects of his disguise seems almost supernatural.

In addition to war masks, Eliade further discusses the nature of certain practices among the Eskimos, that of using masks to affect magico-religious transformation. "The Eskimos," he writes, "believe that the wearer is mysteriously impregnated with the spirit represented by the mask: to put on the mask representing a totem is to become that totem" (65). Like the Eskimos, Siberian shamans use costumes featuring animal motifs such as the bird, deer, or serpent.

> The shaman possesses, among other powers, the ability to identify himself with an animal or magically to transform himself into an animal.... Mask or dress, the function is the same: to proclaim the incarnation of a mythological figure—a god, ancestor, or mystic animal. The mask effects the transubstantiation of the shaman, transforming him before everyone's eyes into the supernatural being he is impersonating [66].

Scott Bukatman discusses the use of mask in 18th century novels.

> The masquerade permits an uncanny return to an earlier animism. Identity is hidden, but upon this act of disguise something of the earlier talismanic power of the mask can again emerge [Bukatman, 213].

There is a certain resonance between these practices and the donning of the Batman costume. Bruce Wayne's diurnal nature subsides as the nocturnal

Batman "emerges" to pursue criminals. This perception of Wayne "becoming" the Batman is one of the most consistent traits of the stories. Rarely does Wayne perform any heroics. When danger arises, he somehow slips out of sight to reappear as the awe-inspiring Batman. It is as if the costume allows the Batman's complex nature to arise and do what Wayne cannot do. This transformation is understood by the adaptors of the character into animation. In *Batman: The Animated Series*, there are two distinct voices for Wayne and Batman, although the same actor performs them. Wayne's is masculine but pitched higher as the youthful voice of a rich playboy. As Batman, the voice is suddenly deeper, more raw and menacing. This is true of Batman even when he speaks to his confidants, Robin and Alfred, with whom he has no need to disguise his voice.

Dionysian Dualism

In addition to the dualistic liminality of Batman's character, a second type of duality emerges in Batman's personality. There is, first of all, the obvious difference between Wayne's role as playboy philanthropist wherein he is congenial, concerned, and businesslike on occasions, but not very compelling, and his other role as Batman, which brings forth the expressions of his darker passions. It is not always clear who is playing whom. Is Batman a means for Wayne to pursue his obsession with justice, or is Batman using Wayne as a harmless front to keep track of the city's criminal doings through his relationship with Commissioner Gordon? This is never clarified in the stories, which contributes to the character's enigmatic mystique. However, a more striking contrast with mythical overtones is the way in which Batman's character reflects the dualistic qualities of the Greek god Dionysus. The author of *The Dark Knight Returns,* Frank Miller, describes Batman as a "dionysian figure, a force for anarchy that imposes an individual order" (quoted in Sharrett 44). As the god of the vine, Dionysus possesses two natures reflecting the effects of drinking wine: a beneficence and joyfulness as well as cruel savagery (Hamilton 56). The only god who is the offspring of a god and a mortal, Dionysus was snatched from his dying mother and raised by nymphs. Later he would venture into Hades to retrieve his mother, Semele. Also known as the suffering god, Dionysus was each year torn apart at the coming of winter and his yearly resurrection brought the coming of spring.

Like Dionysus, Batman/Wayne has two natures, which, in his case, could be termed diurnal and nocturnal. Wayne is publicly perceived as a generally bright and carefree person who spends his days overseeing social functions and committing his wealth to good and charitable causes through the Wayne Foundation. Yet, when night falls, he descends from his manor home into the Batcave. In Greek myths, it was said that some of the entrances to Hades were found in caverns (Hamilton 39). Here Wayne changes his appearance to that of a black bat and journeys "down" to the streets of Gotham, where lawlessness runs rampant. The Greek myths recount that several heroes, such as Hercules and Orpheus, made their way to Hades to bring back those lost to its dominion. The traditional name for the mythical Hades has today come to refer to the scenes of modern urban criminal activity: the "underworld," the site of Batman's salvific activity. As Tarzan journeyed down into the valley of the lost city of Opar, following the classic pattern of a descent or *katabasis* into the netherworld (as noted in Holtsmark), so Batman makes his nightly descent. He descends to Gotham not only to fight evil but also to rescue its helpless victims of crime, surrogates for his slaughtered mother and father. Here he remains a liminal being, not officially recognized by the law but indispensable to it in a city overrun with corruption and disorder.

In addition to his liminal appearance, Batman's ambiguous nature also intimidates his foes because he is neither an official part of the legal establishment (and thus of society in general) nor a criminal like them. Not bound by due process, judicial restraints, or procedural technicalities, Batman is a wild card, a free agent who uses naked fear, threats, and violence to obtain information. His use of the bat motif mystique is calculated to render him terrible in the collective mind of the underworld, an effect far greater than he could achieve as a mere vigilante. It is also a real means of expressing the nature of his fearful relentlessness: he is one who battles darkness by taking on aspects of darkness. As Bruce Timm and Paul Dini, producers of *Batman: The Animated Series*, remarked in an interview, "He looks like a villain" (Dini and Timm). Eschewing daylight, he has made himself a mythic night-creature who is more fearsome than the criminals he pursues.

Like Dionysus, Wayne somehow grew up without parents. He, too, is a suffering figure, the traumatic memory of his parents' murders never far from his mind. These dionysian patterns in the Batman stories need not exactly reflect details of the Greek myths; it is enough that mythic significance resonates through allusion in the mythic actions of the Dark Knight.

As mentioned in the Introduction and Chapter 1, the Batman persona in itself is dualistic, divided into a highly sharpened human rationality on the one hand and a fierce predatory drive to pursue evildoers on the other. This is similar to the dualism of Tarzan, as mentioned in Chapter 1. Holtsmark has remarked, "Tarzan is repeatedly said to have a dual nature, one human and one animal ... Like the best heroic types, Tarzan fits into a genealogy that has roots in human and nonhuman worlds" (92). Unlike the relatively simple Superman, Batman carries within himself two extreme natures borne of his obsession with fighting crime. Only occasionally is the balance of these natures upset, and it is usually when the lower animal nature drives Batman to his limits. In 1993, the writers of the Batman comics decided to focus on the consequences of this imbalance. Over several months, Batman's near fanatical pursuit of criminals begins to result in physical and mental exhaustion, yet he refuses to draw back and pace himself. The "Knightfall" stories tell of the results of Batman's out-of-control relentlessness and his temporary forced withdrawal from battle after he is severely injured by the villain Bane.

Finally, Batman's duality extends to his mission. It is never made very clear to what degree he is motivated by the competing goals of justice and vengeance. The ratio of these goals has never been plainly fixed. There are times when Batman's mission seems focused solely on the detection and prevention of crimes and allowing the captured wrongdoers to be picked up by the police. At times his quest has seemed more like a sport than dangerous crime-fighting, especially in the earlier era when Batman and Robin merrily swung down upon hapless thugs, dispatching them in the midst of their caper. Only occasionally during this period did Batman's original craving for vengeance resurface, such as during a story when he saw a police photo of criminal Joe Chill, and recognized the killer of his parents (*Greatest* 66–78). Leaving Robin at home in this story, Batman strikes out alone to track down Chill. He finds his quarry, and is determined to deliver Chill to the authorities; however, he can find no proof of a specific crime with which Chill may be charged. Approaching Chill alone, Batman accuses him of killing the Waynes and unmasks himself before Chill to prove to him that he is an eyewitness. Still not taking the law into his own hands, Batman warns Chill he will always be watching him, waiting for a mistake. After delivering a left hook to his enemy, Batman leaves the room. The terrified Chill runs out to his cronies telling them what has happened, whereupon the enraged thugs shoot Chill, before he can reveal Batman's secret identity, for his responsibility in creating Batman, their chief nemesis.

Thus, Wayne's parents' killer is punished and his vengeance is obtained only indirectly and without his direct causation. DC's code against Batman killing is upheld while achieving a satisfying conclusion to Batman's "first case." In this story, Batman has suppressed his desire for vengeance against the single person responsible for his mission. Given that this story takes place during the more domesticated era of Batman's characterization, it appears that the writer and editor had Batman sublimate his desire for vengeance through the accomplishment of the ironic justice Chill receives from his cronies. Later, after

O'Neil and Adams had revived the original concept of the dark pursuer of criminals, Batman's tendency was to mete out a little punishment during the apprehension of criminals. Through his use of savage fighting techniques and skillful non-lethal devices to disarm and subdue, was he responding commensurately to the criminals' violent instigations or seeking to punish as well as subdue? Again, this is never clarified. To keep the legend fresh, DC retold the Joe Chill story at least once (*Batman: Year Two*) but, in a later revamping of the Batman historical time-line,[3] editors declared that Batman does not know who killed his parents. This revision kept Batman's quest for justice the focus and makes vengeance against the underworld generalized; that is, every criminal is symbolic of the original transgressor, and Batman pursues each as if he or she were that first destroyer of order. This justice vs. vengeance opposition, another aspect of his duality, is obscure, adding to the character's mystique.

Frank Miller's *The Dark Knight Returns* is a study in the nature of modern heroism in which, at one point, Commissioner Gordon explains to a female police captain, who dislikes Batman's vigilante ways, how the Batman transcends ordinary structures of order and behavior. Reminding her of how, in the 1940s, the U.S. populace was terrified by the bombing of Pearl Harbor, he points out that Roosevelt's leadership had inspired hope by "taking fear and turning it into a fighting spirit" (40). Discussing allegations that Roosevelt had known of the Japanese attack beforehand and had allowed it, Gordon concludes that the allegation

> wasn't *proven*. Things like that never are. I couldn't stop thinking how *horrible* that would be ... and how Pearl was what got us off our duffs in time to stop the *Axis*. But a lot of innocent men *died*. But we won the *war*. It bounced back and forth in my head until I realized I couldn't *judge* it. It was too big. *He* was too big [Ibid., original emphasis].

Gordon's inference is that some individuals defy normal categories and are of a different order. Batman, Gordon implies, is one of these individuals. This is one of the few moments of reflexivity in which the text of a Batman story overtly comments on its own evocation of his mythic nature. This mythic character's actions, to possess internal logic, must occur in a narrative environment where he will be appropriate, for in the "real" world, as with other romantic heroes, Batman would be impossible.

Sacred Time and Space

The necessary narrative environment for Batman is a location where values are highlighted and clear, where characters take on greater and more obvious symbolic meaning than in a realistic setting. It is helpful to refer to Mircea Eliade's concept of sacred time and space as described in *The Sacred & the Profane: The Nature of Religion* to build a conceptual framework for this mythic setting.

Eliade's description of archaic man's concept of sacred time pictures him invoking such a time through ritual retellings of the acts of gods and great heroes. Through this retelling, archaic man could move from profane, everyday time to sacred time. Ancient religious peoples viewed the world as chaotic until order is brought through ritual reenacting of the work of the gods in a place. The concept of sacred space involves the recognition that a certain earthly site has witnessed a breakthrough from another dimension, whether through ritual invocation or through the unilateral action of divine beings. This site is recognized as holy and, here, altars, temples, and other acknowledgments of the sacred are constructed. Some form of consecration, the expression of that group or tribe's beliefs, expressing a cosmological paradigm, occurs which creates sacred space, apart from the profane space without. Eliade notes that "if every inhabited territory is a cosmos, this precisely because it was first consecrated, because in one way or another, it is the work of the gods, or is in communication with the world of the gods" (30). Similarly, religious societies entered into sacred time through ritual evocation of a primordial moment. "Religious participation in a festival," Eliade states, "implies emerging from ordinary temporal duration and reintegration of the mythical time reactualized by the festival itself. Hence sacred time is indefinitely recoverable, indefinitely repeatable" (69).

This process survives today both in religious ritual and, as noted in Chapter 1, in modern man's immersion in compelling stories, which seem to take him out of real time.

If, as Eliade maintains, a sense of sacred time survives in a secular age through our involvement in compelling narratives, then perhaps, similarly, we may perceive certain fictional locations as a form of sacred space. Archaic man invoked sacred time and space for the ordering of his world after the pattern of the gods. Modern people experience something like this in a limited, secularized sense when they seek the diversions of literature and other entertainments. There are differing goals for both activities, the archaic practice being focused on the sacred and the modern one on the diversions offered through stories, but they share something of an experience of being taken out of a sense of profane or mundane time. Eliade, in his essay "Survivals and Camouflages of Myths," after his discussion of the mythical underpinnings of the Clark Kent/Superman myth discussed in Chapter 1, notes how the detective novel also follows a mythical pattern.

On the one hand, the reader witnesses the exemplary struggle between Good and Evil, between the Hero (=the Detective) and the criminal (the modern incarnation of the Demon). On the other hand, through an unconscious process of projection and identification, he takes part in the mystery and the drama and has the feeling that he is personally involved in a paradigmatic—that is, a dangerous, "heroic"—action [45–46].

Obviously, Batman, like Superman, a comic book superhero who is also a detective, partakes of this same heroic struggle heightened above the more realistic setting of the mystery story through the more symbolic nature of the stories' characters, and, thus, arguably is even more strongly mythic.

For the purposes of distinguishing the formally religious functions of archaic man's practices and beliefs from the psychological experience of modern audiences, I'll use the term "displaced time and space" rather than sacred time and space. Northrop Frye used the term "displacement" to describe how mythical content may be manifested in more realistic settings, and it is in this sense that the settings of romance narratives may partake of the sense of a place and time set apart from the everyday but not actually "sacred."

For many people, certain stories create vivid descriptions of the meaningful sites of significant action. These are the places where beloved or esteemed characters perform their great deeds of valor, love, and sacrifice. Readers may wish to "visit" that "place" repeatedly. J. R. R. Tolkien alludes to this in his essay on fairy stories when he speaks of man as a sub-creator of fictional worlds, his "sub-creations." Such storytelling usually involves the appropriately tailored construction of a setting in which characters may act. Tolkien's Middle Earth is such a displaced space, an imagined world, filled with wonder, described in great detail, and clearly distinct from our mundane environment. In the same way, one of the chief attractions of *Star Trek* is arguably a fully realized fictional universe that lends credence to the perception that we are viewing a future place, as well as a future time, extrapolated from our own, full of amazing technology and fascinating worlds and founded on the myth of scientific and social progress. This preferable reality can inspire cult-like followers whose attachment to *Star Trek*'s universe or Middle Earth, as well as Harry Potter's Hogwarts, surpasses mere appreciation of the stories themselves.

It is the displaced space of Gotham City, existing in the displaced time of the Batman stories, that also establishes the mythic nature of Batman. This displaced time is distinct from the reader's profane or mundane time in several ways. This story's time of course takes place in a different time from that of the readers', even if dates like "November 5, 2013" are given as story details. It is not always clear how much time has passed in a given story unless the author makes a point of keeping exact account of time's passage, such as in the Batman story "Death Strikes at Midnight and Three" (*Greatest* 249–263). Yet even that story does not tell us the date or year of the action. Time is also of a different order in that its passage has little or no effect on the characters. Batman/Bruce Wayne has been around for over 70 years, and is still going strong. The details of his world may change, such as fashions, technology, and slang, yet the main characters remain in chronological stasis.

Recognizing the limits of audience credulity for a Boy Wonder who lives for decades in Wayne Manor, Robin/Dick Grayson has shown the most concession to real time. For a time in the 1960s and 1970s he became the "Teen Wonder," grew a little taller, attended college, and finally decided to strike out on his own as the young adult crimefighter, Nightwing. Yet Batman, Commissioner Gordon, the Joker, and the rest of the cast stayed the same. Of course, this is partly due to the editorial decision to continue giving the public more of what they want, as long as the demand lasts. This is similar to decisions made about many comic strip characters, such as Dick Tracy or Dagwood Bumstead. On the other hand, this timelessness is inherent in forms of the romance, as Frye's comment, quoted in the Introduction, points out. The main character exemplified in comic strips "never develops or ages," Frye says, and goes through endless adventures, "until the author himself collapses" (*Anatomy* 186). Fortunately, comic book companies early on began distributing the work of producing comics broadly among their creative staff.

Throughout the history of the Batman comics, writers have occasionally offered stories that posit "imaginary" futures in which Robin has grown up and replaced Batman after Bruce Wayne has retired. An example would be the 1960s' "The Second Batman and Robin Team" (in *Batman: From the 30s to the 70s* 246–254). However, the most renowned speculative story of Batman's future is *The Dark Knight Returns,* which imagines Bruce Wayne going through a midlife crisis of grand proportions before he re-dons his cape and cowl. DC has been careful to characterize such stories as merely possible futures, not the authorized end of the character's history. The comics' chief focus remains the eternal present of the displaced time and place in which the characters live out an infinity of adventures. This sense of displaced time is resonant with the indeterminate "great time" of mythological narratives in which great events take place in a misty past. For example, when reading Greek myths, one is struck with a sense of the inexact nature of the sequence of events. Many of the characters' adventures cross the paths of others' and the great heroes all seem to be contemporaries, all members of perhaps one or two generations. So it is with Batman's world, except we have yet to see the end of Batman's career—the end that so many classical heroes meet, sometimes tragically.

Even in the displaced world of superheroes, where time is essentially static, in another sense, time marches on as the countless adventures and incidents of its characters accumulate over the decades. With so many characters, the continuity, or accrued history of the DC universe, creates narrative conflicts and contradictions as well as increasingly complicated character storylines as one can see when reading any longstanding Marvel or DC character's biography. This creates both a forbidding density for writers and editors to keep track of and makes attracting new readers prohibitively daunting. In 1985, DC's mini-series, the 12-issue *Crisis on Infinite Earths* resulted in a great reduction in the number of characters and a rebooting of its surviving characters' history. While this solved some problems, it didn't solve all, and, in fact, created new ones with un-reconciled character histories. Almost a decade after *Crisis on Infinite Earths*, DC sought to address these in another mini-series and crossover, *Zero Hour: Crisis in Time,* which reset various historical events, including several points in Batman's history, and there have been subsequent chronal crises since which supposedly altered and simplified DC's continuity. But it's hard to keep even an imaginary universe with a myriad of character written by many authors spinning evenly, so in 2011 DC Comics relaunched all of its comics titles in an event titled "the New 52," which allowed it to negate most of the continuity of its characters, in an effort to allow most of its characters, including Superman, a fresh start. Batman's continuity was partially affected but he still had acquired four Robins over his career, including, most recently, his son Damien, the youngest holder of the title. It's an indicator of the resilience of the Batman narratives that he was one of the least affected by this latest editorial makeover.

Umberto Eco, commenting primarily on Superman, and by extension other comic book superheroes, sees such mythic characters as caught between the need to embody "a law, or a universal demand, and, therefore, must be in part predictable and cannot hold surprises for us," contrasted with a novelistic character "and what could befall him is as unforeseeable as what could happen to us" ("The Myth of Superman" 15).

"He must necessarily become immobilized in an emblematic and fixed nature which renders him easily recognizable," Eco continues, "but since he is marketed in the sphere of a 'romantic' production for a public that consumes 'romances,' he must be subjected to a development which is typical, as we have seen ... of novelistic characters." Thus, the writers and artists who have sustained Batman over the decades have taken sometimes radical means to balance the character between his unchanging essence and the need for the appearance of living in time.

The Classic Quest Pattern

"In the meantime," which is where all Batman's stories seem to take place, the character's adventures fulfill another aspect of mythic expression, the classic heroic quest pattern described by Frye and discussed in Chapter 1. The three stages included the "*agon* or conflict, the *pathos* or death-struggle, and the *anagnorisis* or discovery, the recognition of the hero" (*Anatomy* 187). This pattern applies to the basic Batman adventure, repeated countless times, with adjustments made for the aforementioned ageless and endless nature of the cast.

Alerted to some new threat to order, often by Commissioner Gordon, Batman embarks upon a series of minor conflicts as he investigates the crimes in question. This would correspond to the struggle or *agon*. Encountering the guilty parties, a fight ensues, usually with the antagonist meaning lethal harm to Batman, and Batman seeks to violently subdue the villains without killing them. This corresponds to the death-struggle or *pathos,* although it is the villain who usually intends death, not Batman.

The typical pattern involves alternately the capture of the criminal, his escape to fight another day with his most recent plot foiled, or his apparent death. Batman is nearly always triumphant and his antagonist rarely dies (although he or she is usually pretty well beaten up). Within the context of the story the *anagnorisis* or recognition of the hero is rarely overt, since Batman prefers to avoid publicity and attention, nevertheless it is clear to the reader, whose pleasure is derived from having his hero's superiority affirmed yet again.

It should be noted here that Blythe and Sweet, in their article, "Superhero: The Six-Step Progression," offering a formal description of the conventional comics superhero story structure, describe a multi-stage process in a typical adventure. The story "usually opens *in media res* ... like in the Classical epic, which was in itself heavily formulaic. A menace attacks" (182). Step two features the call, by authorities, for the hero; step three, the hero's appearance; step four, his investigation of the menace; step five, his confrontation with the menace; and step six, the restoration of order.

Aside from the reference to the classical epic, the purpose of the Blythe and Sweet article was to offer structural terms toward constructing a vocabulary of the comic book medium and not a linking of superhero stories to classical sources. Nevertheless, it indicates an analysis other than Frye's that describes the "superheroic" story arc, which elaborates upon the basic mythical pattern.

Batman's Mythic Function

Frye characterizes the romance as being the closest of literary forms to the wish-fulfillment dream. As such, the characters and plots of romances contain reflections of the "hopes and desires" found in its audiences (*Anatomy* 186). In that the Batman stories fit Frye's description of a "naïve" romance, the Batman stories, as comic book romances, offer this wish-fulfillment function to readers. Batman functions as a projection of his audience's hopes, fears, and values. As ancient myths were ways in which archaic man sought to express an understanding of the world, of what things meant, so mythic figures today find their meaning as attempts to express what audiences believe to be consonant with reality. The use of mythic language is not meant to be an expression of empirical fact, but rather of deeply held beliefs about the issues of life. Where mythologies could be much more comprehensive in entailing a worldview, albeit more mythopoeic than ideological, mythic figures today, not being true myths, may offer only a partial expression of a particular set of concerns. Thus, Batman is "about" certain societal concerns entailing the problem of crime and chaos.

Arthur Asa Berger's essay on Batman attempts to explain Batman as a reflection of a national trait in which Americans, unbounded by the limiting traditions of their European ancestors, experience a nagging sense of guilt similar to that experienced by children who know no parental discipline (Berger 166–167). This vague guiltiness leads to an obsessive perfectionism that seeks to right all perceived wrongs. Batman, Berger argues, exemplifies this crusading American impulse to assuage our guilt by attacking evil. "He will help regenerate the world," Berger writes, "and his heroic labors take a load off of our backs" (Berger 168). Batman relieves our collective guilt-inducing neuroses by vicariously warring on wrongdoers. This psychoanalysis of Batman as therapeutic hero sounds similar to Terrill's Jungian perspective of "Batman as Schizophrenic Savior," wherein the Dark Knight functions to relieve psychic pain in his audience. As discussed in Chapter 1, this psychological approach, which presumes to analyze the mental dysfunction of millions of audience members, contrasts sharply with an approach to Batman as a figure who functions mythically for the audience.

Batman was created during an historical period of concern with domestic criminal activity and the international growth of fascism. This had followed an earlier period in the 1930s when outlaws such as Bonnie and Clyde and John Dillinger had been romanticized or had at least captured audiences' imagination in cinematic versions such as *Little Caesar* (1930) and *The Public*

Enemy (1931).[4] That public opinion was now turning away in disgust and fear from outlaw heroes was exhibited in popular culture by such anti-gangster films as *G-Men* (1935) and by pulp heroes such as those described in Chapter 1. Batman's tragic origin, borne out of his parents' callous slaughter by a gunman, reflected commonly held fears that anyone was vulnerable to sudden disaster at the hands of the criminal element. Young Bruce Wayne's vow to prey on all criminals was a typically childlike response, "getting back" at anybody who could destroy someone's family. Rather than living in fear, he would personally act to ensure that he himself induced fear in criminals. In a typically American response to terror, he transforms himself in this case into a terrible figure that need never fear a gunman again. Thus, as a wounded protagonist who has suffered personally from crime, he is peculiarly compelling as a hero who reflects societal concerns.

News reports, facts, and statistics about crime are a routine ingredient of journalistic content. In a 1995 *Atlantic Monthly* article, "The Crisis of Public Order," Adam Walinsky provided numerous statistics on the alarming increase in crime since the 1960s. As murder has increased, the number of police officers per murder has fallen far behind. The pain of victims who have been assaulted or have lost loved ones to crime leads to a lingering state of numbness. "We experience the crime wave not as separate moments in time," Walinsky writes, "but as one long descending night. A loved-one lost echoes in the heart for decades." Though crime statistics generally have improved since this time, troublesome urban crime in such cities as Detroit and Chicago demonstrate that urban crime continues as a major threat to the social order and creates a cumulative effect from murders and other crimes traumatizing American communities.

But one does not have to have experienced a violent criminal act to find the Batman story compelling. Our own awareness of the crisis in public order grows from news stories and from our friends and family and provides us the psychological context for an appealing urban hero such as Batman. People fear to walk city streets and are angry that they should have to be afraid. News stories horrify us because we reason that the victims might just as well be us on an unlucky day. Out of fear grows anger at our potential, if not actual, victimization. In the "long descending night" of a fearful and angry society, it is inevitable that cultural expressions will reflect our fears, hopes, and values. As Frye points out, every society has its wish-fulfillment dreams expressed in its romances. The Batman story encapsulates, for many readers, the particular fears, hopes, and values arising out of the crisis of crime. In this dark social milieu, Bruce Wayne's tragedy becomes archetypal and he responds by transforming his loss into a crusade, which is the core of his mythic appeal. Marc

Edward DiPaolo notes another dualism, seeing the wealthy and privileged yet victimized Wayne in medieval terms as "the feudal lord and Batman as the 'Dark Knight' who carries out Wayne's will, acting as his sword of justice" (204).

Being a romantic figure, Batman is neither completely mythical nor completely realistic; he partakes of elements of both. Functioning as a mythic figure, he is the recipient of displaced qualities such as Frye refers to when qualities of myth are expressed in the less elevated setting of the romance. Wayne is a victim of urban street crime who has transformed himself into a strange night creature. Like a modern sorcerer, he uses science and technology to empower his nocturnal forays into criminal detection in ways that amaze and baffle city police. He possesses not only the cool intelligence of a great detective, but he has the strength and passion to succeed where normal law-enforcement has failed.

It is characteristic of a wish-fulfillment figure to encompass conflicting or opposing qualities not occurring in everyday experience. Thus Levi-Strauss's concept of myth's function as reconciling opposites is reflected in a figure such as Batman. The wish for someone who can ignore legal technicalities to apprehend criminals is expressed in a figure who, if he could exist in reality, would be ineffective as a witness, expert or not, since the credibility of a masked man in court is inconceivable.[5] If nothing else, the evidence he obtained by breaking and entering would be inadmissible. Yet, in the comic books, he is the bane of evil, although he is a contradiction in terms: a legitimate vigilante. As this contradictory figure of projected hopes, fears, and values, Batman embodies not only social desires for justice but also fury at criminal offenders. This thirst for revenge, though at times muted, is still projected onto the character, which is capable of savage action in that pursuit. His saving grace is that no matter how savage he may be, he will not kill. However, Gordon and Batman's arrangement creates a conflict in the state's role as maintainer of law and order. Tony Spanakos, in discussing the theory of government that requires a singular vigilante to fight crime, notes, "The irony of the Batman's relationship with the state is that the more he reduces crime and contributes to the public order, the more he challenges the state, as it becomes obvious that the state's use of violence is ineffective" (69). It is Gordon and Batman's mutual trust that makes the arrangement work.

Writing in *The Weekly Standard* in 2012, Jonathan V. Last argues that Batman is a necessity in upholding the liberal order. Where a superhero like Captain America or Judge Dredd may be seen as projecting ideological ideas, "Batman is different. He is not an avatar for a particular political argument or idea. Batman is about the liberal order itself—specifically about the durability of classical liberalism in the face of modernity." More than merely helping police catch bank robbers and other crooks, Batman is dedicated to upholding the social order from the agents of chaos that seek to terrorize the city. Last notes Batman's commitment to not just capturing former district attorney turned Two-Face, but his rehabilitation, symbolic of restoring order and providing healing to his fractured psyche. If Batman's methods are extra-legal, Last notes, "Sometimes maintaining order requires illiberal actions, such as those undertaken by Batman." Between law and criminality, Batman stands as a liminal figure necessary in maintaining civilized society through ordered aggression.

The apparently random nature of much crime (embodied by Two-Face and the Joker, both insane in their own way), such as the stranger murders Walinsky describes, is part of the larger uncertainty of a modern life subject to such crimes as car-jackings, serial killings, physical and sexual abuse, and more recently, terrorist bombings of public places and mass shootings by disturbed loners. This sense of encroaching social disorder was also a concern displayed by archaic man, as described by Mircea Eliade in *The Sacred and the Profane*. Archaic man viewed the natural world as mundane space characterized by a formlessness that became ordered by consecration after the pattern of a mythological paradigm. Through the ritual of consecration, the order of the gods was replicated on earth, and that place became sacred space (32–36). Unconsecrated space remained in chaos, something not of "our world." To live in sacred space was to live in an ordered cosmos. Cities were consecrated so as to include them in sacred space. Outside of the city lived the enemies of the gods, i.e., the enemies of order—the demons and the dragon who had once been defeated by the gods. Eliade states emphatically:

> "Our" enemies belong to the power of chaos. *Any destruction of the city is equivalent to a retrogression to chaos. Any victory over the attackers reiterates the paradigmatic victory of the gods over the dragon (that is, over chaos)* [48, emphasis in original].

Batman's Demonic Foes

As Gotham becomes, for the reader, the sacred space or displaced narrative space of Batman's actions, so any incursion into that space by criminals is a violation. These enemies of the city face a savior who fights to ensure the city's ordered existence and to stand against its being profaned by demonic elements. This defense of the city by the mythic figure of the Batman is a classic romance that, as Frye points out, pits a hero with whom all the values of the reader are bound against an antagonist with demonic mythical qualities. Batman's role as successful defender of the city offers assurance to an audience concerned over the threat of public disorder. He also reinforces audience values, confirming their hope in the triumph of order over chaos.

Batman's many enemies represent encroaching chaos threatening the ordered city. None is more chaotic, as Chapter 2 demonstrated, than the Joker, who delights in the disorder of random death. In the Joker, a mocking humor is joined to the destruction of human life, spreading sacrilege in his wake. Other antagonists exemplify different aspects of lawlessness. For example, Harvey Dent, formerly Gotham's crusading district attorney, has himself been driven mad by a criminal act that horribly disfigured half of his face. A particularly bleak victim of the city's struggle against crime, Dent has become that which he hated: a crime boss, Two-Face. Emphasizing the randomness of existence, Two-Face decides whether he will do good or evil by the flip of a coin, thus giving a modernist twist to his brand of disorder. These villains and others are demonic threats to the city, and the legitimate overseer of the city's law and order, Police Commissioner Gordon, must often resort to the ritualistic calling of Gotham's guardian by projecting the totemic Batsignal into the night skies.

The most noteworthy aspect of Batman's character is that, being Gotham's savior, he fights the darkness by taking on aspects of darkness. Looking more demonic than his foes, he uses fear and surprise to give himself the advantage in his attacks. This is also the most problematic component of the Batman character. It is difficult to find a precedent for a mythical hero who combines a righteous mission with such dark signifiers. The Furies (or Erinyes) of Greek mythology, who were not mortal heroes but mythical beings borne of the shed blood of the Titan Cronus, may be one such precedent in mythology. Known as "those who walk in darkness," they were terrible to behold: they had snakes for hair and wept blood for tears (Hamilton 65). Committed to justice, their mission was the relentless pursuit of sinners. Likewise, Batman incarnates a spirit of public justice and vengeance against wrongdoers, yet he is not a purely other, as were the Furies. Some have suggested that Batman's demonic appearance is inspired by classic renderings of such beings. Batman writer and editor Denny O'Neil remarked to an interviewer that part of Batman's appeal is that his iconography resembles that of medieval devils and demons. Graeme Newman, discussing the social impact of the Batman character, also notes Batman's resemblance to the flying demons of a pre–Renaissance Italian fresco (303–304). O'Neil considers this hellish image to be created for effect and not definitive of a hero who descends into the underworld to fight evil, whereas Newman seems to confuse the character's appearance with the evil he fights. Nevertheless, the image of the dark medieval avenging angel certainly resonates with certain aspects of Batman's mystique. It is not difficult to be a little confused as well as fascinated by such an adulterated figure.

It is this adulteration, this dual motivation, that captures the mixture of public idealism and anger arising from the fear of crime. Batman's pursuit of justice while cloaked in darkness reveals the impurity of our desires. Batman appeals to both the sense of justice and the impulse to achieve it through less than righteous or legal means. A DC senior editor, Mike Gold, acknowledges this impure mixture in the public consciousness: "The Batman was the combination of two different beings locked up in our soul: the shining knight ... and Mr. Hyde" (*Greatest* 13).

There is also an alternative way of thinking about Batman's mythic function. Duncan and Smith, in their text on comics, see superheroes as modern myths in their ability to offer narratives of hope during times of social upheaval. Both Superman and Batman arrived after years of the Great Depression. "Superhero tales are not so much a fulfillment of a wish for power as they are an optimistic statement about the future and an act of defiance in the face of adversity" (242). This role model function recalls the way ancient Greek mythology offered people role models in Perseus, Theseus, Jason, and other heroes. The mythic hero as role model is also the theme of *Wisdom from the Batcave,* written by a rabbi, Cary A. Friedman, who culled moral insights from Batman stories and has applied them in lectures as a spirituality consultant to the FBI and other law-enforcement groups.

Partaking as he does of the mythical end of Frye's narrative continuum and containing elements of divinity, Batman also shares traces of the demonic. Readers admire his hunger for justice as well as his ability to be scarier than the villains. Being both noble and fearful, he is a romanticized reflection of his audiences' ambivalence over the means of achieving desirable ends. In the next chapter, the elements of comic book art and narrative will be discussed and applied to Batman to discover how sequential art effectively expresses the character's mythic aspects.

• 4 •

Comics Art and Batman

The medium of sequential art is uniquely suited to mythic portrayals and Batman's enduring appeal is largely due to his resonance with his audience's mythic impulses. The principles and techniques of comics—or sequential art—that govern this medium enable mythic depiction and thus enable the success and endurance of the Batman character.

Eisner, McCloud, and Sequential Art

While it is necessary to note the social and cultural implications of the Batman mythos, my main concern has been to examine how qualities in the comic book medium itself establish Batman as a mythic figure. This naturally entails the study of comic book technique and style—the subject of this chapter—but such a study is hampered by scarcity of theoretical materials. In 1979, comics scholar Thomas Inge noted the difficulty of studying comics strictly as an art form, rather than for their sociological or cultural importance, commenting that "we lack the critical vocabulary and have not even begun to define the structural and stylistic principles behind successful comic art. Instead we tend to rely on terms borrowed from other areas of creative expression" (Inge, *Introduction* 637). A few others have written on the study of the comic book as an art form, however. A doctoral dissertation in speech communication by Randy Duncan, entitled "Panel Analysis: A Critical Method for Analyzing the Rhetoric of Comic Book Form" examines how the comic book creator's personal history figures in the work. It also uses micro and macro analyses and psychological principles to further discern the meaning in a given comic book's panel composition. Likewise, Lawrence L. Abbott "attempts to formulate the concepts of visual-verbal relationships in comic art that are needed for evaluating the artistic potentialities of this narrative medium" (155). His article applies a structuralist perspective to comic book studies. Along the same general lines, Robert C. Harvey, a cartoonist and author, believes that comics are an art form without a clear aesthetic, as he states in his article "The Aesthetics of the Comic Strip." The chief characteristic of the comic strip, as he sees it, is that "it is a narrative of words and pictures, both verbal and visual, in which ... *neither words nor pictures are quite satisfactory alone without the other"* (his emphasis).

Two major contributions to the creation of a vocabulary of comic book studies are *Comics and Sequential Art* by Will Eisner, and *Understanding Comics* by Scott McCloud, both of which frame my examination of how comics convey mythic expressions. Eisner created the Spirit character in the 1940s and is respected as a master in the field for both his comics stories, which include graphic novels, and his teaching at the School of the Visual Arts in New York City before his death in 2005. Likewise, McCloud is known among comics fans for, among other work, his *Zot!* comic book series. His book on sequential art was published to much critical praise and excitement, being the first volume of its type to attempt to offer a theory of comics using the comic book form, a unique wedding of theory and practice. In an interview, McCloud confronted the tendency Inge had noted, of studying comics as a cultural artifact rather than as an art form in its own right and for its own sake:

> Pop culture studies of comics have centered around comics as pieces of evidence to give us clues about the culture that created them. But that sets up an unconscious hierarchy: that the culture itself is more important than the products of that culture! ... Very few people ... have seen comics, in and of themselves, as a field worthy of study. Since there is that vacuum, I feel that I do not have to so much investigate this science, as *invent* one [Wiater and Bissette, *Comic Book Rebels* 7 (original emphasis)].

In *Understanding Comics,* McCloud explains his ideas by using words *and* pictures, in comic-book style rather than solely through the standard vehicle of prose. McCloud, in fact, uses a cartoon version of himself to serve as the book's narrator and guide. Eisner and McCloud's work supplies a vocabulary and theoretical foundation that explains how Batman is evoked mythically.

Concepts of Sequential Art

While both writers discuss various aspects of comics, Eisner takes an applied approach to his theorizing, offering examples of his art to illustrate his text. McCloud's goal, on the other hand, is to develop a more comprehensive set of unified theories of sequential art using his own art and facsimiles of other artists to demonstrate his points. It is Eisner, however, who pioneered a formalized theoretical approach to the technique of comic book art and coined the term "sequential art." McCloud, in turn, took Eisner's work as a platform and worked through basic questions about the nature of comics to arrive at theories that identify comics as a distinct medium, a form rather than a content (defined by superheroes and funny animals, etc.). McCloud maintains that only by freeing itself from a content-bound mentality can the comics medium realize its tremendous potential.

Comics or Sequential Art

Eisner offers no formal definition of sequential art despite the fact that the term is in the title of his book. Nevertheless, it is clearly used as a technical term for the aesthetic technique of comics and was invented perhaps to provide a more objective term less associated with silly or sensational content than the standard term "comics." Scott McCloud, on the other hand, spends the first chapter of *Understanding Comics* working out a definition of the medium that he usually refers to as "comics." Acknowledging Eisner's contribution, McCloud articulates a definition for the medium of comics in dictionary form:

> comics (kom'iks) n. plural in form, used with a singular verb. 1. Juxtaposed pictorial and other images in deliberate sequence intended to convey information and/or to produce an aesthetic response in the viewer [McCloud 9].

Wherever images are juxtaposed in deliberate sequence for these purposes, it is sequential art or comics. This deliberately broad definition excludes the common associations connected with comic book stories. That is, comics is a medium that is distinguished not by its content, which historically has been much broader than the genres long associated with it, but by its singular formal nature. This definition is followed by an account of the occurrence of sequential art in history, with examples including Egyptian wall paintings, pre–Columbian painted screenfolds, and the Bayeux tapestry, among others. McCloud makes the case that comics, or sequential art, as he has defined it, has been present in the world's art as long as there has been human culture.

The Icon

In Chapter 2 of *Understanding Comics*, entitled "The Vocabulary of Comics," McCloud begins describing the symbolic nature of comic book art

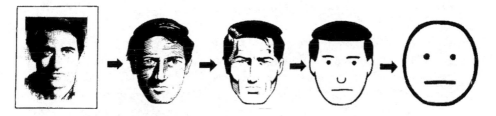

Figure 4.1: One version of the Scale of Iconic Abstraction showing "Levels of Abstraction" (from Scott McCloud, *Understanding Comics*).

by using the term "icon" to mean "any image used to represent a person, place, thing or idea" (27). Distinguishing non-pictorial icons or symbols from pictures, he points out that non-pictorial icons tend toward having fixed meanings since they represent invisible ideas; whereas, with pictures, meaning is "fluid and variable according to appearance" (28). "Pictures differ from 'real-life' appearance to varying degrees" (Ibid.). These images or icons may be depicted in degrees of detail and realism ranging from photographic realism at one extreme through degrees of increasing abstraction to the completely abstract at the other extreme (see Figure 4.1). The further from photorealism an image moves, the more detail is excluded.

In Eisner's book, he describes the process by which a realistic object, such as a face, is adapted by the cartoonist showing how by exaggeration, simplification, and the exclusion of details the object becomes more accessible (148). Eisner presents two depictions of a face, one realistically rendered and the other with a cartoon rendering. The realistic one retains more details and similarity to real-life human features; the cartoon version lacks these details and is more exaggerated. Picking up on this distinction, McCloud creates what will be called here a "Scale of Iconic Abstraction" that renders a human face across the iconic scale from a photograph of a man's face to a realistically drawn version of the face, to a less detailed depiction of the face as it might appear in an adventure comic, to a more simplified version that is minimally recognizable as a man's face, to a circle with two dots for eyes and a horizontal line for a mouth (28–29, see Figure 4.1, adapted from it). A comics reader still sees each version or level as a human face and, in fact, the more abstract levels can be more meaningful than the photorealistic one. It is in the context of this Scale of Iconic Abstraction that McCloud discusses the phenomenon of the icon's ability to involve the audience through what he calls "amplification through simplification" (30). He explains the term as follows:

> When we abstract an image through cartooning, we're not so much eliminating details as we are focusing on specific details. By stripping down an image to its essential "meaning," an artist can amplify that meaning in a way that realistic art can't [Ibid.].

As iconic representation moves from the more detailed specificity of a photographic image toward greater abstraction, it increases in capacity to carry and convey meaning. We no longer see the singular features of a particular person, but rather the more generalized and simplified ones of an abstracted character. It is the very elimination of detail that allows for the increase in meaning because the image can now represent abstract ideas instead of just one person. The less specific the image is, the greater its capacity to describe more people, thus increasing a reader's involvement in the character.

There is a further rationale for the involving, evocative nature of the iconic images found in comics and cartoons. People are drawn to see, in natural and man-made images, reflections of human features. An automobile's headlights and grill form a face, as does an electrical outlet or a cloud formation. "We see ourselves in everything," says McCloud. "We assign identities and emotions where none exist. And we make the world over in our image" (33). This phenomenon can be accounted for by noting that, though individuals can observe the detailed facial features and expressions of others with whom they interact, they cannot similarly observe their own. When we think of how our faces must look at any given moment, it is likely to be a vague, simplified version of ourselves, more like a *cartoon* image than a realistic one. "Thus, when you look at a photo or realistic drawing of a face, you see it as the face of *another*," McCloud states, "but when you enter the world of the *cartoon*—you see *yourself*" (36).

This imputation of self into the cartoon image as well as "universal identification, simplicity and the childlike features of many cartoon characters" are reasons for the reader's involvement with such images (Ibid.). "The cartoon is a vacuum into which our identity and awareness are pulled," McCloud writes, "an empty shell that we inhabit which enables us to travel in another realm. We don't just observe the cartoon, we *become* it" (Ibid.)! McCloud challenges the notion that the simple graphic rendering of cartoons limits their ability to convey the complexities of modern literature, thus consigning comics to the level of children's literature. The simple elements of comics, he argues, can combine to form much more complex and powerful expressions because they are empowered by the reader's mind (45).

Along the Scale of Iconic Abstraction, there is movement from the left, the area of photographic realism, rightward, toward greater abstraction. There are different ways this change may be expressed. To demonstrate this, McCloud develops a series of scales with several left-to-right progressions, as follows:

complex————>simple
realistic————>iconic
objective————>subjective
specific————>universal [46]

Figure 4.2: An extended version of Scott McCloud's Scale of Iconic Abstraction (adapted from Scott McCloud, *Understanding Comics*).

In these progressions, as one moves to the right and away from the simplest rendering of a face, one also moves away from resemblance to the original object and closer to the most abstract realm of conveyed meaning: words (see Figure 4.2). At the left end of the scale is the "reality" of photorealism. At the right end is "language." Comics style renderings may occur anywhere along the continuum to the right of the photograph.

The comics creator chooses the level or levels of abstraction suitable for his or her creative purpose and may combine levels within the panels. Finally, as shown in Figure 4.3, McCloud posits a second dimension of abstraction that moves upward at 45 degree angles from both ends of the scale to form a triangle (50–51). Movement in this direction is non-iconic and involves the goal not of resemblance or meaning, but rather of artistic depiction as an end in itself, on what McCloud calls the "picture plane." Here, style predominates. In a two-page spread, McCloud presents his three-vertice scale of "reality," language, and the picture plane with 116 heads of characters drawn in their respective artists' distinctive manner, locating them in their approximate places on the triangle. This two-dimensional charting of iconic qualities encompasses all the aesthetic possibilities within which any type of art may be expressed. The essence of iconic abstractions is their ability to draw in the reader. They convey the artist's invitation to participate in the work by doing the work of imagination necessary to engage it. In this context, McCloud refers to Marshall McLuhan's concept of hot and cool media, noting that cool media require audience involvement. We are reminded that comics is one of the several cool media, including television, named by McLuhan. In his book, *Understanding Media,* McLuhan stated that, like the woodprint, in comics the "viewer or reader, is compelled to participate in completing and interpreting the few hints provided by the bounding lines" (148).

It is at this point that the expression of the mythic through comic book technique becomes possible. The mythopoeic expresses that which transcends the prosaic or materialistic. Although comics can address realistic areas quite well, the medium is also able to depict stories in which characters become believable as mythic figures because the audience is freed to perceive them as such by their nonrealistic mode of depiction. When McCloud discusses photographic realism as limited to referring to one person and the comics' depic-

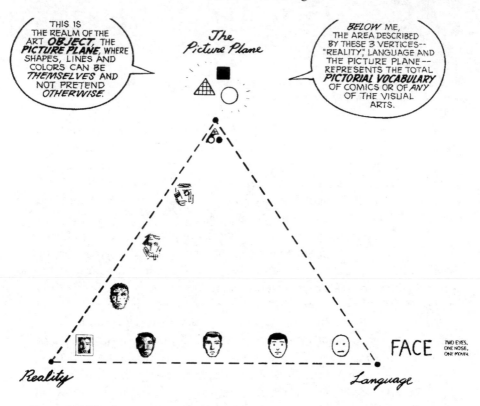

Figure 4.3: The three-vertice scale adapted from Scott McCloud's *Understanding Comics*.

tion of someone as symbolizing many, he is demonstrating how readers can be drawn (via their engaged imaginations) into an involvement they would have found difficult or impossible otherwise. By eliminating the details of realism, imaginative space is created for larger meaning to inhabit. The meaning suggested by iconic depictions is so great that it transcends our sense of what is known empirically. The more abstracted content is perceived to be, the less specific and more conceptual it is and, therefore, the better able to convey mythic content. Thus, the content of the mythic is enabled though the iconic abstractions of sequential art.

Between the Panels: Closure

The second major concept discussed by Scott McCloud is closure. As applied to comics, closure uses the reader's imagination to supply the missing action between the successive panels of a comic strip or comic book. Time, space, and action may all be implied based on our inferred meaning of the relationship between any two sets of juxtaposed panels or images. Although McCloud refers to McLuhan's concept of a cool medium's demand for the participation of the audience, there is another source of insight (not mentioned by McCloud) that contributes to an understanding of closure. Gestalt psychology, as applied to the perception of forms, describes the compulsion we feel to complete that which appears partial. In a book applying principles of Gestalt to the art of photography, Richard D. Zakia explains the appeal of closure. "Man derives satisfaction," he states, "from being able to form a closure that allows him to become an active participant in the visual experience" (77). Whether in a child's connect-the-dots book or in a jigsaw puzzle we enjoy the challenge of completing the partial or determining a whole out of parts. We routinely construct something greater out of the clues and cues that imply something greater.

McCloud, in explaining the concept of closure, resumes the theme of participation to explain how even the simple line drawing of the circle, two dots, and a line are seen as a face because of the compelling need to see something in the figure (64). (And this is, of course, the basis of typed emoticons: (;-).) Likewise when comics use a sequence of as few as two juxtaposed pictures to indicate some action or concept, the meaning for a reader is derived from what the reader's imagination supplies *between* the images. The images cue readers as to what may be inferred, but the actual or the entire event is unseen on the page and takes shape only in the reader's mind (see Figure 4.5). McCloud states that closure may be used to indicate change, time, and motion (65). In an interview, McCloud sees closure as

> the heart of comics, and I think it's a much neglected area. Critics tend to see only what's in the panels—not what's between them. And what's between the panels is the only element of comics that is not duplicated in any other medium [Wiater and Bissette, *Comic Book Rebels* 13].

Comics as a medium derives its power through its enlistment of the reader's imagination in supplying what is only implied by the writer and artist. Not only is action suggested, the panels can, through varieties of techniques, indicate changes in time and space. "Comics panels fracture both time and space, offering a jagged staccato rhythm of unconnected moments," states McCloud, "but closure allows us to connect these moments and mentally construct a continuous unified reality" (67). The ability to infer meaning from seemingly unrelated juxtaposed images testifies to the power of human imagination. Closure enables the depiction of the mythic among other ways by creating the effect of fantastic feats such as flying and incredible acrobatics. What would be impossible to believe in real life becomes credible within the internal logic of the comics' narrative world. The wondrous deeds of a mythic figure seem somehow possible because, through the use of closure within a series of static images, the deeds have taken shape in the reader's imagination.

Though McCloud claims that closure is unique to comics, his discussion recalls the concept of film montage expounded by Russian director and formalist film theorist Sergei Eisenstein. The editing of two different images together to create a new meaning based on their perceived relationship was the core concept of Eisenstein's theory. "From the collision of two given factors *arises* a concept" (Eisenstein 35, his emphasis). In *Understanding Comics*, McCloud describes the similar process in comics. "By creating a sequence with two or more images," he says, "we are endowing them with a single overriding identity, and forcing the viewer to consider them as a whole" (73).

Discussing which type of drawing style works best for guiding the reader through the series of panels, McCloud suggests that a realistic drawing style that emulates photographic reality works against closure because such a sequence seems "more like a series of still pictures" (91). Being to the far left of McCloud's continuum near the "reality" end, photographically realistic drawings are more engaging for their own sake as works of art. The less detailed, more "cartoony" style to the right of the reality end of the scale has, by excluding details, made more room for ideas, thus, we are more drawn to them as an engaging series of images that collectively create narrative meaning.

The Reality-Picture Plane Scale

McCloud discusses yet another concept in comics art, a scale that runs from photographic reality up diagonally to ever more abstract forms. Whereas the scale of iconic abstraction dealt with how the image moves from the specific to the more general, this scale moves from realism toward "the non-iconic variety where no attempt is made to cling to resemblance *or* meaning. This is the realm of the art object, the picture plane where shape, lines and colors can be themselves and not pretend otherwise" (50, 51). Along this scale a photo-realistic face moves up and long, changing into ever more concentration on the constituent parts of the image, increasingly emphasizing form over resemblance to real things, or form for its own sake, with no intended meaning. Along the first half of this scale, cartoon characters become ever more stylized and indeed strange as they move away from reality. In the gallery of images McCloud uses to illustrate the wide variety of renderings possible within the three-vector chart described earlier, he places an image of Batman drawn in the style of Frank Miller's *The Dark Knight Returns* about halfway up the scale connecting "Reality" to "The Picture Plane," or apex of his triangular scale and left of center of his Scale of Iconic Abstraction. Adding this dimension increases our understanding of the dynamics of comics style's potential and variety.

Color and Other Elements

McCloud also discusses the function of color in comics. In comics history, the four-color printing method that characterized Sunday comic pages and comic books was both a limitation and an avenue for developing a new way of rendering images. Because comics were printed on cheap newsprint, which caused colored images to be dulled, artists gave their heroes bright costumes in primary colors to counteract the dulling effect. This turned out to be an advantage in the iconography of the comic book because certain characters became known for their costumes' colors. McCloud suggests that color contributed to the superhero as a mythic expression.

> [The colors] were fixed with a new iconic power. Because costume colors remained exactly the same, panel after panel, they came to symbolize characters in the mind of the reader. Many see the superhero as a form of modern mythology. If so, this aspect of color may play a part. Symbols are the stuff of which gods are made [188].

When a drawing is in black and white, the viewer tends to focus on the lines that make up the figures. The addition of color to the image shifts the focus to form and shape. The best artists in comics, McCloud points out, have excelled at form and composition. Thus, though an artist may seek to enhance figures with shading and modeling effects, the form of a figure in comics is still typically a flat one consonant with the simplicity of the style in general.

There is another aspect of comics technique that contributes to its effectiveness in economically evoking meaning. When, in Chapter 5 of his book on sequential art, Will Eisner discusses the use of the drawn human form in expressing attitudes and emotions, he points out that there is a sort of "body language" depicted by the artist to externalize the internal attitudes and reactions of characters in an exaggerated fashion. Eisner describes how, with such a body language, both gestures and postures of figures may achieve a fluency based on their widely understood meaning. The use of facial expressions becomes especially important in quickly communicating the emotional states of characters.

Bodily and facial expressiveness and conventions in the use of color both contribute to comics' expression of the mythic. Mythic narratives are characterized by personalities who are typically symbolic and clearly embody specific values, whether virtuous or villainous. A comics superhero is identified with his or her costume in such a way that the costume signifies the character. "Costume is the sign of individual identity," comments comics scholar Richard Reynolds. "A costume can be 'read' to indicate an individual hero's character or powers" (26). The usually colorful costume marks out the superhero as a different order of being from an ordinary human. Superhero comics present a distinct order of heroic characters set apart by costumes that signal their mythic standing within their fictional world.

As we will see in the chapters on filmed adaptations of comics characters, this emblematic use of color becomes a challenge in rendering such flamboyant costumes in a photorealistic medium designed to appeal to a mass audience. Characters in primary-colored costumes invite incredulity and smirks from audiences and, thus, we have seen adaptive strategies in Marvel's rendering of Captain America in his first Marvel Studios film, *Captain America: The First Avenger* (2011) and *The Avengers* (2012) with a more functional design for each film than the classic comics design. Though the World War II era and modern versions differ, neither uses the bright flat blue tone from the comics. The modern costume is a darker blue without being too muted. Similarly, in *The Man of Steel* (2013), Superman's costume loses the red trunks entirely and also gains a darker shade of blue and red tones and deeper yellow on the iconic chest shield. In Christopher Nolan's films, it was relatively easy to retain the dark tones of Batman's dark gray comics costume while adding much more in the way of texture.

The Mythic Rendering of Batman in Comics

These theories and techniques of sequential art explain how comics can communicate the mythic qualities of the Batman character and saga. In seeking to explain the survival and endurance of Batman, DC Comics senior editor Mike Gold credits the singular medium of comics. "The vitality of The Batman," he explains, "lies in its primary story-telling medium: the graphic story, the so-called 'comic book,'" and also that it is because Batman is the product of the collaborative efforts of many artists in a periodical format that enables the character to be renewed monthly (*Greatest* 12). Born at the start of the modern comics era, Batman "grew up" with the medium as the comics writers and artists learned how the art form could best tell a story. Even with this being the case, when one examines the depictions of the character since his inception in 1939, it is noteworthy how little has actually changed in the depiction of Batman. This relative changelessness is attributable to the simplicity of Batman's original conception both in characterization and appearance. The character design's elegant simplicity fits neatly in a medium that draws its strength from what McCloud calls the principle of "amplification through simplification" (30). It is here that the basis of Batman's mythos lies.

Iconic Abstraction and the Mythic

One way to demonstrate the relationship between comics' use of the icon and the evocation of the mythic is to focus on how iconic abstraction functions as a doorway into the mythic. It is generally acknowledged that fictional narratives require the suspension of disbelief to engage the story. Stories with mythic content, i.e., those containing story elements that transcend the ordinary, realistic mode of narratives, arguably require more authorial effort to create a narrative which facilitates the reader's suspension of disbelief. Creators must find ways to make the fantastic seem believable within the story's context. One of the tag lines on posters for *Superman: The Movie* (1978) was "You'll believe a man can fly." Everyone knew Superman could fly—in the comic books. The ads drew audiences with the promise that what was believable in a comic book would be believable on the movie screen as well. The film was attractive because it promised to make us "believe" in the impossible through the use, in this case, of special effects. Comics accomplish the same effects as such movies but not by expensive and elaborate special effects. The power of the comics medium lies in its ability to draw in the reader by engaging the imagination in a singular manner. Characters who can be termed mythic are, by definition, extraordinary. They are unrealistic in that they usually possess mental and physical qualities rare or nonexistent in the real world. There is nobody like Tarzan in the real world; likewise, it is difficult to imagine actually being in the same room with Batman, as he is known in the comics. Yet he is perfectly acceptable as a mythic character within the medium of comics. Indeed, the physical, emotional, and mental qualities that make him who he is are so outsized that he is most believable in the comics medium. Comics characters, distanced as they are from realism through iconic abstraction, can be perceived as the mythic creature the artists and writers intend them to be.

Iconic Rendering of an Impossible Being

As rendered in comics, Batman is not only an incredible character, he is also an impossible one. Although his fictional appeal lies in his being a mere mortal who through sheer drive achieves superhero status, it is plain that, in reality, such achievements are beyond the realm of the possible. His acrobatic feats far exceed those of the most trained acrobat and his deductive powers equal those of Sherlock Holmes, another impossible, if more realistically situated character.

This surpassing of the possible is visibly illustrated by the artistic rendering of Batman. In action, in his graceful combat and acrobatics, Batman rarely missteps. His thrown batarang always finds its mark and he swings through the cityscape from a rope seemingly attached to a cloud. What would be too incredible to believe in real life is made credible through its expression in the comics medium. The secret is that such art enlists the imaginative cooperation of its readers in achieving such amazing exploits.

Such an employment of imagination is, of course, not unique to comics. The power to suggest certain qualities and actions resides in other media such as radio drama and theater. Both can use words and sometimes sounds to cue the audience's imagination to envisage something not actually seen.

Peter Coogan's history of the superhero genre addresses how the development of the comics medium allowed for the expression of an evolving fantastic character type, including Popeye and Alley Oop, whom he refers to generically as comic strip strongmen.

> Comics offer a possibility for depicting the superman that was seemingly not available to the prose fiction writers or to the artists working in other narrative media, such as radio or film. Comics can depict the fantastic with equal realism as the mimetic, so things that might not be acceptable or might look ridiculous in another medium do not appear so in comics. In comics, everything—whether a building or a talking tiger—can have the same level of surface realism [167].

Coogan uses the superhero costume as an example, noting that "no matter how well described, cannot appear as striking when described in words, as when it appears in pictures" and thus serving in comics to distinguish the superhero from "civilians" (Ibid.). And "because they are made out of the same material (ink, paper, color)," a superhero costume, so difficult to render believably in live-action media, is perceived as realistic in the comics medium (168). The unique ability of comics is in its ability to *seem* to visually depict the dynamic action on its static panels. What may be effectively suggested by a theatrical or radio character's words is even more dramatically realized in comics form. Thus it is that a character such as Batman becomes such a powerfully mythic figure in the comics pages. A systematic examination of different aspects of Batman's depiction reveals the accomplishment of comics' iconic expression of him.

The Figure of Batman

As typically rendered, Batman possesses a magnificent body: a wide chest, thickly muscled torso, with sinewy arms and legs. Yet this Herculean body is as agile and limber as that of an Olympic gymnast. His costume covers all parts of his body except around the mouth and chin. The gray stretch fabric clings to legs, arms, and chest in a way no real material could. This sheer tightness, common among superhero costumes, makes it a literal second skin that displays the character's physical attributes as if he were uncovered, while maintaining the costume's function of suggesting a nocturnal creature. To all intents and purposes, the costume *is* Batman's skin. Though often exerting himself to the maximum, the costume never shows the sweat stains of normal clothing worn next to the skin. It rarely if ever wrinkles or puckers or shows signs of being anything other than a smooth, hairless, and very resilient epidermis.

His utility belt is of similarly elegant design. Usually drawn as thin, and studded with narrow tubes tapered at the ends, it is somehow able to carry a vast collection of tools, weapons, and other applications such as the batarang and a lengthy rope hidden inconspicuously within its tiny compartments. The cape Batman wears is made of a material that appears leather-like and that, at times, is bulletproof, yet it is often shown wafting in the wind behind its wearer as if made of parachute nylon (which, in fact, the Nolan films employed in building their Batsuit). Sometimes long enough to drag on the ground, the cape still billows lightly into the air as Batman vaults obstacles, never getting caught on such impediments as chain link fences or protruding nails. It is one of Batman's most distinctive features, an extension of the bat motif that usually spreads out wing-like as he swings into action, yet never slows his movements.

The mask and face. The head of Batman is the centerpiece, so to speak, of his iconic significance. From the beginning, when Bob Kane and Bill Finger were conceiving his design, the decision was made to replace the human eyes that would normally peer out of a mask with mysterious white slits. When the hood or cowl is off of Wayne's face, the eye holes usually appear as just that: holes. When he puts on the mask, however, a transformation occurs and the white slits somehow appear.[1] Perhaps more than any other single feature, Batman's eyes contribute to the dualistic eeriness that is the basis for his mythic status. It is the most immediate indication that this being is not merely a man but something else as well—a sort of night creature whose eyes glow in the dark.

Artists use the eyes to suggest not only the strangeness of Batman but also to indicate his stronger emotional reactions. Despite whatever thick material makes up his mask, it becomes, like the rest of his attire, a second skin that changes with his every expression. The white slits may widen in surprise or horror, narrow in anger or droop in grief. In this manner they fulfill Eisner's descriptions of how facial expressions cue readers to the emotional states of a character. Batman's mask, as depicted in comics, functions *as his face* to express his mythic nature in a way a real-life mask never could.

At Batman's inception, the bat ears of the cowl were long and horn-like, befitting his original nocturnal mystique. Upon Robin's arrival, the ears shrunk to match his less eerie persona. When he was returned to his grimmer depiction, decades later, the ears once more grew longer, sharper, and more demonic. It is here that remarks such as those by Denny O'Neil and Graeme Newman about Batman's resemblance to the demons of medieval art are pertinent. His ears, particularly, suggest the demonic rather than the angelic. When conceiving of Batman's appearance, Bob Kane had originally given the figure stiff black bat wings and a simple black mask, like Zorro's. Les Daniels relates that Kane then asked Bill Finger for advice. Finger showed Kane a dictionary picture of a bat, pointing out the ears. "Kane's simple mask was transformed into a black cowl with the distinctive points that were echoed in the wings and eventually in the design of the gloves that Finger suggested," Daniels writes. "The repetition of the triangular motif made for an immediately memorable image and may have helped to account for Batman's success" (21). Philosopher Tom Morris, commenting on Batman's costume, remarks, "Batman has always been very honest about his costume.... It was a piece of theater for a purpose. His outfit was meant to effect something in the minds and emotions of his adversaries," Morris continues, "something supportive of his mission, giving him perhaps a split-second advantage that might make all the difference to the outcome of an otherwise well-matched fight" (253).

The only human portions of Batman's face are the mouth and chin which are those of Bruce Wayne, who is typically portrayed as a generically handsome, square-jawed, brunette male with no other distinguishing features, drawn in the standard comics style. Bob Kane's version of the Wayne/Batman jaw line recalled Dick Tracy's sharp features. Later, more realistic artists such as Carmine Infantino and Neal Adams kept the square jaw, opting only for a more natural depiction of it.

Heroic posture. Another feature adding to Batman's mythic depiction is the heightened style of his body's posture in various stances. As Eisner has shown, body postures do much to determine the interpretation of the character's words, attitudes, and emotions. But more than that, it has become common in superhero comics to render such characters in exaggerated positions. In a book on comic book art, Marvel Comics' Stan Lee describes how a normal gesture and stance are depicted in a larger-than-life manner befitting a character's heroic nature. Thus, a superhero who is standing and pointing does so not as an "ordinary" person would, but rather with legs spread wide and finger forcefully thrust forward. A running figure becomes crouched and tilted forward almost 45 degrees. The rationale for such exaggerations is that they give the static images the dramatic force necessary to achieve the required superheroic status. This, of course, borrows from the manner in which classic representational art, such as paintings and sculpture, depicted gods and heroes in distinctly commanding poses and postures such as, for example, the statue of Poseidon of Melos (*Larousse Encyclopedia of Mythology* 152). In Batman's case these devices simply add to the sense that he is a being of heightened physical form, ability, and gracefulness.

Besides striking various heroic postures, Batman (as well as many other superheroes) is commonly depicted in action scenes at the height of a particular movement. A scene depicting a right hook to a thug's jaw will show Batman's fist at the furthest reach of its swing. The same would hold for a martial arts kick; the foot is shown at the highest point of its travel. Whether or not the "moving" figure is accompanied by the dynamic indicator of speedlines, a comics convention, the reader views the image as the end stage of a swift and powerful action, a sort of closure within the frame. This type of rendering of the hero's actions, typical throughout a Batman comics story, contributes to the overall sense of his physical prowess. All of these techniques of idealization in the presentation of comics superheroes are distinctive to the medium. Comics writer and editor Jim Shooter describes how a certain action in comics would differ from the same one on film. "Cartoonists are not limited by reality," Shooter writes. "They're also not limited by motion, as movies are" (quoted in Sassienie 6). Shooter continues his description of the manner in which comics are more easily able to convey what live-action film finds more difficult:

> In the comics Superman stands tall, proud and powerful—*just so*.... In every single image his posture conveys his nature and personality. In the movies, inevitably, the camera will catch that awkward protruding-butt moment as the actor sits down. And it is an actor isn't it? You know where to find the real Superman, whose cape is always blowing just so [Ibid.].

Comics' control over the presentation of characters is so total that Batman's mythic nature may be expressed with a consistency and effectiveness that creates the internal logic necessary to maintain the believability of the character.

Batman's shadow. Batman's iconic significance is also expressed through the long established motif of the shadow that he casts, sometimes from no particular light source. This is often displayed as a sort of living Batsignal playing along the ground or against a wall as he plunges down onto terrified crim-

Figure 4.4: A rough approximation of the Scale of Iconic Abstraction using various images of Batman from photographic to increasingly abstracted.

inals. A variation on this is the heavily backlit perspective of Batman as he advances, so that only his black silhouette and the white eye slits are seen. Despite the theatricality of this device, it is the more effective for its distance from reality, being for that reason all the more able to enhance Batman's mysterious nature. Functioning as an indicator of the character's true nature, the shadow sometimes appears in illogical places within the scene. An interesting variation on this convention, and one borrowed from the comics, is the final scene of an episode of *Batman: The Animated Series.* The episode, "Nothing to Fear," has Bruce Wayne visiting his parents' gravesite. As he walks way from it, the wind blows against his trench coat, and the large shadow that follows is seen to be not Wayne's, but that of Batman. With this comics device, Wayne's dominant identity is instantly and powerfully indicated.

Batman's Depictions on McCloud's Scale

To appreciate the iconic power of comics art, it helps to understand just how abstracted the art of Batman is. By locating Batman's various depictions along McCloud's Scale of Iconic Abstraction, it can be more clearly seen how the power of the character is presented as a mythic figure, one who possesses liminal, dualistic traits and employs a strange appearance in a compellingly believable way. Any such locating must be viewed as tentative and approximate, but given the comprehensive nature of McCloud's scale, such an attempt is useful. As it is pursued, the most important factor to consider is that on McCloud's horizontal axis, whose poles run from "reality" on the left to "meaning" on the right, anything to the right of reality or photographic depiction begins to lose detail and gain iconic meaning. In Figure 4.4, four depictions of Batman have been arranged from the most realistic on the far left to the most iconic on the far right. The first image on the left is of the cinematic Batman, played by Val Kilmer in *Batman Forever,* and it features the modeling and photorealistic texture of film. Kilmer's eyes peer through the vinyl mask, emphasizing the person behind it. The next image is a Neal Adams's drawing from 1970. Adams was noted for having depicted his characters with features more realistically proportioned than the highly stylized Golden Age artwork. Nevertheless, Adams is able to render Batman as a more mysterious figure than he had been since the first year of his inception. Les Daniels's description explains that Adams "delineated a Batman whose face and figure reflected the influence of realistic illustrations, but whose wildly expressive cloak and melodramatic poses were pure romanticism" (Daniels and Kidd 136). The third image is that of the Golden Age Batman created by Bob Kane with its distinct block-like jaw and half-moon eye-holes. The fourth example is the furthest removed from realistic rendering and is the Batman depiction from the animated series. Here the character design has synthesized elements of both Adams's grim adventurer and Kane's square-jawed classic version but in a more simplified, flat style.

These various depictions of a single character show the range of possible successful renderings of the Batman character as well as the range of possibilities of the comics medium itself. Although meaning and, therefore, mythic potential, increases as depictions move to the right of McCloud's scale, it is premature at this point to offer evaluations of which versions are the most mythic. In the Appendix, a new scale incorporating both McCloud's scale and Frye's Scale of Literary Design will enable a more complete basis for judgment of degrees of mythic evocation among varying versions of Batman depictions as well as among media generally.

Closure and Batman

As an impossible character, Batman does impossible feats. His thrown batarang never misses. His grappling hooks always catch on a pole or ledge to brake his fall. His somersaulting leaps over oncoming cars are always precisely timed to land him neatly on his feet behind the car. Of such exploits are superheroes made. (Attempts to show such actions on film are both costly to produce and unconvincing because a photorealistic medium demands certain concessions to our experience of physical reality.) It is comics' special ability to communicate such action by suggesting it in a series of two or more images that allow the imagination to supply the unseen—unseen on paper, that is, since, to willing readers, the action takes place in their imaginations. An otherwise

Figure 4.5: Closure is how he did it. Closure both between and within panels (from _Batman Adventures_ #9).

improbable feat becomes, in the imagination, another demonstration of Batman's extraordinary abilities as illustrated on page 94. This does not mean comics creators may suggest whatever they can imagine and that credulous readers will automatically gasp in amazement. Successful comics art demands a careful balance between apparently realistic actions and absolutely impossible jumps in credibility. An example of an imbalance in this sense is found in *Batman: Year Two*, in which Batman is standing on a street when the villain, the Reaper, appears. As the Reaper's bullets fly toward him, Batman, in the next panel, seems oddly suspended, horizontally, in the air. The panel's perspective is so unclear that we are not sure from where and to where he is leaping. In the third panel of the sequence, he is suspended over the high metal framework of a building under construction.

Readers have been given no cue or clue as to what has happened between the panels to connect these last two seemingly unrelated images. This is a case of the artist and writer demanding more imagination from his readers than it can provide because he has not provided the means for them to participate in the action. This is an atypical case, however. Normally the comics' writers and artists carefully provide just enough information in the panels for readers to follow the unseen, fantastic, but somehow credible "action" between them. Thus is Batman, an ordinary human, able to transcend his mortality and possess truly mythic prowess.

Color in Batman

In McCloud's chapter on color, he discusses how certain colors come to symbolize certain characters through the colors' consistent application. By showing blocks of the colors dark blue, gray and yellow, proportionate to their respective representation on Batman's costume, McCloud illustrates how colors are part of comics' symbolism, and it is here that he remarks that this symbolic association may play a part in a "modern mythology" of the superhero (McCloud 188). Such a colorful graphic representation evokes the character. The ability of colors (purple for royalty; white for purity; red, white, and blue for the United States) to carry strong emotional meanings is generally recognized and the use of these particular "color codes" in Batman's costume contributes to the iconic power of his comics' depiction. Not only are the iconic abstraction and closure of comics key ingredients in evoking the mythic sense of the Batman character and stories, but color is also used to set Batman apart as the singular fictional being he is.

The Mythic Evoked in Other Comics

The action/adventure category of comics and the superhero genre in particular both fall into the broad category of romance narratives, creating many opportunities for stories and characters that may evoke the mythic to varying degrees. Both the characters of ancient myths and today's superhero characters are figures that, for their respective times and audiences, became symbolic of deeply held cultural values and beliefs. Whereas ancient myths explained the meaning of the world for entire societies, comic book heroes are significant symbols for devotees of the genre. (Nevertheless, such a character impacts the larger culture through adaptations into popular films and television shows.) In this context, Superman, for example, functions as a latter-day version of Hercules in the sense that both characters' common appeal lies in their being heroic ideals of physical strength. Marvel Comics' character Thor is a canny translation of the Norse god into a situation where he may straddle both the mythical Asgard and a modern urban setting. In this case the comics character is no longer a figure of worship by his followers but an adventure hero with mythological origins whose exploits are enjoyed by readers attracted to stories that exploit mythic trappings. In the case of Wonder Woman, her stories are drawn from some details of Greek mythology, yet she herself is not a mythological creature like Thor. While the mythopoeic elements of these respective adaptations may vary, it is still arguable that it was the original mythic content that made the superhero comics' depiction compelling enough to gain its following, although they were obviously adapted to the superhero conventions of the genre. In other words, creators of comics superheroes, as in Batman's case, consciously or unconsciously borrow elements, patterns, and archetypes of mythology to construct appealing and intriguing characters. To illustrate how the mythic is evoked in comics other than Batman, two other significant examples will be briefly discussed.

The Marvels

The 1960s was the time of Marvel Comics' innovative entry into industry leadership through the creation of such titles as *The Fantastic Four, Spider-Man, The Avengers,* and *The Uncanny X-Men.* In 1994, Marvel Comics released a limited series of prestige-style issues called *Marvels.* Printed on thicker, high-quality paper than that used for an average comic book, they consisted of stories already well known to Marvel aficionados, now retold from the perspective of fictional photojournalist Phil Sheldon. Since the 1940s Sheldon has covered the exploits of those he refers to as the "Marvels." For several decades these superhuman beings have been the leading citizens of the "Marvel Universe." Two of the *Marvels* issues retell major storylines from this mid–1960s period. One of these, "Judgment Day," concerns events surrounding the invasion of earth by a giant planet-eating superbeing, Galactus, and chronicles the battle against it by the Fantastic Four. Throughout the story the point-of-view is that of Phil Sheldon as he covers the news concerning various Marvels and then the events of the invasion. At no time is conventional interaction and dialogue among any superheroes featured. The stories anticipate that readers will have some knowledge of the original stories from which they can supply details of plot development as the story is retold from Sheldon's perspective. The theme of how the general populace reacts to the presence of superheroes guides Sheldon's commentary.

The most striking aspect of the series is that, rather than being drawn and inked as usual, the artwork is painted in a semi-realistic manner by Alex Ross. The use of painting techniques that suggest lighting and depth of perspective creates an added sense of spectacle not possible in the comics' conventionally inked comics artwork. Faces of characters are detailed enough to suggest that actual persons served as models. The rendering of some of the superhero figures reflect what such characters might look like in real life; costumes fit rounded forms and wrinkle at joints rather than becoming a second skin, for example. The move of the depictions toward the left of McCloud's Scale of Iconic Abstraction creates a startling sense of spectacle, a "fleshing out" of familiar two-dimensional characters into more realistic-looking three-dimensional ones, yet the sense of the mythic remains. One reason for this is that the paintings, while definitely more realistic than conventional comics art, are still artwork rather than photography. They are therefore able to render a three-dimensional world while retaining a distance from photorealism, a distance that emphasizes and expands upon the fantastic qualities of a comic book adventure story.

Another reason for the retention of mythic qualities in this series is the device of the photojournalist's perspective. In effect, Sheldon is the proxy for the audience. He is usually shown on the streets amid other ordinary citizens of the city, observing amazing events. Readers, in a sense, see the story through his single eye (his other eye was lost in the first issue of the series) in the same way Sheldon sees the events through the eye of his camera lens. Distanced by this perspective, the actions of the superheroes take on mythic import. The awed perspective of an ordinary onlooker compensates for the increased realism of the painting style. These elements, plus the ironic resonance of reading twice-told tales, complete the effect necessary to present a comics story in a new way while, if anything, increasing its mythic evocation.

The Sandman

Another example of a comics series that sought to evoke the mythic in an unconventional way was the Sandman series, written by Neil Gaiman and illustrated by various artists. A mini-series within the larger series has been collected into a published book entitled *Sandman: Season of Mists*. In this collection, the Sandman series can be described as, among other things, a myth about myths. Its central character, Morpheus, is the Sandman. The Sandman is known as "Dream" to his siblings, who are referred to collectively as "the Endless." Frank McConnell describes this metaphysical brood as "anthropomorphic projections of the essential human fears and aspirations, who are projections of our own condition and therefore are the origins of all gods and mythologies" (22). Their names are Destiny, Death, Desire, Delirium, Despair, and Dream. The figure of Morpheus is tall, gaunt, and pale, with a tousled thatch of black hair and black pools for eyes, sort of a Goth version of a Romantic poet. Awake or in their dreams, ordinary people may find themselves visited by the Sandman or appearing in his half-lit realm. Such a metaphysical scenario allows for a broad, multilayered canvas extending back in time and into both Heaven and Hell.

In *Season of Mists*, Dream goes to Hell to redeem a woman whom he'd sent there after she had rejected his love eons earlier. There he encounters Hell's lord, Lucifer Morningstar, who announces that he has decided to quit the infernal region. He then evacuates its inhabitants, leaving the key to Dream. Soon, figures from the world's mythologies converge on Hell to lay claim to possession of the dark realm. Two angels arrive to observe. After a series of encounters, intrigues, and confrontations, Dream bestows the key to Hell to the two angels, who convert the realm from a place of endless torment to a place of eventual redemption where "the flames of hell Remiel [an angel] muses, have become refining fires, burning away the dross, leaving purity and repentance and good" ("Epilogue" 8). Dream frees his lost love, an African woman named Nada, and sends her away to be reborn as an infant in a Hong Kong hospital. Lucifer is last seen sunning himself on an Australian beach.

This synopsis does not begin to communicate the unsettling strangeness of this story, which draws upon Homer, Dante, Milton, and numerous mythologies. The most immediately striking component of the stories is the artwork, mostly by Kelly Jones, that ranges from weird depictions of the dream world to horrific imagery of the denizens of Hell. The conventional comics renderings of figures is replaced by Jones's Gothic style, a cross between El Greco and Hieronymus Bosch. Gaiman's storytelling allows Jones and other artists to explore the depiction of surreal images rarely before seen in comic book pages, creating a sense of a mythopoeic universe. Being less action-oriented than the typical comicbook story, the narration depends more on the rendering of images within panels rather than closure between them.

Gaiman's Sandman tales plumb the depths of mythology, literature, and history by mixing fantasy tales with contemporary urban locales to offer up what might be termed a meta-myth. The darkly romantic Sandman stories move out of the superhero genre altogether to tap into a surreal metaphysical vision employing images and characters appropriated from classical literature and myth. The *Marvels* series evokes the mythic through a changed perspective on familiar characters and stories. Both series hint at how broad the possibilities are for the evocation of the mythic through this medium. At the same time, as Scott McCloud frequently argues in *Understanding Comics,* the comics medium has within it an untapped potential for varieties of storytelling of which the mythic is only one; the comics' potential should not be constrained by its long-time association with the familiar superhero genre (22). The point is that there is more than one way to evoke the mythic in such a medium.

Summary

It is due to the comics' often "invisible art," to use McCloud's term, that Batman achieves mythic expression. We are able to move beyond our "received" view of material reality, in which Batman's existence, not to mention his particular qualities, would be impossible, on to the "perceived" view of iconic representation in which deceptively simple line art and four-color printing render the preposterous compelling and thrilling. McCloud frames his discussion by describing the common closure we all apply to everyday life. As children we learn that just because something is out of sight does not mean it is not there. Gradually, this inference of a whole from evidence of the parts, which is closure, becomes a way of life, and this also becomes the way we encounter comics. The comics' creator depends on our ability to supply that which he has withheld but implied. "All I ask of you is a little faith," states McCloud, speaking as an artist, "and a world of imagination" (93). Such a proposition, the basis of all fiction, is the particular foundation of mythic expression. Seeking to depict more than material reality, such romances make particular demands on their readers. Readers must have faith that there is more to the world than "reality" and must be willing to engage their imaginations in the perception of another world of meaning. The comics' iconography of Batman evokes meaningful mythic expressions because the reader's imagination is engaged in those works. Batman here is no silly crime fighter in tights but rather a complex figure of dual (and dueling) natures. Here, in the art form of comics, he is best realized as a carrier of meaning through his iconic significance.

This dualism, so well realized by the comics medium, raises a question: Is comics the best medium for Batman's realization because, like Batman, the medium itself is liminal? The medium itself combines what are generally two different modes—words and images—into one that is interstitial, or that at least combines two distinct categories, not necessarily opposed but certainly at two ends of the symbolic scale. Noel Carroll's view of the nature of horror is that that which is interstitial can be fascinating because it defies categories. So if liminal means "on the threshold," between two rooms, not just this or that, then comics may be likewise fascinating and compelling because it is a liminal medium. Like Batman, the comics medium itself does not fit neatly into conventional categories.

Comics, both in the form of comic strips and comic books, has gripped the imaginations of readers for a century, often using the simplest and silliest subject matter to confound some of the loftier critics of culture with their persistent popularity along all social strata. Though waxing and waning in his relative public visibility, the character Batman is now more prominent than ever while other heroic comics characters, such as Flash Gordon or the Phantom, have faded from their earlier glory. Naturally, both the company that owns the character and those working in other media have long sought to exploit Batman's potential for adaptation, with mixed results.

• 5 •

Adapting Batman
and the Mythic into Film

One of the earliest "trick" films was *The Dream of a Rarebit Fiend* (1906), directed by Edwin S. Porter and based on a 1904 comic strip by Winsor McCay. One visual medium's content being adapted into another is a recurring pattern in American entertainment; the transporting of comic book superheroes to Hollywood blockbusters is the culmination of that affinity. The 21st century goal of corporate synergy has been realized less often than attempted, but one successful example of this is the Time Warner project of adapting its DC Comics division character of Batman into various media expressions.

The study of film adaptations, whether from literary or other sources, involves several levels of analysis. One of the first such studies, George Bluestone's *Novels into Film*, pointed out the formative differences between literature and the cinema. Whereas film presents its content directly to our perceptions in its creation of visual and aural representations of its content, literature requires an intervening symbol system. Each, Bluestone writes, represents "a different mode of experience, a different way of apprehending the universe," and these differences affect the way each medium handles "tropes, affect beholders, render states of consciousness (including dreams, memories, feelings, and imagination, to their respective methods of handling conventions, time, and space" (20). This acknowledgment of formal differences between media anticipated by several years Marshall McLuhan's famous dictum, "The medium is the message."

The process of adapting prose fiction into film has long occupied theorists. In discussing issues of "fidelity and transformation" in film adaptations,

Dudley Andrew addresses to what degree a film follows the original source. Too literal an adaptation constrains the artistic freedom of the filmmaker to transform the source material into a filmic entity. "The skeleton of the original can, more or less thoroughly, become the skeleton of a film" (100).

"More difficult," he continues, "is fidelity to the spirit, to the original's tone, values, imagery, and rhythm, since finding stylistic equivalents in film for these intangible aspects is the opposite of a mechanical process" (Ibid.). In the process of creating a fictional world, Andrew asserts, writers must employ "signs (graphemes and words) building to propositions which attempt to develop perception," whereas film "is found to work from perception toward signification, from external facts to interior motivations and consequences, from the givenness of a world to the meaning of a story cut out of that world" (101). Spanning the gap between written prose and filmed narrative is a challenge for any type of fiction, but with the literary, authors' use of symbolism, metaphor, similes, and other meanings increases the dangers of forcing literary devices into a visual medium.

This process becomes even more daunting when the literary source is a story that contains mythic elements, such as J. R. R. Tolkien's *The Lord of the Rings.* Rather than working in the style of the naturalistic fiction that characterized 20th century writing, Tolkien sought to return to an epic narrative set in an imagined world with character and creatures from various ancient races whose traits were exteriorized; that is, unburied and directly accessible to the reader. Moreover, one of these races, the immortal Elves, were something above mortal mankind in the story's hierarchy and possessed qualities evoked through Tolkien's language rather than being described in physical terms. Discussing the difficulty of translating such mythic elements in a prose work is important preparation for the shift to discussing how Batman's mythic qualities are rendered, successfully or not, in other media's adaptations.

Fantasy Prose Novel into Film

Peter Jackson's 2001 film adaptation of the first book of the trilogy, *The Fellowship of the Rings,* was widely embraced by critics and audiences alike. A fantasy novel that had been considered unadaptable by many found a new audience of filmgoers. Critical reaction, though generally positive, remarked on the heavy emphasis on action at the expense of character development, but this was considered a necessary cost of fitting an epic story into feature-length running time. One aspect that received less attention was the disjunction between Tolkien's depiction of the more mythic elements of his story and those same elements when rendered on film. To the degree there is a discernable deficit of mythic evocation in the film, the adaptation demonstrates an inherent limitation of the film medium. The film adaptation serves as a case study in what happens when a photorealistic medium attempts to capture qualities that resist such depiction.

Mythic Evocation in Narratives

As with the discussion of Batman, I use the term "mythic" not in a formal sense like mythological, i.e., the mythic object is part of a complete cultural narrative system. Rather, it is used to describe characters and stories with traits that resemble the mythological patterns that have endured through centuries. These characters and stories may be mythic in that they are *myth-like*. They function like myths without the formerly religious aspects of classical mythologies, in that they offer stories and characters which embody an audiences' hopes, dreams, and fears, and offer a resolution to personal or social conflicts. Mythic evocation expresses that which transcends the prosaic or materialistic. It employs archetypal characters and situations to address profound issues of meaning and existence. In the case of the Tolkien trilogy, the author drew from Norse legend and Gaelic culture in inventing a vast history and mythology. The power of words alone, crafted artfully, can evoke mythic resonances in the reader's imagination in ways that mere images cannot. The continuing status of Tolkien's high fantasy testifies to the mythopoeic potential of prose.

Returning to Northrop Frye's concept of myth and displacement discussed in earlier chapters, we can better analyze the nature and challenge of adapting Middle-earth to film. Frye, describing mythopoeic literature, organized narratives along a scale with myth on the upper end, realism at the lower end, and the broad area of romance in between. He discerned clear patterns of heroic action in the romance. Frye situated romance in the broad area between realism and myth (*Anatomy* 136). In order for myth to be expressed through the form of the romance, Frye maintains, the device of displacement must be used. "In a myth," writes Frye, "we can have a sun-god or a tree-god; in a romance we may have a person who is significantly associated with the sun or trees" (137). Thus, the romance may draw upon myth without being itself a myth. As with the comics depiction of Batman, Tolkien locates the mythic in the upper reaches of the romance section of Frye's continuum between realism and myth. Here characters, places, and situations may, through displacement from myth, "borrow" from myth and thus resonate with the mythopathic imaginations of readers.

Figure 5.1: The Scale of Literary Design adapted from Northrop Frye's *Anatomy of Criticism*.

Frye wrote of prose and poetry's treatment of romance and myth, but other media have long sought to depict mythic subjects. From the statuary of ancient Greece, to Wagner's *Ring* cycle that presented a version of Norse myth through the music and characters in operatic form, the various arts have sought to capture the mythopoeic.

As mentioned earlier, Scott McCloud explains how the comics medium utilizes the iconicity of comics art to increase the level of meaning. Comics art is typically simplified compared to photorealistic images. McCloud illustrates this concept with his Scale of Iconic Abstraction showing increasing levels of meaning from realism to pure meaning.

The scale (See Figure 4.2) begins on the far left with realism, exemplified by photorealistic illustration and moves to the right toward increasingly abstract drawings characterized by decreased detail and by increased potential for reader-provided meaning. As iconic abstraction increases and any semblance of realism disappears, the scale crosses over into the area of pure abstraction, i.e., the realm of language or words. Whereas pictures of relative abstraction had represented an object or idea, now words represent them. Thus, in McCloud's scale, a face moves from photorealistic depiction increasingly toward the abstract until it becomes the word "Face" and then is described rather than drawn: "two eyes, one nose, one mouth," and finally a literary rendering demonstrated by use of a quoted poem ("Thy youth's proud livery, so gazed on now ..."). On McCloud's scale, comics and cartoons begin where enough detail has been removed to allow for the involvement of the reader's imagination in a way not possible through photorealistic depiction.

The depiction of objects in the photorealistic medium of film is heavily weighted toward realism or toward what McCloud calls "the world without," whereas cartoons portray "the world within" (41). Film must use other techniques to mitigate its inherent realism, such as the many formalistic techniques developed over the past century, including editing, lighting, music, and special effects.[1]

Film's Strengths and Weaknesses

The history of film has been a record of the medium's development of its potential for both realistic and formalistic style. This preeminent art form of the 20th century could, on one hand, become the mirror of everyday life, producing documentary actualities of diverse lands, peoples and events. But it could also impose a form that alters its perception of reality with changes in lenses, filters, lighting, and color, or by extending or compressing real time through editing. In all cases, audiences are presented with the physical detail, movement, and spectacle that only the print medium can suggest. Film is perhaps the most inclusive of the arts in that it incorporates other art forms: drama, photography, dance, music, and so forth. Being a visual and aural medium, employing a large "canvas" of the theater screen, film can depict spectacle in ways that mere drama, and of course prose, cannot.

In film theory, style has been a central concern. Film itself runs along a spectrum of style from realism to formalism, according to Louis Giannetti. His chart of film style features a line with arrows at each end pointing toward the two directions cinematic style may take. On the left is direction of realism, and on the right is formalism. Strongly realistic narrative films are further to the left, with documentary (and perhaps security camera footage) films furthest out. "Realism is a particular *style,* whereas physical reality is the source of all the raw materials of film, both realistic and formalistic," Giannetti writes. "Virtually all movie directors go to the photographable world for their subject matter but what they do with their material—how they shape and manipulate it—is what determines their stylistic emphasis" (2). Thus, a realistically styled film such as *Tender Mercies* (1983) tells a story such as we might experience in everyday life. Other films, like Bergman's *The Seventh Seal* (1957), with its striking black and white photography and highly allegorical characters, is well into the formalistic direction of the scale. This would also include highly stylized films such as *The Matrix* (1999) with its reality-warping special effects. The ultimate formalistic end of a film style would be the Avant-Garde, wherein form for its own sake is emphasized. Realist directors stress content or style, whereas formalists stress technique and expressiveness (4, 5). Giannetti asserts that most classic cinema, such as Hollywood films of the 1930s, is in the middle of the scale, literally in the mainstream. This realism-formalism scale seems to approximate Scott McCloud's reality-picture plane as both scales start with reality and move toward ever more abstracted forms.

Thus, when filmmakers adapt a comic book character into live-action film, they have a range of style upon which to place their vision. This range of style will become important when analyzing various versions of Batman on film.

André Bazin, the French theorist of film realism, recounts how the coming of film changed painting. Whereas for centuries painters had sought to capture the spiritual qualities of their subjects, such as religious paintings and icons, the Renaissance introduced such elements as perspective and lighting in the search for greater realism. "Thenceforth," Bazin writes, "painting was torn between two ambitions: one primarily aesthetic, namely the expression of spiritual reality wherein the symbol transcended its model; the other, purely psychological, namely the duplication of the world outside" (Bazin, 196). Painting's search for ever more realism ended, Bazin argues, with the arrival of photography, a mechanical process that automatically recorded reality, hence freeing painting to explore abstract areas such as color, form, and implicitly, spiritual qualities. Film's proper sphere was realism, since it was based in a scientific process for capturing the world. Painting was the sphere of the spiritual and the imagination. As such, the material world, being the proper sphere of cinematic content, did not present the challenges of capturing spiritual content. The enlisting of formalistic, non-photorealistic special effects or abstract elements, such as musical scores, added subliminal artistic qualities.

Bazin's ideas might explain to some degree the problem C. S. Lewis had with film's limitations in capturing certain types of story elements. In his essay, "On Stories," Lewis discusses how stories often achieve their greatest effects when they transcend the literal elements of the plot to evoke spiritual qualities. As mentioned briefly in Chapter 1, Lewis uses a scene in H. G. Wells's *First Men in the Moon,* in which a character, Bedford, is shut out on the moon's surface. Bedford (and, vicariously, the reader) experiences, not just the predicament of being left to freeze or suffocate, but a profound sense of eternal separation.

> That airless outer darkness is important not for what it can do to Bedford but for what it does to us: to trouble us with Pascal's old fear of those eternal silences which have gnawed at so much religious faith and shattered so may humanistic hopes: to evoke with them and through them all our racial and childish memories of exclusion and desolation: to present, in fact, as an intuition one permanent aspect of human experience [Stories, 96].

It is a strength of literature that, with words alone, it may create, using plot elements, a sense of otherness in the reader's mind. The use of fantastic narratives is often the means by which readers are drawn in to experience this sense of having encountered such varieties of the other. Thus the fantasy, or science fiction story, becomes a route for readers to contemplate the most profound spiritual dangers and joys. "To construct plausible and moving 'other worlds,'" Lewis continues, "you must draw on the only real 'other world' we know, that of the spirit" (98).

It is here we see how books like *The Lord of the Rings* may become a means of drawing readers into an encounter with the mythopoeic, and beyond the plot elements of adventure stories alone. Further on in the essay, Lewis discusses the manner in which certain readers who enjoy adventure fiction may, in fact, be deriving from it "certain profound experiences that are, for him, not acceptable in any other form" (101). Adventure stories, for example, may be able to evoke in the "unliterary" reader emotions and ideas that transcend the story's clichéd settings and formulas. Rather than receiving mere thrills from such stories, the "untrained" reader with an active imagination may find himself attaining the same rewards as trained partakers of great art. "He will, at a mere hint from the author," Lewis writes, "flood wretched material with suggestion and never guess that he is himself making what he enjoys" (102). Contrasting film and literary versions of adventure stories that have mythopoeic content, Lewis maintains it is the form of the written romance, however hackneyed, that is the most effective vehicle of the mythic, leading to his remark that there is "death in the camera."

It is film's very ability to depict material verisimilitude that diminishes the degree to which our imagination will be engaged. Because film supplies so much detail, both visual and aural, it leaves little to the imagination. Its tendency toward literalism works against the evocation of the mythic. As a literalizing, rather than literary, medium, film often requires the aforementioned formalistic devices that will move the filmic narrative from the too-literally concrete to the more abstract, where the imagination may be more open to evocation of the sense of the spiritual or otherness.

On the other hand, film succeeds in other areas of narrative. The movie screen excels in rendering qualities important in storytelling, including spectacle and drama. By spectacle is meant the ability to effectively render the visible both in scale and detail. It is these qualities that may come to the aid of an adaptation of an epic story, even while film's limitations may diminish or deprive the story of its mythopoeic qualities.

This is in accord with both McCloud's and Bazin's ideas regarding the image, realism, and symbolic evocation of non-material qualities. McCloud's scale of iconic abstraction starts from literal photo-realism on the left end of the scale, where the image captures only the thing itself with low potential for encouraging the imagination. As detail is eliminated in gradual movement on the scale to the right toward increasing abstraction of the image, through elimination of texture and detail, the potential for evoking greater or larger meaning increases. In words we find the complete transition to pure non-representative symbol, freed now to convey whatever meaning an author is able to create. In Bazin's scheme, painting's strength in depicting spiritual qualities is strong to the degree that it avoids the realism only photography can capture. It is this "spiritual reality" described by Bazin that would include the realm of mythic depiction as seen in Tolkien's *The Lord of the Rings*.

The Diminishing of the Elvish

If what McCloud, Bazin, and Lewis seem to agree is true about photography's inability to capture the mythic on film, we should find this borne out in the film adaptation of Tolkien. This process of diminishment, or discarding, of mythic elements is most apparent in the rendering of Tolkien's Elves. This can be established by a comparison of pertinent passages of text with comparable sequences from Jackson's *The Fellowship of the Ring* and may serve to illustrate how literary descriptions more simply and effectively capture mythopoeic qualities.

The Elves in Tolkien's "sub-creation" are an ancient, immortal, isolated race. *The Hobbit* and *The Lord of the Rings* described the Elves as tall, slender, resistant to extremes of heat and cold, and possessed of heightened senses. It is what Tolkien *doesn't* tell readers that contributes to the Elves' mythopoeic nature. More is gleaned by other characters' accounts of these singular creatures. Two passages from *The Fellowship of the Ring* illustrate this. In the first, from Book I, Chapter 3, "Three Is Company," Frodo and Sam have departed Hobbiton for Bree and have been joined by Pippin. One night the Hobbits realize a Black Rider has come near, searching for the Ring. Suddenly, voices are heard; it is the singing of a party of approaching Elves. The dark figure hears and vanishes into the night. The Hobbits listen to the Elves singing until

the song ended. "These are High-Elves! They spoke the name of Elbereth!" said Frodo in amazement. "Few of the fairest folk are ever seen in the Shire. Not many now remain in Middle-earth, east of the Great Sea. This is indeed a strange chance!"

The hobbits sat in shadow by the wayside. Before long the Elves came down the lane towards the valley. They passed slowly, and the hobbits could see the starlight glimmering on their hair and in their eyes. They bore no lights, yet as they walked a shimmer, like the light of the moon above the rim of the hills before it rises, seemed to fall about their feet [*Fellowship*, 99].

The Elves invite the Hobbits to join them for the night, and as they continue on to their destination, Tolkien recounts, "Sam walked along at Frodo's side, as if in a dream, with an expression on his face half of fear and half of astonished joy" (*Fellowship* 90). Whereas Tolkien has opened his epic tale with a 15-page prologue, "Concerning Hobbits," which gives a detailed description of Hobbits' appearances, customs, and history, readers learn of the Elves mainly through the perspectives and reactions of the Hobbits.

Another means by which Tolkien establishes the mythic status of his Elves is his use of elevated language. In Book II of *The Fellowship of the Ring*, we again encounter the Elves through the Hobbit's point of view, specifically

Frodo's, when he joins the wizard Gandalf at the Elvish home, Rivendell, for a feast presided over by the Elf Lord Elrond. Rather than using the detailed descriptive prose of naturalistic novels, Tolkien shifts his writing into an epic, even poetic, mode. In the following passage, Frodo observes the High Elves gathered at table:

> Frodo looked at them in wonder, for he had never before seen Elrond, of whom so many tales spoke; and as they sat upon his right hand and his left, Glorfindel, and even Gandalf, whom he thought he knew so well, were revealed as lords of dignity and power.
>
> Gandalf was shorter in stature than the other two; but his long white hair, his sweeping silver beard, and his broad shoulders made him look like some wise king of ancient legend....
>
> Glorfindel was tall and straight; his hair was of shining gold, his face fair and young and fearless and full of joy; his eyes were bright and keen, and his voice like music; on his brow sat wisdom, and in his hand was strength.
>
> The face of Elrond was ageless, neither old nor young, though in it was written the memory of many things both glad and sorrowful. His hair was dark as the shadows of twilight, and upon it was set a circlet of silver; his eyes were grey as a clear evening, and in them was a light like the light of stars. Venerable he seemed as a king crowned with many winters, and yet hale as a tried warrior in the fulness of his strength. He was the Lord of Rivendell and mighty among both Elves and Men [*Fellowship* 280–281].

It is worth noting that neither of the above passages is depicted in the film.[2] How instead does the film visualize the Elves? We first see them fighting alongside armies of Men in the opening prologue sequence. The Elf Lord Elrond (Hugo Weaving), the most prominent of the Elves in the scene, is distinguished from the men by his lack of a beard, and by his pointed ears, features not mentioned in the book. Other than that, there seems to be little difference in his depiction of the warriors. There are no scenes that parallel the Hobbits' point of view of the Elves, particularly Sam's excitement.

Later, when the Hobbits have reached Rivendell, we see Gandalf and Elrond discuss what is to be done with the Ring. Here it becomes all too apparent that no special quality other than a high sense of dignity characterizes Elrond. The camera has no ability to bestow the qualities Tolkien has evoked through both the Hobbits' perspectives and his elevated prose style. Instead, we get costume design, and whatever appearance the actor brings to the role. Elfish make-up mostly consists of the pointed ear prosthetics. It is a prime example of the limits of cinema when attempting to evoke the mythic.

Similar observations can be made of the Elves of Lothlorien. When the Fellowship first encounters Elf sentries, they appear more androgynous than mysterious. When Galadriel is offered the Ring by Frodo, what in the book is a moment of high drama, is in the film a special-effects moment as the actress's performance is augmented by aural and (apparently) digital effects which turn her a strange shade of green. Rather than capturing the drama of temptation, the scene is distracting in its excess use of effects.

The diminishing of the mythic elements of Tolkien's epic when adapted to a photorealistic medium, as demonstrated herein, raises again the differing natures of media as discussed by Marshall McLuhan, Neil Postman, and Jacques Ellul, among others. Although respective media may, in adapting content from another medium, seek their own equivalent version of a given element from the original source, the result can often strike those familiar with that source as a distressing departure from what had worked so well. Whereas print's strength is in its ability to explore character psychology through passages of description and the internal monologue, film is geared toward spectacle, and, therefore, character psychology must be communicated through dialogue and action. In many ways Peter Jackson's finding of content equivalents succeeds brilliantly, if one is open to the sometimes wrenching changes in approach, particularly pacing, that cinematic adaptation requires. But finding equivalents or correlations for the mythic elements of the text version shows us the boundaries of film's abilities when depicting mythopoeic figures.

Having established that there are boundaries, we may be at the point in time when we could see changes in the potential for mythic evocation of various media. With the continued expansion of digital animation into ever more intricate renderings of visual information, a new look at Bazin's assessment of the distinction between photography and painting is in order. If, as Bazin asserted, the burden of realism carried by painting from the 15th century on prevented it from doing what it did best, i.e., portraying the esoteric qualities of the spiritual, and that cinema liberated painting from that, then what happens when cinema goes from film to digital, from a photorealistic medium of chemical-emulsion on celluloid to one of digital cameras and processed pixels? Does the growing fusion of digital photography with digital animation and effects change the potential for mythic evocation in live-action narratives? In an article in *Film Comment* discussing the implications of George Lucas's conversion of the filmmaking process to a totally digital one, Gregory Solman recalls Bazin's discussion.

> But Bazin's aesthetic/psychological distinction between photography and painting can also describe the tension between live-action film and digital fabrications. CGI in particular is created like painting, by the collective hands of artists. Indeed, the proliferation of digital imagery (and now digital video projection) should rekindle an argument that has raged throughout cinema history. It mandates a reconsideration of Bazin's phenomenological theory, which viewed the cinema as an extension of the perception of nature, rather than a radical alteration, because photography refers

profoundly to the actual object or person photographed, representing for Bazin a "transference of reality from a thing to its reproduction" [Solman 26].

So, does digital technology rewrite the rules of cinema's potential for capturing qualities that have been the province of painting? Does "painting with pixels" promise the reunion of the spiritual and material in the cinematic image? So far, in terms of the depiction of human figures, we have seen some attempts such as *Final Fantasy: The Spirits Within* (2001), a totally computer-animated film with human figures, as well as many other films featuring numerous CGI-augmented scenes and characters, including the aforementioned *Lord of the Rings* film trilogy. Thus far, such efforts have managed to approximate human movements and features, or those of more fanciful creatures, but have not attempted to create mythic characters such as Tolkien's Elves. Can computer pixels render that which words evoke in the imagination? Can numinous qualities be digitally represented? To refuse to believe it is possible may be to betray a bias toward prose's mythopoeic ability, but thus far, computer-generated imaging's struggle toward ever more specific depictions seems to put it in competition with photography in achieving realistic textures, which, according to Scott McCloud's argument, are the very qualities that diminish meaning. The work of painting prior to the 15th century didn't aim for realistic depiction—it sought to render the spiritual qualities. Will CGI seek to move in a less realistic direction that seeks to capture the mythopoeic?

Jacques Ellul, in an essay in his book *The Humiliation of the Word*, states clearly that the written word is best able to capture the mythopathic human imagination. For all the pleasure a faithful cinematic adaptation of Tolkien's book can offer filmgoers, it is his literary strategies that remain the more satisfying.

Issues in Adapting Comics into Film

Comic books, long a culturally marginalized medium and not sharing the cultural status of the novel, nevertheless have carved a niche in the public consciousness, first as a juvenile form of entertainment, and more recently as an increasingly sophisticated form of narrative for adult readers. The basic principles of adaptation, whether from traditional literary sources or comics, must take into account the particular biases of each medium, the original and its intended new one. As McLuhan and others have discussed, content changes from one medium to another, and just as one cannot simply create a word-for-word film script version of a novel without accounting for the formal differences between the two narrative forms, the adaptor must grapple with finding how to translate the original content into its cinematic equivalent.

The success and endurance of Batman over 70 years is partly due to his adaptability into various narrative scenarios and stylistic modes in the comics medium. Writing in 1999, Les Daniels, after recounting the character's evolution through various comics eras, remarks, "At this point it seems that Batman can enter any world he wants" (Daniels and Kidd 202). Over the decades, Batman has been a time traveler, space explorer, fought magical forces, robots, zombies, other superheroes, and fantastic elements other than the bizarre criminals most associated with him. Because of the way in which comics art iconography calls for the imaginative response from the reader, two-dimensional imagery makes Batman's adventures more varied than virtually any other character in popular culture history.

While this has certainly been demonstrated in the comics medium, moving Batman into other media has proved more challenging. If Batman's effectiveness as a character hinges on the evocation of his mythic aspects via the comics medium, what happens when adaptations are attempted in movie serials, television series (both live-action and animated), and feature films as well as novels and video games?

Comics and Film Contrasted and Compared

For the sake of this analysis, "film" refers to any use of the film medium in live-action or animated feature-length or short features, live-action feature films or television programs. Throughout its history, the film industry has used the comics as a source of material. Comic strip characters such as Li'l Abner, Blondie, Flash Gordon and Popeye have inspired their own live-action film adaptations. Similarly, Superman, Wonder Woman, and the Flash, among others, have become the subjects for feature film or television adaptations, with varying degrees of success. The 1990s saw other, lesser known, comic book characters becoming the subjects of movie adaptations, such as *The Rocketeer* (1991), and *The Mask* (1994), *Tank Girl* (1995) and *Judge Dredd* (1995). It is evident that Hollywood producers perceive some affinity between the two media and, put quite simply, both feature dramatic storytelling through a combination of pictures and words. And since 2000, various comic book franchises, mainly from Marvel Comics featuring the X-Men, Spider-Man, the Fantastic Four and others have become profitable studio tentpole features. Since the Christopher Reeve Superman series of features ended with *Superman IV: The Quest for Peace* (1987), DC has struggled to successfully translate their premier hero as well as Green Lantern for modern audiences. The summer of 2012 saw a critical mass of comic book-based blockbusters, *The Avengers, The Amazing Spider-Man,* and *The Dark Knight Rises,* indicating just how committed Hollywood studios are to this genre. Similarly, the summer of 2013 saw more blockbuster releases with *Iron Man 3, The Man of Steel,* Warner Bros.' latest attempt at making Superman fly at the multiplex, and *The Wolverine.*

Similarities

In considering the relationship between comics and film, there are several notable areas in which they resemble each other. Both media manipulate visual images to control narration, to speed up or slow down the perception of time and space, and to indicate the relationships of characters and objects. The superficial resemblance of a movie storyboard to a comic has long been obvious: both feature the graphic depiction of pictorial and aural information, including viewer perspective and dialogue.

In a book on the basics of filmmaking, *Moviemaking Illustrated,* authors Morrow and Suid demonstrate the similarity between storyboards and comics panels by using examples from comic books to illustrate filmic devices such as camera movements, editing, and narration. Besides this similarity, both media make use of changing perspectives or "camera angles" to suggest relationships and to vary the presentation of a scene. Similarly, both comics (using closure, in the sense described in Chapter 4) and film (by editing techniques) have established conventions of arranging the sequence of images so that the action depicted is matched from image to image, providing a sense of seamless temporal continuity. This study has already referred to the similarity between comics' use of closure to convey meaning and film's use of editing as expressed in Eisenstein's theory of montage. Both media juxtapose images—comics in space and film in time—to create a new meaning arising from the juxtapositions. Though comics are "silent" in that no audible sound emanates from them, the use of the convention of "sound effects" through stylized lettering ("Pow!," "Thwack!," etc.) are the comics' counterparts to film's sound effects.

Mutual Influence

Throughout the development of both comics and film there have been enough mutual influences that each medium is beholden to the other for devices and effects. Film historian John Fell notes that even as far back as the early part of the 20th century, when both film and the comic strip were burgeoning art forms, comic strip pioneers, such as Winsor McCay, preceded filmmakers in the ingenious use of shifting perspectives to depict movement through space (Fell 92). Credited as a unique feature of film, this technique was actually anticipated by comics. This mutual influence was particularly evident in the case of the Batman stories, according to two men on the creative team. Dick Sprang, one of the Batman artists from the Golden Age, readily credits the movies as a chief influence: "I really soaked up the movie technique," he stated, "and I've always used that" (quoted in Darnell 35). "Movies were a great influence," he said elsewhere, "simply because they had movement.... But a comic artist works in a static medium" (quoted in Desris 57). Referring to filmmaking technique, he commented, "What I tried to do was get into my work a dramatic highlight, to isolate peak action in what moviemakers call the frozen frame, the equivalent of a comic page panel" (Ibid.). This echoes the classic editing practice of "cutting on action," i.e., at the point where a dynamic movement, such as a swinging fist, expresses the greatest sense of action, followed by cutting to the reaction of the blow. Both comics and film use changes in "shots," or images, to suggest and magnify the sense of movement for the greatest dramatic and visceral impact.

Finally, the discussion of Bob Kane's and Bill Finger's repeated viewings of *Citizen Kane* in Chapter 2 underlines the impact of film art on comics art. Comics historians George Perry and Alan Aldridge trace the cinematic devices made famous by Orson Welles in *Citizen Kane* and maintain that they "echoed the work of the comic-strip artist and created a new library of film clichés" (254). The same authors also point to the influence comics had on such French filmmakers as Alain Resnais and Jean-Luc Godard. They report that Resnais used "the whiting out of backgrounds to throw the foreground characters into relief," and that Godard used the comics narrative convention of titles to announce sequences of the story (Ibid.).

Differences

The most obvious difference between film and comics is that comics images are static and film images move. The "movement" in comics is only implied, being communicated through such conventions as speed lines, indicating motion, or through the device of closure, signaling action between sequential panels. The chief appeal of film is, of course, its ability to reproduce motion. Likewise, one cannot really hear sounds when reading comics, but must read descriptions of them. However, it is in the unique blending of these elements—movement and sound—that the real nature of film emerges.

Words and Sound

Because of its mechanical nature as a recording medium, film is equipped to capture pieces of life in a more complete fashion than any other medium. Combining the photographic process with the recording of synchronous sound, film offers what appears to be reality. It is this ability to offer multiple sensory inputs that creates the unique mediated experience of film and constitutes its greatest contrast with the medium of comics. Though comics may seek to render images that offer high degrees of verisimilitude, by its very nature sequential art is comparatively constrained. A comic book illustration of a man and a woman walking down a city street would indicate enough detail for readers to know what was happening in the panels, whereas the same scene on film would obviously contain far more detail because of its ability to photograph exactly what was there. In addition to providing photographic realism, film's sound recording captures the natural effect of complex sound (footsteps, conversations, traffic, and other machinery, etc.). In contrast, a comics rendering would have to depend on devices such as word balloons or narration (much like a novel's expository and descriptive passages) to indicate the same cluster of complex ambient sounds.

This contrast in complexity is even more evident when one compares dialogue in comics and in film. On film, the soundtrack in the scene of the man and the woman walking down the street could, of course, enable the audience to hear in the actors' voices whatever tonal qualities, accents, and inflections are there. The same conversation in comics would use written words for the dialogue and for whatever vocal qualities could be indicated. Comics lettering of dialogue has developed its own codes of expression, using all uppercase letters, italics or bold print for emphasis, with the occasional exaggerated stylization for the more unusual vocal and verbal expressions. Dialogue in comics tends to be concise and limited to the essentials, as opposed to film's more expansive, back-and-forth verbal exchanges. Conversely, film, being dependent on the naturalistic reproduction of sound, has difficulty indicating the thoughts of its characters, whereas through the simple device of the thought balloon or narrative captions comics readers are made privy to the musings and internal monologues of comics characters. Film only sparingly uses voiceover for such expressions.

It is film's use of its most abstract element—music—that lends the photorealistic medium the necessary abstraction to keep it from an excess of literalism. That is, music can be used to add or amplify emotional qualities that the photorealism of film inherently lacks. Film uses music to underline or indicate moods or emotions and other qualities that have no direct counterpart in comics. For indicating and underlining mood and emotion, comics may depend on illustrations that stylistically serve as indicators through perspective changes, exaggerated facial expression, and body postures, to name a few possibilities.

Iconic Abstractions vs. Photorealism

For the purposes of this study, the most crucial distinction between comics and film is the contrast between comics' drawn depictions and film's cinematography. Describing essential features of film content, film theorist Siegfried Kracauer noted that "the nature of photography survives in that of film" so that film, being a mechanical extension of photography, partakes of photography's ability to capture the details of physical reality (9). McCloud showed how meaning in a comics pictorial icon grows as the icon moves away from photographic realism. The subsequent loss of such detail "makes room" for the reader to impute cued meaning for that icon. Referring to photorealism as occupying the "received" end of his scale, McCloud posits that readers grow in their involvement with comics characters as the characters become less specifically realistic, moving increasingly toward the other end, the "perceived." The effect of the different depictions is perhaps best seen when examined using the example of a film adaptation of a comics character. In the comics depiction, characters are always themselves; no actors take the parts of the characters in order to bring them into the photorealistic "realm" of live-action. However, when a comics character is depicted on film, what is up on the screen is always the character as portrayed by an actor.

As Scott McCloud noted, a photographic image of someone represents one person, that particular individual, but as one moves toward increasing levels of abstraction through drawings, depictions represent increasing numbers of people as details diminish and generalizability increases. Speaking of this universality of the cartoon, McCloud stated, "The more cartoony a face is ... the more people it could be said to describe" (31). So an actor playing a cartoon character is, to some degree, reversing the process that creates the distinctive appeal of that character. By tearing the character away from its relatively generalized iconicity, the character's appearance is forced to "describe" fewer people; the actor's specific features replace the comics character's generalized ones. Other techniques must be employed to simplify and abstract the characterization away from the realistic setting of the photographic medium in order to find some filmic equivalent for the simple appeal of the comics character.

By attempting to portray a comics character—that is, a pictorial icon— an actor necessarily brings his or her own specific three-dimensionality to the role, thus lessening (if not negating) the iconic effect. Photorealistic film performance highlights the particular nuances and traits, bodily mannerisms, and facial details that an actor can bring to a role—expressions that constitute the actor's distinctive filmic style and presence. At the same time, audience members carry the memory of an actor's past performances to the viewing of each new one. Thus, a performance by a prominent film actor in one film reminds us of another of the actor's roles in a different film and, if the new performance is compelling, it becomes part of that actor's cumulative cinematic persona. Also, over time, most established film actors become known for the general types of roles they play or the particular persona they bring to a part. (Thus, casting a certain actor in a role very different from the types he or she has been in previously is known as casting against type.) These type associations are an almost ineradicable part of their public selves, and the audience expects to see them in each performance. This specificity is a major factor that sets film characterizations apart from comics characterizations. In contrast, to see a character in a comic book is, as in literature, not to see a performance but to see the character itself, unmediated by an actor. The only "performance" in this case is that of the artist and writer as they bring their distinctive style to their depiction of the character.

The producers of *Superman: The Movie* cast the then-unknown Christopher Reeve as the title character. Because he brought no prior filmic associations with him, audiences could more easily accept the unfamiliar actor as the very well known comics character. It may be inferred that producers realized that the casting of a well-known leading man would have taken away from the credibility of the performance because audiences would necessarily recall earlier "incarnations" of the actor. The involvement of the imagination enabled by comics' deliberately generalized and simplified characters is greatly mitigated, if not lost, when human actors portray the characters. Film's virtue is that it offers such vivid, realistic detail of both characters and scenery that it seems to be showing us reality, even when using a highly formalistic approach. And it is precisely these qualities that set it apart from the comics medium, which deliberately reduces the detail of its images, particularly of its characters, in order to increase their significance in their readers' imaginations by focusing on only a few telling details.

This distinction is further defined when it is related to the theorizing of Parker Tyler, who posits that film itself is a sort of mythic depiction. Through the film-watching process, the audience seated in the darkened theater engages in what Tyler asserts is passive daydreaming. Characters on the screen resonate with unconscious universal patterns, reenacting a mythic role and serving much the same function as dreaming. Tied to psychoanalytic concepts of dreams and archetypes, Tyler's theory posits film stars as gods and goddesses, who, though human, die and return to life with each succeeding film experience. Therefore, it is not the particular story's character the audience responds to as it is the gods/stars who persist through each cinematic incarnation. "Even as the gods do, they undergo continual metamorphoses," Tyler writes, "never losing their identities, being Rita Hayworth or Glenn Ford no matter what their movie aliases" (xxvii). If, as in this view, film's strength is mythic rather than aesthetic, then film's true power lies in mythologizing its stars, and in the stars' ability to function as mythic figures for the audience.

These distinctions between comics and cinematic characterizations apply to any consideration of negotiating adaptations between the former and the latter. As in all aspects of adaptation, the need to find some sort of suitable cinematic equivalent for a given quality in the original comics is the greatest challenge.

The Literal vs. the Mythopoeic

Many superhero comics tend toward the mythic in content, suggesting beings with the powers of gods and heroes of classical mythologies. We have seen why such exalted figures are difficult to depict photographically. The actors playing them look too much like normal people, except of course they are usually Hollywood handsome. The camera is too good at capturing the mundane details of the material world. It can only with great effort suggest the transcendent. Compared with photographic media, comics share with C.S. Lewis's "popular written fiction" the greater ability to draw on our imaginations, enabling us to believe in worlds and beings beyond the prosaic. This is largely due to the aforementioned simplicity of comics' depiction, which eliminates detail in order to focus on universal qualities of character and personhood.

Those attempting to adapt a subject and/or story from one medium to another must determine what particular qualities or components of the source medium constitute its appeal. To successfully adapt the story and characters into another medium, equivalents in the adaptive medium must be found for the appealing components of the source material. Simply put, what interests and appeals to the audience of one medium's artifact must find expression in some form in the medium into which it is being adapted or, if missing, or diminished in the adaptation, must be somehow compensated for to allow for a degree of audience satisfaction.

In the case of the adaptation of a comic book character such as Batman, the identification of the appealing components of his stories must precede its translation into other expressions. While research into the adaptation of novels and plays into films is not uncommon, similar degrees of research into the adaptation of comics into film has yet to occur. Those adapting comics into film often fail to comprehend the appealing components clearly enough to find satisfying equivalent expressions for them in the film versions. Comics, being a medium less appreciated and understood than literature or theater is often approached with superficial analysis. By not understanding how sequential art acts upon the imagination of its readers, those attempting to adapt a comic story and character risk losing essential components of the original. Thus, the mythic component at the heart of the Batman stories is often misunderstood if not entirely overlooked. The next two chapters examine efforts to adapt Batman into other media, and focuses especially on how the mythic content of the stories is treated in the process.

• 6 •

Adapting Batman, Part 1
Batman in Film and Other Media

Any discussion of adapting comic book superheroes into other media should take into account the differences between media forms. Comic books themselves have, over the years, between 28 to (currently) 22 pages, a pretty constraining boundary for narratives. Until the 1960s, superhero comics stories rarely extended past one issue, particularly when Stan Lee and his colleagues at Marvel Comics began writing multi-issue stories. The parameters of a story grew and enlarged the potential for more diverse and complex narratives. But the basic unit of a comic book story is still the single issue, whether it's a "one and done" stand-alone story, or a "chapter" in a multipart story, often running as long as six or more issues (often for purposes of later collecting into trade paper format). The single issue serves as pacing for a multipart story similar to book chapters, and these chapters often have cliffhanger endings to keep the reader coming back each month until the story's conclusion. This structural trait means superhero comics tend to take on a particular form with some variations which is distinct from forms in other media, such as film structure. This is perhaps the chief reason there have been few attempts to directly adapt a particular story from superhero comics to film. When these attempts have been tried, the results were rarely memorable. For example, Mark Steven Johnson's 2003 adaptation of Daredevil attempted to compress many issues of the comic title involving the hero's origin, the female assassin and Matthew Murdock's lover, Electra, and their battle against the villain Bullseye, and crime boss the Kingpin into one very busy feature film, resulting in critical and box-office failure. The film attempted to give ardent fans one of the best-known Daredevil stories, but Johnson's overly ambitious project didn't translate into film form.

Similarly, Zack Snyder's 2009 adaptation of one of the handful of masterpieces of comic storytelling, *Watchmen,* was found by many critics to be too literal an adaptation of Alan Moore's 12-part epic while necessarily cutting out one of the story's most ingenious devices, "Tales of the Black Freighter," a comic book read by a boy in the central narrative that comments upon the larger story. As Moore's original story is considered one of the more literary examples of graphic novels, it may share some of the same problems writers have when adapting prose.

Another main reason screenwriters have avoided specific comic book stories is film's three-act structure, running from 90 minutes to over two hours. The prescribed narrative structure for screenplays with its story beats, scene lengths, dialogue requirements and pacing is completely at odds with the comics form. The issue of form also relates to non-theatrical film adaptations. Despite its parodic approach, the 1960s *Batman* television series, which offered two half-hour episodes a week, with a cliffhanger at the end of the first episode, approximated the classic comic book structure described by Les Daniels: "Batman would encounter his opponent three times: losing the first fight, earning a draw in the second and finally triumphing in the third" (Daniels and Kidd 58). Following this pattern rather closely in its three-part structure, the Dynamic Duo initially confront the villain of the week, who escapes them; then they are captured by said villain, who places them in a fiendish death trap for the cliffhanger. In the follow-up episode, Batman and Robin manage to escape, after which they track down and capture their antagonist. The television series' two half-hour episodes per week was able to accommodate the serial nature of the superheroes narratives and remained a ratings winner during its first two seasons.

Though most of the stories in *Batman: The Animated Series* and other episodes produced by Bruce Timm at Warner Bros. were newly created, a few, including "The Laughing Fish," "Night of the Wolf," and "Joker's Millions" were adaptations of specific stories that had appeared in Batman comics. None were literal translations but they did retain the original story outline. "The Laughing Fish" effectively combined plot elements from two different stories from Batman comics. The story time of one or two single issues seemed to translate well into the 22-minute running time of an animated episode.

This chapter will focus on four attempts at adapting the Batman stories: the two Columbia Batman serials of the 1940s; the Batman television series of the 1960s; the first four Batman feature films released by Warner Bros.; and the *Batman: The Animated Series*, which initially ran on the Fox network. Although film is the technical process of production in all these adaptations, they differ in form, style, and production values. Also included in this chapter will be a section on several attempts at adapting Batman in prose fiction.

1940s Serials

With the publicity usually reserved for a feature film, Columbia Studios released the first film adaptation, *Batman,* a serial in 15 chapters, in 1943 (Cline 25). The story pitted Batman (Lewis Wilson) and Robin (Douglas Croft) against a Japanese villain, Dr. Daka (J. Carrol Naish), who used mind-control technology to forward Axis strategy against the U.S. Like many adventure serials of the era, the story's progression was cyclical: protagonists and antagonists repeatedly clashed with one another as they pursued various objects and divergent goals. Each episode ended with the requisite cliffhanger: one or both of the masked heroes facing certain death as the screen flashed to the title card of the next chapter, such as "Poison Peril," and "Slaves of the Rising Sun" (236). Eventually, Batman and Robin discovered Dr. Daka's hidden lair in an amusement park and triumphed over the Axis menace.

In the serial, there were no major departures from the Batman stories as the comic books told them. Batman's costume was recognizable, as was Robin's. Bruce Wayne and Dick Grayson lived in Wayne's mansion above the Batcave. Alfred, the butler, served as comic relief, nervously seeking to aid his employer's detection efforts. Missing was Commissioner Gordon, who was replaced by an ineffectual police chief. Batman did not work with any liaison of law enforcement in the serial, preferring instead to drop off the trussed-up crooks at police headquarters with an explanatory note, ending with a bat symbol. Bob Kane writes of his amazement when, visiting the set, he learned there was no Batmobile. Rather, the production was using the same convertible used by Alfred to chauffeur Wayne around town. "The least they could have done," wrote Kane, "was rent a black limousine" (*Batman and Me* 127). Such were the constraints of serial budgets. Batman fans, accustomed to seeing their hero defeat a villain in one issue, had to get used to seeing the Caped Crusader endure repeated setbacks and small victories, surviving numerous near-death predicaments, until finally defeating his Japanese nemesis after 15 weeks. Andy Mangels writes that this serial introduced two details that were adapted to the comic books: the entrance to the Batcave via the mansion's grandfather clock and the physical portrayal of Alfred based on the actor William Austin (80).

There is one memorable attempt at an evocative rendering of Batman early on in the serial. Set in the Batcave, it depicts Batman at a large wooden desk with a large bat emblem on the rock wall behind him. As the camera dollies in, Batman sits pensively with his chin in his hands and elbows on the desk. This seems to be an attempt to capture some of the character's mystique by casting a shadow of the hero on the wall to the right; however, it is so brightly lit his gloves and cowl appear brighter in tone than they do in other scenes. The poor production values undermine this attempt to conjure up Batman's mythic style as he looks more puzzled than mysterious.

This first film depiction of Batman served as a harbinger in recreating the comic book character: Batman loses his mystery when played by an actor. The actor playing Batman in the serial looks uncomfortable in the heavy gray tights which have thick rolls appearing with every fold. The horned cowl sits awkwardly on his head with its bat-ears pointing at odd angles. During fight scenes, the actor often had to stop to adjust his mask and cape on camera. Most of all, normal human eyes peer though the loose mask. There is no mystery about this Batman: he is simply a rich playboy who likes to dress in a silly costume and track down criminals at night. What's more, we are never told what motivates his mission. Though the gee-whiz flavor of the serial is very much like that of the Batman comic book stories of the period, the modest production values, typical for a serial, lack the nocturnal style that distinguished the comic book version.

The next serial, again by Columbia, was 1949's *Batman and Robin* with a new cast (Robert Lowery as Batman and Johnny Duncan as Robin), this time featuring a more typical comic book villain, "The Wizard." This new nemesis was cut from the same cloth as so many serial villains whose identity was hidden until the last chapter. The Wizard employed the usual crew of henchmen sent out to steal technology that enabled their leader to control automobiles from a great distance and turn himself invisible. This serial introduced Vicki Vale (Jane Adams), a blonde female news photographer and girlfriend of Bruce Wayne. Kane later put the character in the comic books, modeling her appearance after his friend, Marilyn Monroe, whom he had met years before when her name was Norma Jeane Baker (*Batman and Me* 130–131). Commissioner Gordon (Lyle Talbot) was in this version, and Batman and Robin frequented his office for conferences with him and other officials, among whom the Dynamic Duo are recognized as legitimate crimefighters. The Batman costume was similar to that of the first serial. And once again, we learn nothing about what drives Bruce Wayne to pursue his crime-fighting career. In neither serial were serious attempts made to evoke a sense of mystery or of the mythic in how Batman is presented. Criminals seeing Batman's approach express no fear or dismay; they simply start swinging at him with both fists.

Years later, in the mid–1960s, the Batman serials would become the object of amused entertainment when booked in towns around the country and shown as "An Evening with Batman and Robin." This was the era of pop art; audiences found such dated productions quaint and silly, but enjoyable as a type of camp, reports serial historian William C. Cline (25). It was this revival that led to the next attempt to adapt Batman to a filmic medium.

The Batman Television Series

In the mid–1960s, *Playboy* publisher Hugh Hefner was showing the Batman serials at his mansion when, according to Bob Kane, a visiting representative of ABC television recognized their entertainment value and suggested a new Batman series to the network. The idea eventually made its way to producer William Dozier. Unfamiliar with the source material, Dozier purchased several Batman comics and acquainted himself with the character. Finding the material "so juvenile," he hit upon the idea of deliberately exaggerating its comic book qualities. "If you overdid it, I thought, it would be funny to adults," Dozier explained, "and yet it would be stimulating to kids ... the derring-do and that stuff. But you had to appeal on both levels or you didn't have a chance" (quoted in Garcia 17). Consequently, the decision to present a camp version of Batman determined the subordinate choices about writing, casting, and costume design. Every aspect of the production would serve a multi-layered approach allowing adults or older children to enjoy the parodic attitude and recognizing how quaintly square this Batman (Adam West) was, while at the same time allowing younger children to enjoy a televised realization of the comic book hero. In the era of the anti-hero, this parodic approach proved to be very successful.

Many of the ingredients from the comics were included: Robin (Burt Ward), Commissioner Gordon (Neil Hamilton), Alfred (Alan Napier), the Batsignal, the Batmobile, and other Bat-paraphernalia often used as a staple of running bat-gags. Many of the comics' villains, almost always played by an eager, well-known, Hollywood star, appeared including The Joker (Cesar Romero), Riddler (Frank Gorshin, John Astin), Catwoman (Julie Newmar and Eartha Kitt), Mr. Freeze (Otto Preminger, George Sanders and Eli Wallach), and the Penguin (Burgess Meredith). The over-heated voice-over narration echoed the captions from the comics, breaking in to engage the audience in commentary on the action. The well-known gimmick of superimposing comics "sound effects" ("POW!" or "BAM!") during the fight scenes was a pop-art flourish intended to remind viewers of the show's comics origins.

The series producers set out to make this treatment of Batman patently ridiculous, understanding that, while adults would get the joke, children, being unsophisticated, would take the characters straight. The series' whole conceit was based on the literal transferring of elements from the comic book into a television format and exaggerating them just enough to drive the irony home. Thus comics' bright four-color art is reflected in a set design saturated with primary colors. Batman's costume was designed to be part of the overall comic effect. The costume designer describes how anything serious-looking was avoided. "We were looking for camp," he is reported as saying. "We were looking for it to be funny" (quoted in Garcia 20). Indeed, the series' costume is different from the one used in the serials, but the designer took pains to emphasize aspects that increase its ludicrousness. The chief effect comes from its being worn by an actor with an ordinary build. Adam West's rather average physique did little to suggest the powerful figure depicted in the comic books. The shiny blue satin cape suggests more a garish drape than dark menacing bat wings. The cowl's eye-holes, little semi-circles cut out of the mask, allow the actor's eyes to peer out benignly. And, of course, West's performance was directed as a parody of the noble square-jawed do-gooder.

Parodying Batman

Commenting on the nature of irony and satire, Northrop Frye asserted that irony often takes the form of parody of the romance. Such irony is presented as "the application of romantic mythical forms to a more realistic content which fits them in unexpected ways" (*Anatomy* 223). Thus parody subverts romance by imposing a literal interpretation on it that highlights the contrasts between romantic content and reality. To put it another way, the romance is pushed down Frye's Scale of Literary Design into the realm of realism. Such a collision of the romantic with the realistic demonstrates the alleged absurdity of both the romance's form and its content. By pushing their depiction toward the realistic, the *Batman* series emphasized how absurd the comic book adventures would be if taken more literally, as if to announce, "Here's what a man dressed up in a bat costume really looks like!" Presented from an ironic perspective, that is, standing outside of displaced romantic time and space, there is no longer grounds for accepting Batman's exploits as an idealized quest for justice or for accepting romantic treatments that evoke a mythic quality in his character and story.

Thomas Schatz, writing on film genres, discusses how westerns, musicals, and other genres may move through several stages of development until a point of creative exhaustion is reached. These stages shed some light on how the superhero genre may likewise change in its manner of depiction. Drawing on the works of numerous scholars including Henri Focillon, Schatz identifies four stages: the experimental, wherein the conventions of a genre are developed and established; the classic stage, wherein such conventions become formally understood by both artists and audience; the refinement stage, wherein these conventions accrue embellishments and "stylistic details"; and, finally, the baroque, wherein the form becomes self-conscious and the genre's "form and its embellishments are accented to the point where they themselves become the 'substance' or 'content' or the work" (Schatz 38). The *Batman* parody is obviously at the baroque stage. Louis Giannetti's description of the historic trajectory of genres follows a similar arc: the primitive, the classical, the revisionist, and the parodic (271–272). In both Schatz and Giannetti's progressions, the end-stage of a particular genre is an ironic mode of self-reflexivity that ridicules the genre's conventions. This approach arises out of overfamiliarity with the genre and a change in the social attitudes concerning the values the form once celebrated. In the 1960s, Batman comics sales had ebbed and prospects for the character were not promising. The television series took up the function of parodying a known storyline with characters familiar from the viewers' childhood. The distance many of these viewers felt from the comic book character allowed the ironic mode to function as a successful one-joke parody. Irony and satire, opposed as they are to the romance, cannot sustain the presence of the mythic whose objects they exist to debunk. A legend cannot be debunked and revered at the same time. There was nothing mythic about Batman in the *Batman* television series.

The series' popularity encouraged ABC to bring another character from prior decades to television. The Green Hornet had first appeared on radio in 1936 and movie serials in the 1940s. Like Batman, the Green Hornet was a wealthy heir who moonlighted as a masked adventurer. Britt Reid, inheriting his father's newspaper business, decides he needs to do more than expose crime journalistically. He therefore creates the persona of the Green Hornet as a purported crime boss who actually fights criminals. Also like Batman, he has a sidekick, Kato, who is Reid's valet. When ABC's Green Hornet series arrived, it was a departure from Batman's parodic approach by playing the stories as straightforward updates of the original adventures. Gone was the tongue-in-cheek humor and gags of the Caped Crusader as the series, even though each episode opened with an introduction using the same announcer from the *Batman* series setting up the show's premise. In March 1967, the Green Hornet and Kato guest starred on that week's Batman two-parter and it is a study in clashing tones as the campy style of *Batman* collides with the seriousness of *The Green Hornet*'s sensibility.[1]

The popular response to the new *Batman* program ironically revived the sagging fortunes of the comics, and the influence of the show on the Batman titles was noticeable. Mark Vaz reports that DC's Batman editor, Julius Schwartz, responded to the series' success by making Batman "a campy, lighthearted figure" (95). Schwartz injected a lighter tone into the storylines, although they lacked the tongue-in-cheek self-mockery of the series. "It was successful as long as the show was successful," Schwartz reported, "and once that was enough, the readers wanted the previous type Batman" (Ibid.). It was at this point that the Batman titles began their transition back to the original concept of Batman as a grim, mysterious avenger. The end of the television series led to the comics' eventual return to the classic vigilante mode, with artist Neal Adams innovating a dramatic style of presentation that met with broad popular approval among its fans. This was a case of a particular story form reinventing itself through a return to something close to its primitive or experimental stage. This would be the general style of depiction in which Batman remains to the current day.

The Warner Bros. Feature Films

In his book on film adaptations, Thomas Leitch discusses the manner in which certain directors take pre-existing literary sources and impose their signature style upon the work to the extent that the story assumes, in the finished film, new authorship. Citing men as diverse as Alfred Hitchcock, Stanley Kubrick, and Walt Disney (the latter a non-director whose creative vision emanated throughout his studio productions), Leitch discusses how each of these auteurs often radically shaped their material—be they novels, fairy tales or other sources—into a work displaying the author's distinctive touch. Throughout their handling of the Batman feature film franchise, Warner Bros. executives have sought directors who could contribute, not just their filmmaking competence but their particular stylistic touch. This strategy served to make the films artistic achievements as opposed to merely live-action versions of their comic book source. The studio then sought directors who were being hired to work on their first blockbuster film without having an established reputation that would require superstar-director salaries. In both cases, this strategy paid off.

In the mid–1980s, film producers Michael Uslan and Ben Melnicker, believing in the viability of Batman as feature film material, selected Tim Burton to direct what they envisioned to be a serious depiction of the character. After numerous script changes, the filmmakers cast Michael Keaton as Bruce Wayne/Batman and Jack Nicholson as the Joker. Pre-release publicity, much of it generated outside of the studio system, raised public awareness of the film, and moviegoers, curious to see this new version of a well-known character, made the film the biggest box-office success of 1989.

Batman's production design was one of its most dramatic elements. Expressionistic lighting and huge sets created a dark, dystopian Gotham City—an appropriate stage for Batman's exploits. Danny Elfman's booming operatic score, performed by an oversized orchestra, enhanced the heightened sense of comic book dynamics the filmmakers were seeking. Likewise, the picture's art design sought to create a world in which a character such as Batman would be believable on film. As to the film's time period, that was uncertain. Much of the clothing seemed to date from the 1940s, the era of comics' Golden Age. Yet the automobiles were more recent and, of course, all of Batman's equipment represented the height of modern technology. Many of the comics' "cast members" were present: Commissioner Gordon (Pat Hingle), a pre–Two-Face Harvey Dent (Billy Dee Williams), and Alfred the butler (Michael Gough). Vicki Vale (Kim Basinger) served as the love interest. Batman was intended here to be seen as a shadowy, grim predator of criminals, driven to this strange mission by the murder of his parents. At first a strange, marginal figure who baffled police, by the film's end he was established as Gotham's savior after foiling the Joker's mass-murder schemes.

The film departed from the comics mythos in numerous ways, both large and small. A particular standout is the Dark Knight's costume and its molded vinyl physique. Bypassing the necessity of finding an actor with Bruce Wayne's height and muscular build, the film's designers opted to "add" the muscles as part of the suit, creating a defined musculature impossible in an Adam-West-style cloth version, even if worn by a bodybuilder. In the story, the vinyl suit functioned as body armor, a more logical feature for a character constantly dodging bullets. The mask and cowl of the movie costume has the comics' demonically long bat-ears but the rest is wider and bulkier than the comics' sleek version and, of course, Michael Keaton's eye's peer out of the large eye holes, surrounded by black mascara to lessen the amount of skin visible. The whole costume was reportedly bulky, heavy, uncomfortable, and stiflingly hot. In the thick cowl, Keaton could not turn his head or hear very well. The actor's distinctive mouth is just one of the specific human details that remind the viewer that this is a Hollywood actor in the vinyl suit. Publicity stills brightly lit to display details of the costume make the character look frankly silly. Careful cinematography was implemented to prevent this perspective from making the hero unintentionally funny. For example, the film's gloomy, expressionistic lighting casts Batman in dramatic perspectives that often cause his eyes to remain in shadow. Michael Keaton's lack of Bruce Wayne's square jaw also served to detract from a resonance with the comic book model. The cinematic Batman is most effectively exhibited in long shots where less detail allows him to more closely resemble the Batman of the comics.

Further cinematic concessions to reality were such devices as the grappling hook projectile attached to a cable that Batman fired up at buildings to hoist himself up with a small winch. This served as a cinematic replacement for the simple, thrown, Batarang, it being obvious that such a device would look as ridiculous on film as it did in the *Batman* television series. Even so, the film often resorts to the comics' trick of having an endangered Batman pull a small but elaborate and heretofore-unseen gadget out of his utility belt hidden by the cape.

Filmic Texture vs. Comics Text

The key to comparing the cinematic image of Batman with the comic book is in recognizing the film version's overwhelming sense of texture or physical detail. The comics version relies on line art for Batman's form; between those lines there is only a hint of texture. In a film, texture is unavoidable; it is film's strength and visual substance. In comics, most detail is suggested and what is there is open to the imagination. The figure of Batman in this film is rich with detailed photographic information. The film's designers sought to supply in vivid detail what comics only suggest with lines. But carrying so much visual information weighs this Batman down. Moving stiffly through his scenes, this Dark Knight's armor threatens to sink him. Nevertheless, even without that expensive Hollywood embellishment, Batman depicted photographically would have been quite problematic. The television version demonstrated what a cloth costume closer to the original looks like in the merciless eye of the camera. The comics' romantic distance from realism is eliminated by the technology of recorded physical reality, the camera.

Not only was the physical depiction of Batman mitigated by the photographic representation, the story itself kept underlining, not the mystery but the oddness of such a character. Film's predisposition toward realism forced the writers to reposition the cinematic narrative's stance toward how strange it is that a man would dress up in a bat costume and fight crime. Writing such epithets for Batman as "sideshow freak," used by the Joker no less, derive from an ironic perspective rather than one in which the existence of a bat-man is part of a mythos. The film's writers were unable to take the character as seriously as the comics do in part because the literalness of live-action film makes a straight presentation of the comic book Batman less tenable. An unassimilating translation of content originating from one medium to another will always undermine and compromise the source material.

To counteract its tendency toward the literal, the film's formalistic elements sought to emphasize story elements that highlight the comics' Batman's mythic nature. The aforementioned expressionist cinematography sought to render Batman as a mysterious figure, and Elfman's powerful score provided moody and dynamic aural punctuation that suggests something of the character's mythic stature. These more abstract elements of formalism and music contributed some small measure of mythic evocation, but are unable to carry the entire burden of a nearly impossible task given the film's ironic tone.

Psychological Emphasis

Burton's decision to characterize Batman as being nearly as psychotic as the villain he fights was also detrimental to the mythical evocation of the character. Burton's oeuvre is renowned for its preoccupation with the marginalized, with the misfits of society and their struggle against misunderstanding. *Pee Wee's Big Adventure* (1985), *Edward Scissorhands* (1990) and *Ed Wood* (1994) are typical of his work, in which misfit characters must strive against "normal" society to attain their goals. Speaking of this vision of Batman, Burton remarked, "I love Batman, the split personality, the hidden person. Having those two sides, a light side and a dark one, and not being able to resolve them—that's a feeling that's not uncommon" (quoted in Salisbury 72). It is this delving into the psychological nature of a tortured crime victim and discovering that his psychosis is expressed in his mission that defined Burton's approach. Interestingly, it is Burton's interpretation that makes possible an analysis of the film, such as Robert E. Terrill's "Put On A Happy Face: Batman as Schizophrenic Savior." Terrill posits a Jungian interpretation of *Batman*, wherein Gotham City becomes a psychological landscape of the warring conscious and unconscious. Batman fights the Joker's attempts to push the city's psyche toward individuation and succeeds in allowing the city to remain complacent in its repressed state. Wayne/Batman remain unintegrated as well. "The fissured world of Gotham City requires a madman to keep the repressed contents of the collective unconscious from erupting into consciousness," Terrill wrote, "and Wayne/Batman must protect his splintered psyche to maintain the psychosis of the city" (332). Burton's psychoanalytic vision of Batman invites such interpretations and, as applied to the film, it is a valid one.

Like Terrill, Parker Tyler sees film as a dramatized psychological state playing before our eyes. As mentioned in the previous chapter, Tyler argues that the mythic personas brought to the film by its stars become the focus of the story rather than, in this case, the mythic aspects of Batman. Michael Keaton, known more for his comedic roles, played Wayne as the sometimes befuddled and distracted leading man of a romantic comedy. This style alternated with the more wry, brooding style appropriate for a man living a double life. Keaton's appearance does not resemble the standard comics depiction of Bruce Wayne as tall, dark, and handsome. As Batman, the Keaton persona is suppressed to allow the expression of the grim avenging hero to emerge. To the degree that a character is known by his words, not much is revealed about Batman. His voice is lowered and he usually speaks only when necessary. Despite his flamboyant appearance, the character is played in an understated manner. This is in contrast to Jack Nicholson's Joker, who brought decades of accumulated screen associations to his performance. Often portraying mavericks and rebels, Nicholson's screen persona is known for its cleverness and for its diabolical grin, familiar from his roles in *One Flew Over the Cuckoo's Nest* (1975), *The Shining* (1980) and *The Witches of Eastwick* (1987). As the Joker, Nicholson was allowed to dominate the story with a performance calculated to tap into the public memory of his prior performances. Once again, the story suppressed a comics character's authenticity in favor of the pleasures of enjoying a popular actor in a star turn.

There were several other departures from the original comics Batman worth noting briefly. Near the climax of the film, Batman attacks the Joker's factory hideout by sending the Batmobile into the building by remote control. Stopping, the vehicle is surrounded by several of the Joker's henchmen. The Batmobile drops a small but powerful bomb and retreats as the factory and apparently all its inhabitants are blown up. Batman has just intentionally killed several people. Later he guns down more of the Joker's men in his Batwing aircraft, firing missiles into their midst. Still later, pursuing the Joker, who has grabbed Vicki Vale and taken her up into a cathedral tower, he battles more thugs, pulling one into a long plunge down through the tower. When he finally confronts the Joker, he threatens to kill him, and thinks he has when he throws him off the tower's edge. He finally succeeds when one end of his bolo wraps around the Joker's ankle and the other wraps around a loosened gargoyle that pulls the villain down to his doom on the street below. Batman has killed at least five people by the movie's end: a dark knight indeed. The comics Batman, whose code prevents him from taking life, is subverted by a movie hero out for vengeance.

Other Films in the Series

What has been discussed above applies generally to the two sequels as well: *Batman Returns* (1992), also directed by Burton, and to some degree to *Batman Forever* (1995), and *Batman and Robin* (1997), both directed by Joel Schumacher. In *Batman Returns,* the Penguin (Danny DeVito) and Catwoman (Michelle Pfeiffer) and a new antagonist, Max Shreck (Christopher Walken) are the villains; the story juggles these and other characters in a convoluted storyline. As in the first film, the focus is on the characters' psychoses as manifested by their flamboyant deviance. One characteristic of this as well as the other films is the extended dialogue sequences, particularly between the two villains: Max Shreck and the Penguin. Comics dialogue is typically succinct and direct. Putting movie dialogue in a comic would slow the pacing considerably and make the length of the story prohibitively long. Indeed, all four pictures run over two hours each. In contrast, the two villains in *Returns*— Catwoman and the Penguin—are given detailed origin stories in the script so the audience can learn the source of their psychic pain and see why that pain makes them act out in "anti-social" ways. Both villains are driven to self-destructive acts and wind up being seen as tragic victims of society rather than criminals. *Entertainment Weekly,* in discussing the second film, noted how its defying of Hollywood feature film conventions, made it a more personal if less entertaining film than the first: "Yet for all the wintry weirdness, there's more going on under the surface of this movie than in the original. No wonder some people felt burned by *Batman Returns:* Tim Burton just may have created the first blockbuster art film" (Burr). In comparing the Burton films to their comics source, it becomes apparent that they are not as much about Batman as he is known in the comics, as they are about Burton's themes of lonely societal misfits and their neuroses.

Batman Returns, though profitable, was not a huge blockbuster like the original film, although it was the biggest commercial success of the year (Daniels 214); *Batman Forever* (1995) was an attempt by Warner Bros. to recover and sustain the Batman franchise. Burton was replaced as director by Joel Schumacher, who attempted, in his words, to "make a living comic book ... I wanted people to have an experience of a *Batman* comic, and I wanted to make it fun" (quoted in Lemanna 32). The production design is more colorful, and the action sequences owe a bit more to those of comics, but again the storyline seeks to balance the heavy exposition demands made by two villains: the Riddler (an off-the-leash Jim Carrey) and Two-Face (Tommy Lee Jones, who is eclipsed by Carrey's mugging). Robin (Chris O'Donnell) was finally added to the film's treatment. All three of these new characters' origin stories are included. Yet another new love interest was added, Dr. Chase Meridian (Nicole Kidman), a blonde criminal psychologist, from whom Bruce Wayne (now played by Val Kilmer) seeks counseling for his emotional troubles. As in the first two films, the villains are played by major stars who have brought their screen personas to bear on their portrayals. The film indicates its lighter approach to the material in the first lines of dialogue when Batman is about to drive off into Gotham City. Alfred asks, "Can I persuade you to take a sandwich with you, sir?" To which Batman replies, "I'll get drive-through." This immediate self-parodying reiterates the proclivity of the film series to skew the story away from a straight presentation (as well as offering material for McDonald's advertisements that had offered tie-ins in all three films). Similarly, when Robin examines the metallic surface of the Riddler's island hideout, he exclaims, "Holy rusted metal, Batman!" evoking audience laughter at the amusing reference to the parodic 1960s television series.

With humorous elements undermining the potential for mythic depiction, another quality was stressed in rendering Batman: a not too subtle erotic element inspired by the new Batsuit's sleekly enhanced vinyl anatomy and leathery cape. There is, though, one brief scene that resonates somewhat with the comics' mythic ingredients as discussed by this study. When Bruce Wayne sees the Batsignal from the window of the Wayne Enterprises building, he goes to his office and activates a mechanism that drops him from his office chair into a smooth sarcophagus-like capsule that, in turn, shoots him rapidly through a metal tube to the Batcave. Upon its arrival the upright sarcophagus opens and Wayne emerges into his subterranean base. The sequence, whether intentional or not, is readable as a figurative descent into the underworld, complete with a coffin.

Schumacher's second and final film, *Batman and Robin* (1997), found the franchise with yet another actor to play the main character, George Clooney. Once again, as in the previous two films, Batman faced multiple members of his rogue's gallery, including Mr. Freeze, played by Arnold Schwarzenegger (who received top billing), Poison Ivy (Uma Thurman) and Bane (Jeep Swenson). As in Schumacher's first film, it opens with a joke. Robin (a collegiate-looking young man rather than an early teen) is nagging Batman to let him have his own car, like the Batmobile, for a basic reason: "Chicks dig the car." Batman drives off muttering, "This is why Superman works alone." Picking up on the eroticized costume elements of the previous film, *Batman and Robin* added a subtext of homoeroticism as the film's opening montage of close-up shots of the titular heroes' body parts, including buttocks and the infamous nippled chests as they prepare for a mission. The baroque styling of the earlier films was now fully rococo in over-produced extravagance signaling the creative exhaustion of the series. Widely derided as flamboyantly overstuffed and an updated version of the campy sixties series, it was blamed for effectively shutting down the Batman franchise.

All four Batman films are chiefly spectacular extravaganzas exploiting the attraction of big-name stars playing well-known comic book characters. Despite the producers' and directors' claims to have taken their source material seriously, all the films allow the colorful antagonists to dominate the stories with camp performances that often wink ironically at the material. In film, Batman was now a grim, brooding figure, while his antagonists are merely more flamboyant cinematic versions of the frenetic rogues from the television series, but with better wardrobe and make-up budgets. In terms of Giannetti's realism-formalism scale of style, the films, with their dependence on sound-stage sets standing in for exterior locations, extravagant production design, expressionist cinematography and increasingly camp performances, would fall toward the formalistic end of the scale.

More important, the tonal attitude of the films toward their source text is increasingly ironic and parodic, even embarrassed by the prospect of bringing its comic book character to cinematic life. The underlying sense that the movies are either opportunities for personal auteurist projects (as in Burton's case), or campfests (in Schumacher's) undercut the tonal and mythic elements which constitute the core of Batman comics. Looking back on the first film years later, Burton remarked, "I liked parts of it but the whole movie is mainly boring. It's OK, but it was more of cultural phenomenon" (Crocker 77).

Comics Adaptations of the Films

In order to fully exploit the commercial potential of the core audience of Batman fans, one of the licensed products produced for all four films were comic book adaptations. Comparing one of these to the regular Batman comics is an excellent way to highlight some of the differences between the two media. The comic book adaptation of the 1989 film was written by Batman veteran writer and current editor Dennis O'Neil, and drawn by long-time comics artist Jerry Ordway. Seeking to faithfully reflect the film's look and story, the dynamic fluidity of comics narrative is lost because the artwork is merely an illustration of scenes from the film. Each character is carefully drawn to resemble the actor as he or she appears in the film. Such a realistic style is a dramatic departure from the abstract nature of true comics art. Readers see images of Jack Nicholson as the Joker and Michael Keaton as Bruce Wayne throughout the panels. As drawn here, Batman looks as stiff as in the film. Again, no accommodations were made for comics style—Keaton's eyes still peer through the mask. Even the fine details of his beaded gloves have been captured. The only element not captured is the photographic texture of surfaces. The realistic rendering has, as Scott McCloud described, served to negate the process of reader involvement in the characters as characters because the eye is drawn instead to the fidelity of the artist's rendition of the Hollywood actors (McCloud 36–37).

Even though the problems of adapting Batman to live-action film detracted from the mythic content of the comic book stories, the first three films were, to varying degrees, commercially successful—a success partly attributable to the residual mythic content. But there was also the appeal of a familiar popular-culture figure realized in expensive and extravagant productions.

Batman: *The Animated Series* (1992–1998)

With the success of the 1960s television series, Batman was seen as a good prospect for a Saturday morning cartoon. Filmation, an animation company, produced episodes that ran on *The Batman-Superman Hour* in 1968. Using less-expensive, limited animation, typical for television, the design was based on the comic book characters as depicted by comics artist Carmine Infantino. Indeed, certain drawings looked as if they were directly lifted from one of his panels. Similar to other animated children's programs of the time, the images were often barely animated: repeated sequences of a character talking are drawn from the same angle with only the lips moving; figure movement was stiff and occasional. The stories were simpler than what might be found in the comics of the time and lasted no more than five to ten minutes per episode. Throughout the 1970s, Filmation continued to produce similar animated episodes of *Batman,* placing the stories alongside those of Superman, Wonder Woman, Aquaman, and other DC superheroes in different versions of the *Superfriends* Saturday morning series (Daniels, DC Comics 144–145).

More than a year after the release of the 1989 *Batman* movie, Warner Bros.' animation unit began work on another animated version of the *Batman* stories (Garcia, *Animated* 75). Bob Garcia reports that Warner Bros. animation division president Jean MacCurdy had given producers Eric Radomski and Bruce Timm one stipulation about the design of the series: that it look like the classic Max Fleischer Superman cartoons of the early 1940s (69). The creators of the series were commissioned to produce 65 episodes, to be run or "stripped" weekday afternoons on the Fox Kids Network. Drawing from a number of influences, Radomski, Timm, and others on the creative team worked to have the series ready for the fall of 1992, following the summer release of *Batman Returns.*

The finished product showed the influence of Burton's films, depicting Gotham City as a shadowy, urban jungle in an indeterminate time period. The moody theme and incidental music, borrowed from the Danny Elfman score, could be heard on the cartoon's soundtrack. The character design departed, however, from the familiar Filmation design. At first glance, the animated style was noticeably more "cartoony" in its flatness and its stylized, exaggerated simplicity. Radomski and Timm's design resembled a hybrid of Bob Kane's classic block-jawed muscle man and a simplified rendering of Neal Adams' fearsome vigilante (see page 42). Interwoven throughout the production design was an art deco style, recalling the era of Batman's Golden Age in the 1940s. The finished product was a stylish body of stories that made a virtue out of the production constraints. Timm sought to create designs that would work better in animation rather than imitating comics style art. "The more lines you have on a character," he remarked, "the harder it is to draw over and over. I knew that simplicity would be better" (quoted in Daniels and Kidd 181). Some stories touched on the murders of Wayne's parents that formed his determination to fight crime, but, even so, the series depicted Batman as a wounded hero, not a psychotic vigilante. Timm was familiar with the character from the comics he had read while growing up. "The comics are our biggest influence on which version of Batman we consider to be the definitive Batman," he said (quoted in Funk 60).

Like classic superhero comics, the half-hour episodes told self-contained stories, with only the occasional two-parter. (Today's practice in superhero comics is more often to have ongoing storylines, with several subplots running, sometimes for months.) Rather than being forced to extend a comic book story to a two-hour plus running time, as in a feature film, the animated episodes told compact stories in three acts per episode. All of the ingredients composing the Batman legend remained intact, but the series did not attempt to weave itself into the continuity of the current Batman comics titles. Creating a separate continuity and slightly different versions of several characters, the stories sought to include many of the ingredients that had characterized the Batman comics for over 50 years within a single style. Thus sometimes Batman worked alone; at other times, Robin joined him during a break from college. At no time does the series' take an ironic stance that subverted the main character. Alfred sometimes makes droll remarks about his employer's nocturnal activities, but, in the dramatic context, these are seen as indicating concern for Wayne's well-being by injecting a bit of dry humor into his master's grim mission.

Like the comics, the appearance of Batman is often announced by his silhouette or by a shadow thrown dramatically on a wall or floor. His build is the classical, tall, muscular one adorned by the gray elastic cloth costume first introduced in 1939. The sleek utility belt is able to somehow hide all manner of tools until they are needed. The horned cowl is slightly stylized to fit the animated style, and his eyes are the classic narrow white slits that change in width and shape according to his emotional state.

Because the series created its own separate continuity, there was no discernible influence on the continuity of the ongoing Batman comics. However,

DC Comics did create a new title based on the series, *The Batman Adventures,* about which more will be said below. The animated version in both the series and its comics adaptation received positive comment from comics journalists. "It's ironic," noted writer Mike Tiefenbacher, "that it would require writers and editors outside of DC to rediscover the finer aspects of the original concept" (31).

The most obvious and fundamental difference between the comics character and the animated series is that Batman is put into visual motion in the series. Produced using limited animation techniques, however, the movement exhibited the occasionally jerky effects of that practice. Nevertheless, the show more often transcended these limitations through innovative character design, the adaptation of cinematic devices, and highly dramatic plot structuring. Technical innovations, such as beginning all artwork using a painted black background and painting the images over it, created a consistent mood, borrowing from the Hollywood film noir style of a shadowy cinematographic design and making the series stand out from standard television animated fare.

By animating the Batman saga, the added realism necessarily undercuts the power of the comics medium, which employs the reader's imagination to supply "movement," by mentally completing closure between and within the panels. Being closer to a realistic depiction, the series made changes from the comics version, conceding its inability to maintain plausibility otherwise. Thus, taking cues from the feature films, Batman uses a grappling line projectile device to fix his Bat-rope to a structure. Still, the series stretches the limits of credulity with Batman's spring-loaded leaping ability and his cooperative cape that never catches on sharp objects. Here in the animation of iconic figures, it is evident where the limits of iconic abstraction lie. However, because the animated images remain iconic abstractions, C. S. Lewis's remark about the photographic image's ability to nullify the mythopoeic remains largely inapplicable (*Stories* 102).

Despite these drawbacks, the series succeeded in capturing the Batman mythos better than any of the previous live-action adaptations. The producers found equivalent elements in the animation medium to sustain Batman's mythic status. Comics scholar Thomas Inge maintains that the efforts to adapt cartoon characters to live-action films fails "because the two-dimensional world of comic art allows for things not possible in the three-dimensional world of reality" (quoted in Beck 143). The flatly abstracted world of the cartoon character cannot easily sustain the move toward a three-dimensionally realistic depiction found in live-action film, but animation, adding little more than the illusion of movement and sound to comics' static images, can achieve a "golden mean" between comics and film. "When animation came along,"

Inge writes, "it proved to be a middle ground between the comics and film and made for easier adaptation" (Ibid.). Inge's description of the 1940s Superman cartoons' success in adapting its comic book subject goes to the heart of animation's relationship to comics and could be describing the Warner Bros. Batman animated series that, decades later, sought to emulate its style:

> By paying more attention to design and color than to achieving the effect of dimensionality and by crafting tightly knit plots that could be resolved satisfactorily in minutes, each film came close to reproducing the experience of reading a comic-book story. The Art Deco settings, the flat character designs, and the use of colors to create moods, combine to elevate the films to a level of pure artistry seldom found in animation outside *Fantasia* of the year before [Ibid.].

By retaining the abstract artwork, which allows viewers to participate in the characterizations, and by emulating the qualities that established Batman as a dualistic character, the animated series was able to maintain the comics' mythic evocation.

The Batman Adventures comic book title, tied to the animated series' continuity and vision, effectively returned the *Batman* stories to a consistent art style that had gradually diminished in the regular Batman comics. Particularly since Frank Miller's *The Dark Knight Returns,* DC has allowed its artists to render Batman in their own style, moving further away from the influence of Neal Adams to a multitude of interpretations expressed through the regular continuity and frequent graphic novels. Several artists who drew *The Batman Adventures* maintained character consistency following the show's animation model sheets. For the first time since the "new look" was begun in the mid–1960s, the Batman stories had a consistent look and style, almost as if they were rendered by a single artist—a style characterized by a clean and simplified design with emphasis on graphic form and three-act story structure.[2] In this manner, the character's comic book depiction came full circle, incorporating elements from each era of the character's history, elements that comprise his mythic ethos.

Timm became Warner Bros.' animation overseer of adaptations of sister company DC Comics. The result was a series of shows featuring Batman either as lead character or working with the Justice League. Among the various versions is *Batman Beyond,* featuring an octogenarian Bruce Wayne overseeing a teenaged protégé using a high-tech Batsuit to fight crime in a futuristic Gotham City. For several years, Warner Bros. animation unit, under Timm's supervision, produced a series of direct-to-video movies including *Batman: Year One* (2011), and *The Dark Knight Returns,* parts 1 and 2 (2012 and 2013, respectively), all adaptations of the Frank Miller graphic novels and each mimicking the original comics art according to Timm's simplified artistic approach.

Batman in Prose Fiction

In the wake of the renewed public awareness of Batman, several attempts at adapting the character to prose fiction were made. *Tales of the Batman,* a collection of short stories by mystery writers, is unremarkable in that all of the stories lacked a sense of the mythic. In the Batman comics stories much of the mythic content is expressed in the manner in which Batman enters the action and appears in the panels. The short-story writers, on the other hand, seemed uninterested in finding a prose equivalent of this visual style, opting usually for a straightforward narrative in which Batman must solve some mystery or apprehend a perpetrator. His effect on those he encounters is rarely described in a way that might resonate with readers.

A novel-length effort, *Batman: To Stalk a Specter* by Simon Hawke, pits Batman against a professional super assassin contracted to kill a drug-smuggling Latin-American dictator awaiting trial in Gotham City. Here Batman is presented much as he is in the comic books in his relationship with Commissioner Gordon, his array of technological devices, and his cunning nature. Yet the novel is overly dependent on lengthy conversations and narration for exposition, and Batman does not encounter the antagonist until the final chapter. Readers are more likely to perceive Batman's character indirectly through someone's recounting of his actions than through evocative language that matches the depictions of him in the comics pages.

The most ambitious prose effort involving Batman is Andrew Vachss's *Batman: The Ultimate Evil.* Vachss has an established reputation among mystery readers for his series of novels featuring his character, Burke. These stories are often concerned with the rescue of abused children, a cause for which Vachss, who is also an attorney, has long been a champion. In his Batman book he enlists the Caped Crusader in the cause. The writing skill in the novel is markedly better than other Batman prose adaptations: Vachss seeks to create a character akin to or surpassing what comic book readers experience, as the following passage attests:

> The Batman was a hyperhuman phenomenon, a living ghost, skillfully surfing the whisper-stream throughout Gotham's underworld, a terror to terrorists [5].

During the course of his investigation, Batman discovers that his parents' death was the result of his mother's covert investigations into a far-reaching web of child-exploitation. The Joe Chill character, who for years in the comics had been the Waynes' murderer, was merely the trigger man for this operation. Following the pattern of other consciousness-raising stories, Batman serves as the reader's surrogate by learning of a social evil through a motivated encounter with an expert on the subject and by being drawn into further involvement and commitment to action for the cause. This leads to his successful instigation of a revolt in the fictional southeast Asian country of Udon Khai, the source of the web of victimization, where child exploitation is legal. Evidently a fictional surrogate for Thailand, Udon Khai's revolution is only the start of Batman's new crusade against child abuse in all its terrible forms, and the novel ends when, spotting physical abuse taking place in an apartment, he "swung through the open window to face the ultimate evil" (Vachss 196). Vachss sees a natural ally for his cause in the Batman character, who, like the victimized children he defends, lost his childhood to evildoers. Taking care to include plentiful action in which to display Batman's prowess, Vachss balances the heroics with passages detailing the truly hideous extent of child exploitation. Yet for all his skill, it is this very strategy that works against the evocation of the mythic. By making him a spokesperson for a particular crusade, the level of realism is increased at the cost of the mythic depiction that makes Batman so compelling a character. This is not to say that writers can never recruit the character for a particular cause without risking his mythic aspects; but care should be taken when changing such core material as his origin story. After all, current DC Comics' continuity makes clear that Bruce Wayne does not know who killed his parents, the better to stress the generalized nature of his fight against crime.

Prose writers have yet to successfully evoke the mythic elements in Batman to the degree that comic book depictions achieved. Yet, if McCloud's Scale of Iconic Abstraction indicates that meaning increases as there is movement toward the more iconic end of the scale, then the medium of words alone should be able to best convey the mythic in the Batman story. It could be that the comics medium is simply the best mode of expression for a character like Batman, who requires visual expression to succeed. Or it may be that a writer with skill enough to evoke the mythic aspects of Batman has not yet attempted the task. Mythopoeic prose of this kind requires both an understanding of the character and the ability to write in a way that finds prose equivalents for what the comic book style achieves. A gifted enough writer might feel too constrained by the long-established parameters of the Batman stories and might not be willing to stay within the boundaries required by a sponsoring corporation that seeks to maintain a certain stasis in the character's depiction.

Batman: Arkham Asylum (2009) and its sequel, *Arkham City* (both produced by Rocksteady Studios and published by Warner Bros. Interactive), took the character into the realm of modern video games. There had been previous games with Batman as a character but the two Rocksteady games were highly rendered images with sophisticated gameplay and a storyline by longtime Batman animation and comics writer Paul Dini. Batman's depiction in the games owes something to both the comics style in the character's over-developed physique and the film adaptations with more textured surface detail; realistic human eyes also peer from behind his mask. As such, with the richly detailed design of the various scenes and the dynamically animated action in both cut scenes and gameplay, the result is akin to a high-end CGI version of the animated Batman. The formalistic emphasis of the vivid and lurid production design helps to retain the requisite mythic elements.

Up to this point in our narrative, no live-action representation of Batman had succeeded in presenting the character as mythically as the two-dimensional comics have so routinely done for decades. That was about to change.

Adapting Batman, Part 2

The Christopher Nolan Batman Trilogy

After several years of seeking to find a way to return the once-profitable Batman franchise to the cineplexes, Warner Bros. again reached out to a rising young director. Having started his career two independently made cerebral crime films *Following* (1999) and *Memento* (2001), and then directing a studio film, *Insomnia* (2002), Christopher Nolan proposed a different approach to Batman. In a meeting at his garage with Warner Bros. executives, he showed them a plastic model of his design for the Batmobile that captured his vision for the film. Rather than the elaborately bat-finned models of the earlier films, his Batmobile would reflect a contemporary aesthetic, something practical like armaments producers would design for the military. "It doesn't make any sense in the real world for Batman to stick goofy fins on his car," Nolan remarked in an interview with James Mottram for the published *Batman Begins* screenplay. "I firmly believe that our vehicle is the equivalent of what the Batmobile was in the late 1950s" (xiii). This realist ethos would guide everything about Nolan's adaptation strategy as his vision for a new film was greenlit by the studio.

Restarting Realistically

Before the film's release, Nolan told *Variety* that he wanted a film set in a more recognizable world: "The world of Batman is that of grounded reality" (Graser and Dunkley). By contrast, Burton's and Schumacher's visions were idiosyncratic and unreal. In an interview with James Mottram in the *Batman Begins* published screenplay, Nolan acknowledged Tim Burton's achievement in bringing the character to the screen.

The thing with Burton is that he had the challenge of convincing a cinema audience that you could have a "cool" Batman film. Convincing the audience who remembers that the TV show was ridiculous. And he did it, he succeeded. The way he did it was the make the entire world that he lives in—Gotham—as peculiar and extraordinary as he is ... so that isn't a hurdle that have to get over with this film [xii].

In a 2004 *Variety* article, Nolan said, "Ours will be a recognizable, contemporary reality against which an extraordinary heroic figure arises" (Graser and Dunkley). In discussing the film's look with his cinematographer Wally Pfister, Nolan stated, "I related very much to the other two films we made [*Memento* and *Insomnia*] because I like to shoot things in a very naturalistic style and he knows that. Therefore, you know, he didn't use a lot of filtration. He didn't use a lot of image manipulation" (Murray). The look of the first film, *Batman Begins* (2005), was a reflection of Nolan's goal of making the film treatment of Bruce Wayne's mission less formalistic in style. Kyle Smith's review in the New York *Post* likens the film to crime dramas of earlier eras:

It's great because it's so real. As Batman starts stripping away each layer of Gotham crime only to discover a sicker and more monstrous evil beneath, his rancid city simultaneously invokes early '90s New York, when criminals frolicked to the tune of five murders a day; the "Serpico" era, when cops were for sale; and today, when psychos seek to kill us all at once rather than one by one [Smith].

Michael Uslan, the executive producer whose lifelong mission had been to bring Batman to the screen, had overseen the production of the both the live-action Burton and Schumacher films as well as various animated works. In his opinion, Nolan "realized the way to make Batman work again would be to make him real. The audience had to believe that Bruce Wayne could be a real person in a real city in a real world" (229). Moving the city scenes out of soundstages and onto locations such as the streets of Chicago, the film immediately distinguished itself from the artifice of the earlier attempts. Throughout the Burton films, the characters at times seem to be stepping outside of the story to comment on the strangeness of a world where people dress up in fantastic costume to battle each other. Jack Nicholson's famous question as the Joker, "Where does he get those wonderful toys?" is more of a question from the audience than an admiring antagonist. In *Batman* and *Batman Returns,* the term "freak," is often used (by villains) to describe both hero and villains, suggesting the general deviancy of the plot and characters. When the Penguin says to Batman, "I think you're jealous that I'm a genuine freak, and you have to wear a mask," Batman replies, "Maybe you're right." In *Batman Forever,* when Batman acrobatically drops into the ballroom to stop the Riddler and Two-Face's crime-in-progress, the Riddler remarks to Two-Face, "Your entrance was good—his was better. The difference? Showmanship." This consistently self-conscious tone suggests the unwillingness of the filmmakers to un-ironically depict its characters, or in other words, to play them straight. Burton's obsession with misfits (which often kept Batman as a supporting player in his films) and Schumacher's neon-lit camp style suppressed the mythic elements of their main character.

Speaking for the "alienated fan base," Christopher Nolan remarked of Schumacher's *Batman and Robin* during the production of *The Dark Knight,* "If the people who make the film aren't taking it seriously, why should we?" (Halbinger NYT). In another interview, Nolan addressed the different tone of *Batman Begins:* "I felt that everything we were going to do in terms of translating the story onto film was going to have to be extremely reverent to the history of the character and the mythology of Batman" ("Genesis of the Bat"). Thus, comments spoken about Wayne's theatrical costume and nocturnal persona don't stand outside the story but arise internally out of the psychology of the characters. For example, when picking up Bruce Wayne after his international journey of self-discovery, Alfred expresses curiosity about whether the purpose of his master's new symbolic persona is to protect those in his close circle, Bruce assumes he's referring to Rachel Dawes. "Actually sir," Alfred says matter-of-factly, "I was thinking of myself" (*Batman Begins*). In the published screenplay interview, Nolan states that he drew from several specific Batman stories in constructing the film's script, including the early 1970s-era stories that returned the character to his darker beginnings, as well as *Batman: Year One* (xv-xvi).

Batman as Rationalized[1] Myth

Commenting on the place of superheroes in modern culture, Christopher Nolan told the British newspaper, the *Guardian*:

> Superheroes fill a gap in the pop culture psyche, similar to the role of Greek mythology. There isn't really anything else that does the job in modern terms. For me, Batman is the one that can most clearly be taken seriously. He's not from another planet, or filled with radioactive gunk. I mean, Superman is essentially a god, but Batman is more like Hercules: he's a human being, very flawed, and bridges the divide [Pulver].

To translate Batman's mythic persona, Nolan and co-screenwriter David S. Goyer set out a deliberate strategy to justify Wayne's use of a costumed figure to achieve his war on crime. Knowing that the film medium is inherently more realistic, that the photographic textures and detail make it, in McLuhan's terms, a hot medium where the literal can easily suppress the symbolic, Nolan's

Golden Age logo from the title page of many Batman comics. It featured a literalized image of Batman. Even during the happy "Scoutmaster" Golden Age, this brooding logo reminded readers that this knight was dark (from http://www.batmanonline.com/index. php?gallery;id=2146).

approach was to render Batman as a mythic persona rationally constructed by the protagonist. Hence one of the film's chief plotlines is Bruce's search for a means of effectively attacking Gotham's endemic corruption, which reaches from the underworld through the civic structure of government and law enforcement. The first hour of the film presents that process of mythic construction.

Nolan believed that the new film could take advantage of the part of Wayne's life never before covered in the films, the years between the deaths of his parents and his career as Batman. Nolan remarked in the screenplay interview that Batman had never had a filmed origin story, like Richard Donner's 1978 *Superman: The Movie*, "When Dick Donner made Superman ... it seems odd that they didn't do Batman that same way—with that same epic sensibility" (xii). Screenwriter David S. Goyer noted the importance of rooting the audience in a connection with Bruce Wayne's character. Nolan and Goyer, in an interview with *Empire* magazine, believed "that the [earlier] films were always just marking time until the guy was in the costume. So we thought, 'If we can get the audience to care about Bruce Wayne and not even care or not if he's in the costume, then we will have properly rehabilitated the franchise'" (Jolin 93). In a conversation printed in a volume collecting his three Batman film screenplays, Nolan remarked that it was important to trace the arc of Bruce Wayne's journey from victim to hero: "The whole premise of *Batman Begins* was not just watching how he built the utility belt or what not, but how, step-by-step, he went from an orphaned child to a man who had a hole in his heart, to eventually become this mythic figure" ("A Sense of Ending"). The realistic sensibility controlled the narrative construction, tracing Bruce Wayne's conception of Batman as a means to fight crime and corruption in Gotham. The foundation was laid in the first film and built upon and explored through the trilogy.

Batman Begins (2005)

Adopting a quest journey for the beginning of the film, we first meet the adult Bruce Wayne (Christian Bale) as he awakens in a jail cell in an Asian country and is attacked at breakfast by six toughs. Fighting them off, Wayne is thrown back into his cell, where he finds Henri Ducard (Liam Neeson), a representative of the secret organization the League of Shadows, run by the mysterious mastermind Ra's Al Ghul (Ken Watanbe). Ducard quickly realizes that Wayne has lost his way on his journey toward revenge against the criminal element. When Bruce dismisses the League as a gang of vigilantes, Ducard responds in this exchange:

> Ducard: A vigilante is just a man lost in the scramble for his own gratification. He can be destroyed or locked up. But if you make yourself more than just a man ... if you devote yourself to an ideal ... and if they can't stop you ... then you become something else entirely.
> Wayne: Which is?
> Ducard: Legend, Mr. Wayne.

Challenging Wayne to define what he's really seeking in his wanderings, Ducard tells him how to find the League's mountain headquarters, where he will be trained to fight injustice. Bruce makes the arduous climb up the mountain and is met by Ducard, who, translating for Al Ghul, asks, "What are you seeking?"

Wayne responds, "I seek the means to fight injustice. To turn fear ... against those who prey on the fearful."

Finding a goal, Bruce is trained as a ninja and in other exotic combat methods. Ducard teaches him the value of theatrical effects like stealth and smoke bombs. "Theatricality and deception are powerful agents," he tells his student. "You must become more than just a man in the mind of your opponent."

Step by step, the narrative presents the elements that Wayne will incorporate as tactics in his strategy of terrorizing criminals. Ducard explains that in order for Bruce to use fear as a weapon, he must face his own fears and turn them against his opponents: "To conquer fear, you must become fear. You must bask in the fear of other men. And men fear most what they cannot see. You have to become a terrible thought. A *wraith*. You have to become an idea!"

Earlier, as a college student tormented by the injustice of his parents' murder, Bruce had sought to kill their assailant, Joe Chill (Richard Brake), during his parole hearing. When mob boss Falcone's (Tom Wilkinson) assassin did the job for him, Bruce faces what he almost became, a murderer like Chill, and he throws his gun into the river, vowing never to kill. But when he confronts Falcone to assert that he isn't afraid of him, the crime boss tells him that Wayne has more than himself to be concerned about: "Because you think you got nothing to lose. But you haven't thought it through. You haven't thought about your lady friend in the DA's office. You haven't thought about your old butler. *Bang*!" Another motivation for creating a different persona arises when Bruce realizes the threat his activities could present to his loved ones. At this point, about 30 minutes into the film, all the elements of the Batman mythos have been introduced except the particular form it will take.

When Alfred (Michael Caine) picks Bruce up to return him to Gotham, Wayne expresses his intention to apply the lessons he has learned from Ducard: "People need dramatic examples to shake them out of apathy. I can't do that as Bruce Wayne. As a man ... I'm flesh and blood, I can be ignored, destroyed. But as a symbol.... As a symbol, I can be incorruptible. I can be everlasting." In an interview with Jeff Jensen, Nolan stated, "That was a very important scene for me, not just because I knew it would play out over three films as a theme, but I had to understand why the eminently sensible Alfred Pennyworth would sit there and listen to his employer explain that he's going to dress up as a bat and fight crime as a vigilante. That's a huge leap to make" ("*The Dark Knight Rises* Preview"). Nolan describes the concept of Batman as a symbol:

> So in each film, we talk about the symbol of the character being the key thing. It's not about what he can achieve beating up criminals one by one. We address this again at the beginning of *The Dark Knight,* where you have these copycat Batmen popping up. The idea was to ask: Is *that* the meaning of the symbolism? To raise an army of

these guys? No. Bruce sees himself as a catalyst for change in Gotham, and to me, in that conversation with Alfred, it's very clear to me that Bruce only ever thinks of this as, like, a five-year plan, a short-term thing.... It was the only way we knew to understand the reality of the story of Batman.

When Bruce returns to Wayne manor and explores the cave under the house's foundations, he finds it full of bats. Facing his terror of the creatures, he comes upon the idea that will transform him. Here the comic book origin of Batman intersects with the film's realistic articulation of Wayne's rationale; as the original comics panel depicts Bruce Wayne's epiphany: "I shall become a bat!"

Using his great wealth and the resources of Wayne Enterprises' research, Bruce constructs the persona using body armor and cutting-edge applications of technology to give himself the advantage in his confrontations with criminals. As had been done since Burton's first film, Batman's muscular physique was mostly provided by the vinyl costume with body armor to protect him from bullets. This need for a heavily muscular appearance is given a realistic explanation with Bruce's visit to Lucius Fox (Morgan Freeman), the man in charge of military technology research in Wayne Enterprises. Besides offering an answer to the question of "where he gets his wonderful toys," it allowed the script to provide close-to-plausible technology made possible by Wayne's actual superpower, his great wealth. We see him adapting the body armor originally intended for military use by soldiers, and developing the cape's memory cloth that, when fed an electrical charge from his gloves, will spring into the bat-winged configuration, enabling him to glide across the rooftops. As Bruce is sharpening a piece of steel into a bat-shaped throwing weapon, Alfred asks, "Why bats, Master Wayne?"

"Bats scare me," Bruce responds. "And it's time my enemies shared my dread."

These scenes depict the construction of Batman's mythic identity, based on Ducard's philosophy. Nolan, discussing the armored suit, stated, "The costume has to be frightening or it has no purpose. For it to be intimidating and imposing, it had to have a sense of function that would play into the credibility of Bruce Wayne putting on this extraordinary costume."

Discussing the function of the suit, actor Christian Bale noted, "He [Wayne] really channels this other character. When he's confronting an individual that he wants to take down, he kind of ceases to be human" ("Cape and Cowl"). Recalling the ancient use of masks and (by extension) costumes, the suit combines functionality and theatricality while allowing Bruce to express an aspect of his psyche in ways he never could without it. It remains only for him to make a properly threatening introduction of his persona to the criminal element to begin creating the legend of Batman that will make him effective in his crusade.

In keeping with his tactic of terrorizing criminals, Batman avoids showy arrivals, choosing rather to spook them by picking them off one at a time, or using stealth and sudden attacks to unnerve his prey. His first encounter with criminals is on the docks as they are moving smuggled items from transport carriers. Seeing the action from the thugs' point of view allows the audience to perceive how Batman's tactics create dread in his enemies, giving him a psychological advantage while also establishing his mythic persona in the criminal underworld.

In designing a realistic take on the comic book hero, Christopher Nolan sought, as Burton had done, to give the familiar costume functionality. "For it to be intimidating and imposing," Nolan stated in an interview for the *Batman Begins* DVD, "it had to have a sense of function that would play into the credibility of Bruce Wayne putting on this extraordinary costume" ("The Screenplay"). The design was to be an expression of Ducard's strategy of "theatricality and deception," to unnerve one's opponents. "But," Nolan remarked, "I wanted to combine that with a design that incorporated the more operatic, animal-like, organic qualities of the costume" ("Cape and Cowl").

Those involved in fulfilling Nolan's vision of Batman often resorted to the comics depiction to evoke the character's dual nature, balancing human intellect with animal ferocity. It was Christian Bale's idea to have Batman crouching in the shadows, like a predator. "You just couldn't pull it off properly," he said in an interview "unless you became a beast when you were inside of that suit" ("The Journey Begins").

While evoking the nocturnal predator of Batman's persona, Nolan rooted Wayne's transformation from traumatized victim to proactive crusader in a real world figure. Paul Levitz, then president of DC Comics, in an interview for *The Dark Knight* Blu-ray, noted, "Chris said, 'To me, the key to understanding the character is that Bruce Wayne is Teddy Roosevelt'" ("Batman: Unmasked."). The future U.S. president, having fought childhood asthma by taking up strenuous activities, had, during one day in 1884, lost both his wife and mother. He fought this double tragedy by heading west and re-inventing himself as a rancher before returning to New York to become superintendent of police. Both Roosevelt and Bruce Wayne are examples of the manner in which individuals in America have fought personal tragedy through reinvention.

At the film's end, Wayne's childhood friend Rachel Dawes (Katie Holmes) tells Bruce that when he returned to Gotham City, she'd hoped that their relationship could grow into something more than friendship. "But then," she says, "I found out about your mask."

"Batman's just a symbol," Bruce responds. Rachel touches his face and says, "This is your mask. Your real face is the one criminals now fear. The man I loved ... the man who vanished ... never came back at all. But maybe he's still out there somewhere. Maybe one day, when Gotham no longer needs Batman, I'll see him again." Wayne has so exteriorized his inner predator in the Batman persona that it has become the truest expression of who he is. The "Bruce Wayne" the public sees is a disguise.

Throughout the film, the tone of the narrative stays within the range of urban crime genre. The ironic jokes of the first four features are absent as is the soaring, heroic score of the previous films. When there is humor, it's from within the narrative itself as when, as in the comics, Alfred makes an acerbic remark about his master's secret life, and not at the expense of the story's credibility. Though hardly documentary in style or presentation, Nolan's Gotham is closer to real-world crime films than other superhero features. Even after the triumphant outcome of *Batman Begins,* a new element of realism is introduced. Standing on the roof of police headquarters and discussing the newly installed Batsignal, freshly promoted Lieutenant Gordon (Gary Oldman), Batman's ally, remarks that Batman's activities have changed things. Though Ra's Al Ghul's scheme to destroy Gotham was thwarted, the Narrows neighborhood where his attack began was lost and Arkham Asylum's criminally insane inmates were freed to prey on the city. And now, Gordon says, there will be escalation as the underworld fights back with stronger methods and means. Batman himself has apparently inspired others toward theatricality to mirror his own as Gordon shows him a Joker card found at a murder scene.

Critical reaction to *Batman Begins* indicates that Nolan had achieved his goal of moving the narrative closer to the real world. In his review of the film, Roger Ebert stated that "this is, at last, the Batman movie I've been waiting for," adding, "The movie is not realistic, because how could it be, but it acts as if it is" ("Batman Begins"). This aligns with Giannetti's concept of film realism as a stylistic direction rather than an end point. Noting the lack of ironic distance in the film, *New York Times'* critic Manohla Dargis remarked, "It's amazing what an excellent cast, a solid screenplay and a regard for the source material can do for a comic book movie.... Mr. Nolan approaches Batman with respect rather than reverence" (Dargis, "Dark Was the Young Knight").

In the first four Batman films, the dynamic score balanced the photorealism with music's abstract underlining, sonically embellishing Batman's mythic nature. This complemented the sense of a comic book on film for which the directors were striving. For the *Batman Begins* musical score, Nolan commissioned Hans Zimmer and James Newton Howard to compose a score as different from Danny Elfman's Batman music as Nolan's film was from Tim

Burton's. Eschewing fanfares and soaring orchestral style, the composers sought to create a sound to fit the more psychologically intense perspective. Thus, the use of percussive sources (at times with a metallic element), digitally rendered sonic effects, and a particularly minimalist two-note theme for Batman. In an interview with *Empire* magazine, Zimmer remarked, "When we did *Batman Begins,* we never thought we were going to spread two notes over three movies! The character changes and it's amazing how flexible two notes can become."

In the development of Bruce Wayne's story, the two notes, Zimmer explains, are the beginning of a theme that gets cut off as tragedy strikes: "If there was an arc to be had, it was that he sees his parents getting killed—that's the defining moment of his life—and he feels guilty for it. The theme is interrupted at essentially two notes: it's never completed, because he never gets past this point." To create a sonic image of the devastating interruption of Bruce Wayne's young life, Zimmer added a choir boy's voice. "If you listen really carefully in the first film, there's this little choir boy at one point, and what the choir boy does, through electronic trickery ... his note actually freezes and goes on for about four minutes" (Williams).

The Dark Knight (2008)

The theme of escalation dominates the sequel, *The Dark Knight* (2008), as Batman finds that the Joker (Heath Ledger), a self-described "agent of chaos," will not yield to Batman's methods and challenges his code of non-lethal combat. By the end, citizens of Gotham are calling for Batman's arrest, the unintended consequences of well-intended actions having pushed the Dark Knight to a place the comics never took him—something like real-world ramifications with no simple solution. Yet Nolan's story uses these disastrous results to reassert Batman's mythic essence.

As the movie begins, Bruce Wayne's use of Batman as inspirational symbol results in a misfire when overzealous citizens begin putting on Batsuits and trying to stop crime—using firearms. In a parking garage encounter, Batman must attack both the criminals and the misguided wannabe Batmen. Later when the Joker releases a video of one of the batmen tied to a chair, we hear the villain ask, "Why do you dress like him?"

The terrified vigilante replies, "He's a symbol ... that we don't have to be afraid of scum like you ..."

This is not what Bruce intended, and it almost leads to his revealing his true identity. The Batman's mystique is challenged at another point in the story when, trying to scare mobster kingpin Maroni (Eric Roberts) into giving him information about the Joker, the gangster responds, "No one's gonna tell you anything—they're wise to your act. You got rules ... the Joker's got no rules." To stop more people from dying, Maroni tells Batman, he will have to give in to the Joker's demand that he drop his mask and turn himself in. Thus criminals have begun to realize that Batman's threats will go only so far.

When Bruce Wayne states his intention to give in to the Joker's demands, Alfred tells him, "Endure, Master Wayne. Take it. They'll hate you for it, but that's the point of Batman ... he can be the outcast. He can make the choice no one else can face. The right choice."

Later, after District Attorney Harvey Dent (Aaron Eckhart) claims to be the Batman, Rachel Dawes (Maggie Gyllenhaal) is angry at Bruce for not unmasking himself. Alfred tells her, "Perhaps both Bruce and Mr. Dent believe that Batman stands for something more important than a terrorist's whims, Miss Dawes, even if *everyone* hates him for it. That's the sacrifice he's making—to *not* be a hero. To be something more."

After Harvey Dent, having been driven mad through the loss of Rachel Dawes and his traumatic defacing, becomes Two-Face, he preys on those who are implicated in her death. When Batman, to save Commissioner Gordon's son, knocks Dent off a ledge several stories to his death, it appears that the Joker's schemes have succeeded and Gotham City has no legitimate figure to idolize. Recalling Alfred's earlier admonition that Batman be the one who "can take it," he tells Gordon to publicly blame him for the deaths to allow Dent to be Gotham's "white knight." Batman flees into the night, pursued by the police, as Gordon's voiceover addressed to his son both affirms and reframes the Batman mythos: "Because ... he's the hero Gotham deserves ... but not the one it needs right now. So we'll hunt him, because he can take it. Because he's not our hero ... he's a silent guardian, a watchful protector ... a dark knight."

The greater realism of Nolan's Batman films should not be interpreted as strict cinematic realism of course. The films fit pretty squarely in the classical tradition of Hollywood film narratives but rather than leaning heavily on the expressionistic technique and baroque style of earlier films as an appropriate cinematic frame for such an extraordinary character, Nolan chose to find the cinematic equivalents that would translate Batman from his two-dimensional comic book panels to a photorealistic medium while preserving his mythic characteristics through rationalized mythmaking. Using a straightforward attitude toward the character rather than irony and camp, the content of the Batman narrative makes a cleaner transition between two media with less alteration of the original treatment. This required two things of Nolan and company: a seriousness of attitude to his adaptation based in his appreciation for the history of the character, as he had stated in interviews, and second, the understanding that film, being photorealistic in texture, and with an inherent claim to verisimilitude, must necessarily move the content of comics closer to real-world depiction. *New York Times* film critic Manohla Dargis notes that Nolan's "moody resurrection" of the Batman franchise, "largely by embracing an ambivalence that at first glance might be mistaken for pessimism. But no work filled with such thrilling moments of pure cinema can be rightly branded pessimistic, even a postheroic superhero movie like *The Dark Knight*" ("Showdown"). This ambivalence resonates with the ambiguous nature of Batman mentioned in Chapter 2 as it makes vivid what is implied in Batman's complex nature and mission. "This is a darker Batman," Dargis continues in remarks cited earlier in the Introduction, "less obviously human, more strangely other. When he perches over Gotham on the edge of a skyscraper roof, he looks more like a gargoyle than a savior. There's a touch of demon in his stealthy menace." Such images resonate with the readers of Batman in the comics in which he appears as an almost otherworldly being, indeed sometimes drawn perched high on stone buildings alongside grey gargoyles.

The Dark Knight Rises (2012)

After the record-setting success of *The Dark Knight,* Christopher Nolan pondered how to best end his Batman series. Knowing he needed to resolve the moral predicament he had left Batman in at the end of *The Dark Knight*, he returned to Bruce Wayne's story, and pursued the original motivations that had led to Wayne's creation of the Batman as a symbol that would give hope to Gotham. Screenwriter David S. Goyer had originally commented that Nolan, in taking over the Batman movies for Warner Bros., wanted to do more than make just another installment in the series, the standard practice in blockbuster superhero films. Both men believed, as stated earlier, that the audience needed to care about Bruce Wayne rather than wait for Batman's next appearance. In an *Entertainment Weekly* interview with Jeff Jensen, Nolan recalled the conversation between Bruce and Alfred in *Batman Begins* where "it's not about beating up criminals one by one. It's about being a symbol. Bruce sees himself as a catalyst for change, and only ever thinks of this as a short term thing" ("Behind the Camera" 33–34). Nolan's realist approach demanded that his Batman story have an ending. The themes that began in *Batman Begins* would be tested and pay off in *The Dark Knight Rises*.

Nolan's brother and co-writer, Jonathan, remarked that the artistic cost of ongoing film franchises is a loss of continuity and gravity: "I think with almost every other franchise it's a mistake to try and keep those plates spinning. You want stakes. You want tectonic plates to shift. And as a writer you wanna feel you've worked on a complete story, with a beginning, middle and an end" (Jolin, "It Begins with an Ending," 90). In the first film, Batman, having been introduced to Gotham, hasn't yet inspired the city to dramatic change. At the beginning of *The Dark Knight,* the police have begun to feel that Batman is on their side and do little to follow orders to hunt down the vigilante. But corruption still exists and is exploited by the Joker. Batman's attack on the SWAT team and his subsequently taking the blame for Harvey Dent's crimes make him an outcast while seeming to set Gotham on the path to restoration. Dent's death becomes the stimulant to clean up Gotham, so much so that at the beginning of *The Dark Knight Rises,* the draconian Dent Act, passed to honor Gotham's fallen "white knight," prevents parole for incarcerated criminals. But there is a sense of unease in the two men who promulgated the deception. Police Commissioner James Gordon is about to confess the whole thing at an anniversary event honoring Dent held at the Wayne estate when he suddenly puts his notes in his pocket. Looking down from his mansion, Bruce Wayne, long a recluse from the world, turns and limps away. His injuries are both physical and psychic. He has lost Rachel Dawes, who symbolized a life beyond his crusade as Batman, and his goal of making Batman a symbol of hope to inspire the city's recovery has been replaced by Dent's false idolatry. Now Batman is despised and Wayne knows, as does Gordon, that the city's peace is ephemeral.

Though Nolan's world is more realistic than that found in the comics, characters and places still carry great symbolic weight. Below the city, the rot that was never really expunged, is growing again. The brutal Bane (Tom Hardy), leads Ra's Al Ghul's League of Shadows to finish what their fallen leader began: the cleansing of Gotham's corruption through the city's destruction. With this renewed threat comes the theme of Wayne's original mission to be an incorruptible idea, allowing the city to be restored. In *The Dark Knight Rises,* the damage to the city is so great that Batman's efforts would have to exceed his earlier heroics in order to achieve his lofty goal. In an interview, Christopher Nolan stated, "I never wanted it to feel like another episode of Batman or Bruce Wayne's story. This had to feel like the culmination of all of the things he's been dealing with in the first two films" (*The Dark Knight* Trilogy).

In each of the films, antagonists challenged the hero in different ways. Ra's Al Ghul's strategic attack, using the Gotham water supply, was intended to make its citizens destroy the city in a frenzy of fear. The Joker was determined to give the city "a little push" into nihilistic chaos as he threatened them into mass murder. Two ferries evacuating Gothamites in response to the Joker's threats receive trigger devices and are told that if each doesn't blow up the other ferry by midnight, the Joker will blow both of them up. Batman's faith in the city was rewarded when no one pushes the button and he stops the Joker before he triggers the ferry bombs. In *The Dark Knight Rises,* Bane represents both the bold strategic planning of Ra's Al Ghul and the brute strength that would literally erupt out of Gotham's sewers to bring a reckoning to the city.

Bruce's losses are tied directly to his crushed goals of inspiring the city, not because the city was rid of crime without his getting credit for it, but because he knows Dent's "white knight" myth was based on a lie, at the expense of its dark knight's inspirational myth. His hope for a life with Rachel now destroyed, he is a man on the edge of despair. Even his attempt to expend the Wayne fortune for a clean nuclear fusion energy source is halted until he could ensure that it could not be weaponized. This results in the draining of Waynecorp's earnings, so that now there are no profits to fund his service to the city's orphans. Both Bruce's diurnal life of civic philanthropy and Batman's nocturnal mission are closed off and the mythic function of Batman is thwarted by his own efforts to give Gotham hope. After Bruce learns of Bane's presence in the city, he prepares to put on the cape and cowl again and confront him. (This includes a trip to his doctor, who tells him that one of his knees has no cartilage; he goes on to say that there is "not much of any use in your elbows and shoulders ... and the scar tissue on your kidneys, residual concussive damage to your brain tissue and general scarred-over quality of your body," a realistic assessment of the consequences of being Batman.) Alfred tells him he could do more for the city as Bruce Wayne, but Bruce replies that Batman will succeed where Wayne's efforts failed. "You *can* fail as Bruce Wayne," Alfred says insightfully. "As Batman you can't afford to."

Bruce replies, "That's what you're afraid of—that if I go back out there, I'll fail."

Alfred wonders aloud, "I'm afraid you want to." He thinks Bruce is at a point where he doesn't care if he lives or dies since there is now no life beyond Batman.

Meanwhile, police detective John Blake (Joseph Gordon-Levitt) is chosen by Gordon to investigate the deaths of young men who have outgrown the orphanage system once funded by the Wayne Foundation. While speaking with the younger brother of one of the victims, one boy, while etching a bat symbol on a bench, asks, "Do you think he's ever coming back?" Some of Gotham's citizens still believe in the Batman. This includes Blake, an orphan whose experience of masking his anger at losing his parents to crime helped him see through Bruce Wayne's public mask. The myth of Batman endures, though it is pushed under the surface of official city policy.

Batman responds to Bane's first public attack on the city, when the League of Shadow's invades the Gotham Stock Exchange to hack into the system and run a program that will bankrupt Wayne. Batman responds to the attack, drawing the police to him as television cameras capture the Dark Knight's return. The mixed reaction to Batman's reappearance indicate that he isn't a pariah to every citizen. Bruce's seeming death wish causes the loyal Alfred to tearfully take his leave after he reveals that Rachel Dawes had written him a letter, stating that she had chosen Harvey Dent over Bruce. Now totally alone, Batman hunts for Bane by approaching cat burglar Selina Kyle (Anne Hathaway). She leads him to the villain's lair in the city's sewers but betrays him to Bane, who quickly bests Batman in a brutal fight.

The third film takes the mission of defending Gotham against crime and chaos to the ultimate level as Bane's League of Shadows literally attack the city's foundations and destroys its ties to the rest of the world. Blasting into Lucius Fox's armory of high-tech vehicles, he has almost completely deprived Batman of his de facto superpowers, his fortune, and the technology that gives him the edge against the underworld.

Bruce is carried off to captivity in the great sunken prison where Bane grew up while the city itself is set upon by the League of Shadows. The police are led into a trap in the very underworld of the city's sewers as the entrances are blasted shut. At a Gotham Rogues' football game, the stadium is attacked, and the mayor killed as Bane declares the city "liberated," and that the people are free to topple their rich oppressors. With the tunnels and bridges of the city cut off and Bane in control of the Waynetech fusion reactor, now a ticking time bomb, the city finally descends into chaos, with its Dark Knight protector gone.

Bane has told Bruce that he won't kill him; instead, he will force him to watch a video screen of the Gotham newsfeed as the weeks pass, knowing that watching the city die will be a fate worse than death. As Wayne seeks to recover his strength, he learns that the only way out of the pit is to climb to the top and leap over to a ledge, which only one other prisoner has ever done. After two failed attempts, he recalls what his father had told him many years before when he had fallen into a hole on the family's estate and been attacked by bats: "Why do we fall? So that we can learn to get up again." An aging prisoner tells him that he fails because he doesn't fear death. "How can you move faster than possible?" the old man asks him. "Fight longer than possible, if not from the most powerful impulse of the spirit. The fear of death. The will to survive." Bruce admits he fears "dying here while my city burns with no one there to save it." The man tells him to make the climb without a safety rope. "Then fear will find you again." Bruce must let in the fear he'd fought off in *Batman Begins* in order to complete the leap. Taking supplies with him this time, he begins the climb without a rope, as the prisoners rhythmically chant "Rise!" in another tongue. Climbing to the final level, he prepares to make the leap when out of the pit wall explodes a colony of bats echoing his original "baptism" of fear. Wayne completes the leap across to the ledge and climbing into the bright sunlight, he drops a coiled rope down to the prisoners below. The imagery evokes the Christian story of how Christ, after his Crucifixion, descended into hell, and according to the book of Ephesians, "When he ascended on high, he led captives in his train and gave gifts to men" (4:8). Bruce's "resurrection" has restored his ability to bring others out of the underworld and he proceeds to complete his mission to save Gotham. It also echoes the classic mythic hero pattern described by Joseph Campbell, wherein the hero undergoes a figurative death before rising again in triumph.

Bruce's earlier words to Alfred about how a dramatic example is necessary to jolt people to act have finally begun to take root in Gotham. The idea that Batman inspired of rejecting fear spreads to the captive citizens as James Gordon and John Blake organize a resistance to Bane's army. When Gordon searches for Peter Foley (Matthew Modine), his deputy commissioner, he finds him hiding at his home, afraid. When Foley argues that the resistance should wait until the federal government finds a way to liberate the city, Gordon replies, "This only gets fixed from *inside* the city, Foley!"

Soon thereafter, Gordon is captured and condemned to "death by exile" by being sent across the frozen river where others have broken through into the fatal waters. As he cautiously moves across the ice, Bane's mercenaries are taken out by small bat-shaped darts and Gordon hears Batman's voice say, "Light it up " as the cloaked figure comes out of the darkness. Gordon lights a flare that ignites a trail of flammable liquid and watches the flame rise up the side of the great brick bridge and erupt into a huge fiery bat symbol. Bane stares at it in disbelief while others take heart.

Dark Knight Apotheosis

After Batman has freed the police from their underground prison, Bane's army meets them on the streets of Gotham. As the two factions are about to clash, two Tumblers with roof cannons appear, all but ensuring the defeat of the city's police force. At that very moment, Batman, appearing overhead in the flying Bat vehicle, blasts both cannons, serving as the signal for the army in blue to charge. The city, led by Batman, has now risen to fight.

As the countdown to the bomb's explosion continues, Bane and Batman fight on the steps of city hall. During this altercation, a renewed Batman drives Bane back and damages the face mask that dispenses his pain-killing medication. Bruce's imagined ally, Miranda Tate (Marion Cotillard), is revealed to be Talia, Ra's Al Ghul's daughter, who is completing the mission of and exacting revenge for her father. Driving away in the truck containing the bomb, Batman's pursuit results in her crashing. With only a few minutes until the bomb explodes, Batman prepares to haul it out to sea in the Bat. Recalling Batman's disappearing act, an example of the theatricality that contributed to his mystique, Gordon says, "So this is the part where you vanish, only this time you're not coming back?" He then adds, "I never cared who you were."

"And you were right," Batman replies.

"But shouldn't people know the hero who saved them?" Gordon asks.

"A hero can be anyone," Batman responds. "That was always the point. Anyone. A man doing something as simple and reassuring as putting a coat around a little boy's shoulder to let him know that the world hadn't ended..."

Finally realizing Batman's secret identity, Gordon watches as the Bat rises and carries the bomb over Gotham. Watching an explosion from a bus of the orphans John Blake was trying to save, Blake thinks the bomb has gone off, but one of the boys cries, "No, it's Batman!" The Bat races out over the ocean and soon a bright flash and a mushroom cloud fill the eastern sky.

At the small memorial service for Bruce Wayne, Lucius Fox, Blake, and a tearful Alfred listen as Gordon reads the last lines from Dickens's *A Tale of Two Cities,* one of the inspirations for Nolan's concluding story:

I see a beautiful city and brilliant people rising from this abyss ... I see the lives for which I lay down my life, peaceful, useful, prosperous and happy ... I see that I hold a sanctuary in their hearts, and in the hearts of their descendants, generations hence. It is a far, far, better thing that I do, than I have ever done ... It is a far, far better rest that I go to than I have ever known.

The inspiration for the city's renewal is strongest in the generation whose perspective was most open to the idea Bruce Wayne created to lift the city up and give it hope. John Blake, the one responsible for prompting Wayne to take up his mantle again, is bequeathed an athletic bag with written coordinates. As the city honors their hero by unveiling a great black granite statue of the

Batman at City Hall, Blake (whose complete legal name includes "Robin") follows the coordinates to a waterfall. Swinging by rope under the cascade, he enters the Batcave and, upon entering, he activates the floor mechanism, raising him up to become the next Batman.

Gordon, back on the rooftop of police headquarters, smiles as he discovers a new Batsignal, knowing that someone—it doesn't matter who—will be there to respond to the symbol of hope. Bruce Wayne's narrative arc is completed, his original goals met, and he's allowed himself to return to something like a normal life while the idea, the myth he's created, continues to function on behalf of a recovering, reinvigorated Gotham City.

Christopher Nolan's more realistic approach to Batman included the aforementioned approximation of real-world consequences of a vigilante's actions on behalf of a city. Batman has always been at least an extra-legal figure, working on behalf of law and order, but outside of the legal system. Working to bring criminals to justice while ignoring the letter of the law and destroying city and private property along the way, Nolan's Batman is like a warlord endeavoring to work himself out of a job by making the legal system able to function again.[2] Though Harvey Dent works with Batman and Gordon, he admits publicly that someday the Batman will have to pay for laws he's broken. In an interview, Christopher Nolan was asked if his perspective is pro-or anti-vigilantism. "It's kind of both at the same time," he answered. "It's enjoying something and questioning it" (Holloran).

Batman, a character that fascinates because of his liminal nature, was in the Nolan films a compartmentalized psyche of three personas: the diurnal Bruce Wayne, the mask that the world sees, the nocturnal Batman who is predatory and relentless, and a third, Bruce Wayne in private, known to only a handful. We are never told who the "real" Bruce Wayne really is. In *The Dark Knight Rises,* it becomes evident that the low, rough voice he uses as Batman isn't simply a means of disguising his voice. He uses it when wearing the Batman suit, even when speaking to Alfred, or when he's alone, talking to himself. The Batsuit allows him to *become* the idea he has created, fueled by anger and his relentless commitment to fighting a war on crime. But sticking to a realist approach allowed Nolan to go beyond the "eternal now" of superhero's never-ending battle over decades. As Alan Moore said in the introduction to Frank Miller's graphic novel, *The Dark Knight Returns,* "Miller has also managed to shape The Batman into a true legend by introducing that element without which all true legends are incomplete and yet which for some reason hardly seems to exist in the world depicted in the average comic book, and that element is time" (no page number given). In like manner, Nolan's films created a total history of Batman, a beginning, a middle, and an end, as with so many of the great figures of myth and legend. As Time Warner looks to the future when it may try to further exploit its lucrative franchise, it is difficult to imagine how some future director will be able to match the artistic success of the Nolan films while finding another stylistic avenue for Batman in film.

• 8 •

The Comics Medium
as a Means of Evoking the Mythic

I have argued that much of Batman's enduring popularity may be attributed to the mythic nature of the character and his stories, a nature most effectively expressed in the medium of comics. The mythic dimension of Batman's character, i.e., the dualities constituting his mystique, are most effectively realized when depicted in the comics medium because only in that medium is such a character fully allowed to capture the reader's mythopathic imagination through the powerful comics techniques of iconic abstraction and closure. Whenever adaptations of comic book superheroes are attempted in other media, mythic evocation is usually diminished if not altogether lost. When photographic media such as film seek to depict a comics character, the necessary increase in the realistic detail results in a suppression of an audience's imaginative activity which is essential for mythic evocation. Batman has served as the exemplar for this study, but as the discussion of other comics that evoke the mythic earlier in Chapter 4 indicated, Batman is just one example of how the comics medium is able to evoke the mythic.

This has several implications for further research. Batman, as he has been known in comic books, has gone through numerous modifications and refinements as artists and writers have continually sought to find the right depiction of him for their respective time. Yet, looking at the whole span of Batman's "career," one sees that, although that depiction has varied widely in tone and style, both the basic scenario and the character have changed remarkably little. This is noteworthy considering how rare it is for a comic book superhero to survive without major changes, much less endure for 70 years. Those characters that have lasted are often reinvented with some basic change to the hero's origin, costume, or powers. It may be that the less mythic potential there is in a given character, the more the need to adjust the character to keep it viable. With a character such as Batman, who is in many ways unique, the mythic import was present during the first year of his creation. The creators found the right graphic design for Batman, with the right motivation for his mission. With such a perfect match between the character and his medium, his endurance may be attributable, so to speak, to his good breeding.

Likewise, other superheroes should be studied for their mythic content and whether that element was successfully realized in a cinematic or other adaptations. Here are several characters whose mythopoeic elements found some degree of successful expression onscreen.

Thor (2011)

Marvel's version of the Norse god of thunder was mythological from the start. In the comics he is from a race of gods, but in the film, perhaps to avoid grappling with the task of addressing gods in the present day in film's more realistic rendering, Thor is simply one of a vastly advanced race who, according to Odin's voiceover at the film's beginning, have "fallen into man's myths and legends," because humans in earlier times could only have seen the Asgardians as godlike. As an earth-bound Thor later explains, "Your ancestors called it magic ... but you call it science. I come from a land where they are one and the same." As a strategy to make the character more accessible, perhaps, the script may have avoided an adaptation challenge. Nevertheless, posters for the film featured the words "The god of Thunder" in all caps over the image of Chris Hemsworth's Thor, so the production had it both ways. After the film's prologue, the story proper starts on earth with the human characters encountering the fallen Thor, allowing time for audiences to become oriented in a realistic setting before flashing back to Asgard for the account of how Thor came to be exiled on earth. Balancing the two settings allows audiences to process the mythological elements with the more accessible earthbound story before the climax and ending in Asgard's cosmic city.

Captain America (2011)

That same summer, Marvel released the film featuring one of its oldest heroes, the star-spangled "living legend of World War II." Whereas Thor was inspired by Norse legend, Captain America is the quintessential American hero, more so than Superman. Clothed in the flag, a cinematic depiction of the character could risk looking ridiculous in the move from two-dimensional comics art to film's photorealism. Thus the story carefully and deliberately builds to the final rendition of the costumed character through a series of stages. Steve Rogers is introduced as the ultimate 90-pound weakling with the heart of a champion. Chosen as part of a supersoldier experiment by the Army, the script stresses Rogers's noble character to be his chief qualification as the great American hero. When the supersoldier serum works to produce the ultimate in human physical potential, the government keeps Rogers off the battlefield, opting to let him be used as a war bonds mascot in a costume literally adapted from the original comic book. Performing in a traveling war bonds stage show, the costume reproduced from the comics seems gaudy and impractical for battle. Frustrated and embarrassed, Rogers dutifully fulfills this assignment until he has a chance to prove his mettle in a one-man rescue of POWs in Nazi-occupied Europe. The Army, realizing what they have in Rogers, allows him to wear a more practical version of the costume to attack the menace of the Red-Skull-led Hydra organization. All through the film, the focus remains on Rogers's heroic character as the basis for his success. Like the comic, the film achieves the task of creating a character, who (though wearing red, white, and blue) credibly incarnates the ideal qualities of courage and humility in idealistic form that is still believable onscreen because of the careful scripting and Chris Evans's performance in the title role.

Superman

With the first modern superhero feature film, *Superman: The Movie* in 1978, the comic book film adaptation used high production values to fulfill the poster's tagline, "You'll believe a man can fly." The film itself, directed by Richard Donner, was an interlocking amalgam of three styles that were never reconciled. Beginning on the planet Krypton, Jor-El (Marlon Brando) and Lara (Susannah York) send their only son to earth to escape the planet's destruction. With the setting now being the Kansas heartland, John Williams's powerful score underlines the making of the American version of Joseph Campbell's mythic hero. Clark Kent's (Christopher Reeve) gradual self-discovery of his real identity culminates in his training by a Kryptonian hologram of Jor-El in his Fortress of Solitude. The image of his father concludes his son's preparation in the arctic wilderness with pseudo-biblical language: "They can be a great people, Kal-El, they wish to be. They only lack the light to show the way. For this reason above all, their capacity for good, I have sent them you ... my only son." Thus framed as a caped Christ figure, the film up to this time has expressed the mythic trappings of Superman. Superman soars off to Metropolis and there the film's first stylistic shift occurs. The *Daily Planet*'s hectic newsroom is where we encounter scoop-hungry Lois Lane (Margot Kidder). Perry White (Jackie Cooper), the paper's editor, introduces her to his new hire, the awkward and meek Clark Kent. The film's tone is now that of a screwball romantic comedy as Lois and Clark's interactions play with the audience's sense of comic irony. This tone continues through the middle section of the film until the scene shifts to the underground lair of Lex Luthor (Gene Hackman). There the camp sensibility of the Batman television series comes to the movie's foreground as Luthor boasts of his plans to his incompetent underlings. The jarring tonal shifts indicated the filmmakers' inability to reconcile the thematic and narrative elements of their origin story in translating the comic book to the screen. The subsequent Christopher Reeve films gradually slid further toward camp and smaller budgets, squeezing out whatever mythic potential the films could have achieved in a character who demanded some sustained realization of it. For so mythic a character as Superman, cinematic adaptation has remained problematic. Bryan Singer's *Superman Returns* (2006) consciously sought to return to the first two films' sensibility but, in many ways, felt too beholden to Donner's vision while darkening the appealing tone that had made the Reeve interpretation so attractive. The latest attempt to adapt Superman, *The Man of Steel* (2013), stressed the science fiction elements more while deepening the identity crisis of Clark Kent, caught between the fear of his earthly father that his foster son's exposure to the world will bring only grief, and his Kryptonian father's (again in hologram form) hope that his son can inspire and aid the human race with his great power. There is a suggestion that Superman is like Christ at one point, but rather than follow through on that familiar idea, there is little after that scene to suggest anything close to a sacrificial figure who redeems the world. The film's main goal to find a way for a superpowered alien to be integrated into a world of mortals. Thus, there is less emphasis on the mythic in this latest Superman adaptation.

Other superhero adaptations may call upon Kurt Busiek's idea of metaphor without being expressions of the mythic. In the introduction to a collection of his Astro City stories, Busiek asserts that the concept of superheroes as metaphors is one of the genre's strengths. The popular Spider-Man movies are a case in point. If the character is a metaphor for the passage from adolescence to responsible manhood, Peter Parker as Everyman functions well within fantastic comic book storytelling that doesn't require mythic elements ("Life in the Big City" 8). Similarly, cinematic treatments of The Hulk, Iron Man, and the X-

Men have worked well on a metaphorical or simply adventure level, although some may offer their own argument for the inherent mythopoeic elements.

The Scale of Mythic Design

A fundamental and larger contribution of this study is the juxtaposition of Northrop Frye's Scale of Literary Design with Scott McCloud's Scale of Iconic Abstraction to form the Scale of Mythic Design. It provides a means of understanding why and how various media artifacts are able to evoke the mythic. Although Frye's scale was derived from his description of the range of literary works, when it is correlated with McCloud's Scale of Iconic Abstraction, one is able to locate the relationship of media artifacts other than literary ones to the mythopoeic. Especially now when there is so much mythic content in comics, as well as in other mass media, the Scale of Mythic Design may provide better understanding of mythic expressions in these artifacts.

The Need for the Mythic

Readers have continued to be drawn to Batman because they perceive, consciously or not, his mythic significance, particularly the manner in which certain values and beliefs about justice, crime, and the social order are incarnated in his character and his stories. This and other similar examples of mythic evocation in popular culture are significant in that they point to a hunger for transcendence from the materialistic sensibility that dominates the modern era. In this sense Batman serves as a signpost pointing to the human need for the mythic, that is, for the expression of meaning through narratives featuring extraordinary characters and situations. Though we are the children of the technological age and the heirs of scientific progress, our materialistic culture lacks both the images and the values to create meaning for us and to adequately explain our persistent desire for myth. Therefore, what has been explained away and debunked by materialism resurfaces in the guise of mythic narratives, which continue to build on pre-modern types and ancient archetypal patterns. Even if these contemporary mythic forms lack the richness of their mythological predecessors, they still feed the ongoing human need to view the world in a manner that transcends the material. Strictly rationalistic approaches to meaning are inadequate for addressing the full range of human concerns. Humans seek expression of those concerns in rich narratives that find ways of articulating these values, hopes, and fears.

Batman, being merely "mythic" (i.e., not a myth itself but drawing from mythical patterns), addresses a relatively small portion of human concerns, specifically the problems of crime, disorder, injustice, and vengeance. Batman's endless quest allows for a mythic response to the fear and anger that people feel in what they see as an increasingly desperate social predicament. The Batman stories, as featured in the comic books, reaches a relatively small audience made up mostly of young males, yet we have seen how, over the years, this mythic character has insinuated his way into the larger public consciousness through many adaptations. Although Batman's mythic evocation is usually diminished through adaptation into other media, something mythic and archetypal nevertheless survives. It is certainly true that the corporate owner of the Batman franchise has sought to ensure his prominence through prodigious merchandising. However, one has only to note Batman's perennial popularity and compare it to the short lives or intermittent exploitation of other pop-culture characters (such as He-man or the Teenage Mutant Ninja Turtles) to understand that something more enduring than merchandising must be taken into account.

Comparing other highly merchandised heroes with Batman also brings up the issue of the nature of popular-culture heroes and hero worship today. Many of the biggest commercial successes in contemporary American film are those that draw their form and inspiration, not from the successful feature films of Hollywood's Golden Age, but from the content of that era's Saturday matinee adventure serial, with its cliffhanger endings, melodramatic situations, arch villainy, and dynamic heroes. The matinee serials featured several genres, including jungle adventures, science fiction, and the costumed comic book hero (such as Batman). These multi-part serials and B-movie features were juvenile, cheap programmers that won little, if any, critical respect upon their initial release. In 1977, however, *Star Wars* marked the beginning of a transition in film subject matter in which the content of the old serials, pulp novels, and comic books began to become the inspiration for blockbuster films. *Raiders of the Lost Ark* (1981) furthered the move toward the cliffhanger sequel as another successful model for major feature films. Of course, other kinds of films were not made obsolete: their popularity was simply diminished in the marketplace by the action blockbusters of the 1980s and '90s, as well as current offerings. Although much of this transition to the matinee model was fueled by a new era of greater sophistication in special effects and sound quality, it was also propelled by the emergence of a different type of hero. Movie heroes of the this era were markedly different from the classic American heroic figures as portrayed by such stars as John Wayne, Gary Cooper, or Jimmy Stewart. Although their characters may have resorted to violence, they were not defined solely by this behavior. In contrast, action heroes, including such box-office favorites as Arnold Schwarzenegger, Bruce Willis, and Sylvester Stallone, and more recently, Jason Statham, are characterized by the havoc and bloodshed of which they are capable. The contemporary male hero is a supercompetent killer (with roots in the James Bond films), pitted against incredible odds but who triumphs through his ability to dispatch enemies by the truckload. Of course, the classic Western hero was known for his skill with a gun, but his often reluctant use of the weapon was a reflection of societal morality (and, more significantly, censorship). Contemporary action films exist mostly for the thrill of the pyrotechnic action. If they serve any purpose besides excitement for audiences, it is that they provide wish-fulfillment dreams to an audience seeking rough justice in an increasingly chaotic world. For people who sense a loss of control over their environment, particularly due to the crisis of public order, these film characters offer a fantasy of a hero who is never at a loss, who overcomes the most daunting odds, and whose nerves never fail him.

Perhaps because of a public frustration with the criminal justice system, today's movies became two hours of escapism, in which the criminal gets what is deserved—and more. They are vengeful fantasies offering a momentary sense of satisfaction before the audience must leave the theater, venturing back into a fearful world where justice and security are more elusive. It is in this cinematic milieu that Batman has been adapted as an action hero, one whose proactive mission it is to prey on wrongdoers. Whereas the comic book Batman has sworn not to kill, his Burtonesque cinematic counterpart apparently had no such reservations: in each film, several of his opponents, either directly or indirectly, die while fighting him. Embraced by the huge audiences that have made these feature films such successes, Batman is part of this pantheon of modern heroes who function as surrogates in violent, wish-fulfillment fantasies. Christopher Nolan's more faithful adaptations go easier on villains in that his Batman makes a point of not proactively killing (although his last words to Ra's Al Ghul in *Batman Begins*, "I won't kill you, but I don't have to save you," are a cold justification), but most die as a result of their confrontation with the Dark Knight.

Locating the Mythic: Suggestions for Further Research

Describing and locating the mythic in popular culture remains a challenging task. It is not enough to simply assign the term "mythic" to an artifact:

a study must offer a clear and manageable definition of the mythic and one that is, hopefully, consistent with that of other research. "Myth" and the "mythic" tend to be loaded terms with varying or contested meanings. Perhaps greater progress toward a nomenclature of schools of myth, similar to but more developed than those terms in Chapter 1, would be a first step toward enabling more general discussions of the phenomena. As meanings are refined, better methods for identifying and elucidating the mythic can also be expected.

Continued work in discerning the mythic patterns in different media narratives could build on this study by using the scale developed here. The Scale of Mythic Design discussed in the Appendix is merely the beginning of a concept that could increase knowledge and understanding of how various popular-culture artifacts achieve mythic evocation. Additional work should be done to develop the scale so that it is able to offer a more complex and nuanced analysis of a given example. One thinks of what must be considered one of the central, mythic, popular culture exemplars of our time, the *Star Trek* franchise, with its popular and compelling vision of the future. If one accepts *Star Trek* as a mythic artifact, then do the terms used by the Scale of Mythic Design explain its mythic patterns and content? How is this largely television-oriented phenomenon using photorealism to depict its narratives, able to achieve some measure of mythic resonance?

The same or similar questions could be asked of other media examples. Since prose writing is on the end of McCloud's Scale of Iconic Abstraction where meaning is the greatest, then the potential for mythic evocation should be at its strongest there. Investigations of mythic evocation in individual novels, series of novels, or whole genres could be pursued, using the Scale of Mythic Design. Similarly, movies, television shows, and of course, comics, are other natural objects of scholarly inquiry. Also worth investigating is the burgeoning field of multimedia products such as video games. Many interactive computer-based and console video games feature mythological trappings and may derive their structure and content from some sort of mythic patterns.

In this study, adaptations of *Batman* in various media were compared to the comic book version of the character to better understand how sequential art is uniquely able to evoke the mythic. As such, this was not a comprehensive study of the process of adaptation but rather of in what manner mythic content survives adaptation, if and when it does. Research that undertakes the study of adaptation from comic book to television, film, or other media could focus on many other features of the comic book other than the mythic. William Albert Neff demonstrated that the formulas of comic book stories may be studied in terms of their pictorial and linguistic features. A study of adaptations of comic books might also focus on how comics formulas translate between media—a subject I have touched on—and on the formal and structural links that forge that process.

And since Hollywood has already realized so many billions of dollars in profit from adaptations of superhero characters and will continue to for as long as the cash cow can be milked, studies of how successful or failed efforts translated from the comics page to the big screen can shed light on the artistic process of finding cinematic equivalents for comics stories. McAllister, Gordon, and Janovich note in their article on film adaptions that "comic book companies see themselves in the character-licensing business ... and perhaps even more specifically in the filmed entertainment industry" (111). Indeed, it's widely known that this is where the real money is for Time Warner's DC Comics.

One of the other unique ingredients of comics is the nature of their storytelling. Comic books are one of the few narrative forms in contemporary culture that publishes monthly issues. Any number of perspectives, whether historical (there were once many weekly and monthly publications that featured fictional content), cultural, or economic, would offer valuable insights into this medium as it relates to other forms of popular culture. Similarly, researchers could examine how the comic book narrative has changed over the last several decades as it has moved from the typical single-issue story to the largely Marvel-instigated, multi-part (or continuing) story.

Chapter 1 of this study briefly discussed the manner in which comics, along with pulp magazines and the dime novel, are examples of popular narratives in which the prodigious output of stories is linked to the manner in which the writer functions, which is less as a creator than as a mediator between the audience and its shared fantasies. In this context, the writer seeks to identify with the shared dreams of his readers, reflecting them back in the form of endlessly repeated formulas. Comics is perhaps the chief example of a popular art form in which interactivity between writers and their readership is pronounced. Letter columns have been a longtime convention in comics, allowing readers to praise and criticize, speculate and inquire about their favorite characters and titles. Today, online correspondence through email to editors, chatrooms, and social media all keep the conversations and complaints going.

Several years ago, when the then-current Robin proved unpopular with readers, DC offered a storyline in which the audience could call a 900 (toll call) telephone number to vote on whether the sidekick would live or die. Jason Todd, the second Robin, received a death warrant in the form of a negative majority of votes from callers and died at the end of the series. Later, to revive sagging sales in the comics market, DC and Marvel, in an unprecedented alliance, published a series pitting the heroes of their respective universes against one another. Readers could vote on who would win specific fights, and the results were depicted in the third issue of the series. In these and other ways such interactivity raises questions about the nature of narrativity and authorship and is worthy of research.

Such issues as form, structure, formula, and adaptation involve matters of both aesthetics and craft. It is therefore important to stress the importance of the comic book medium as an art form in itself and not just a means of cultural analysis. Scott McCloud and others have pointed the way to greater appreciation of the comics medium, but further research and debate would illuminate this relatively neglected subject. Further theoretical research along these lines could form a base upon which continued critical studies of the medium may be built. Cultural studies remain valuable, of course; this study has touched on Batman's sociocultural significance, which also deserves more attention. Finally, researchers in the social science tradition might give some attention to the demographic breakdown between male and female readers of comics. Studies could explore what it is in particular that young males like about comics and, perhaps, what it is that young females do not like about comics. (This applies, of course, mostly to superhero comics. Female readership of manga comics is a phenomenon of its own.) A study of the growing segment of post-adolescent males who read comics could also offer useful information about changes both in the comics audience and the content of comic books themselves.

Conclusion: The Uses of the Mythic

A character from the Noel Coward play, *Private Lives* remarks that it is "amazing how potent cheap music is," testifying to the ability of what has been considered a middle- to lowbrow art form—like comics—to evoke deep responses in an audience. Likewise, in his essay, "On Stories," C. S. Lewis points out that the profound effect of certain adventure stories on "unliterary" readers is akin to a literary experience. Here, something "which the educated receive from poetry can reach the masses through stories of adventure, and in almost no other way" (16). The ability of such stories to induce in readers a taste of transcendence will always be a key to their appeal. In a time when the audience for poetry and other traditional literature is declining and the mass media of television, film, and digital media are progressively more dominant, people seek for the compelling but elusive effect of the mythopoeic in "stories of adventure." A debased culture devalues its ties to traditional cultural roots, but audiences still search for something more than cliffhanger excitement and sometimes find it in popular culture. Whether in the projected utopian future of *Star Trek*, the magical adventures of Harry Potter, or in Batman's never-ending quest for justice, audiences connect to a meaningful vision that seems to make sense of an uncertain age. The continuing presence of Batman in his native medium and in other adaptations testifies to the power of comics—a

Batman as depicted at the end of his origin story (from *Batman* #1).

still rather marginalized mass medium—to convey meaning both to its own audience and to society at large. Comics stories are hardly transcendent in the religious or spiritual sense; like the long shadow cast by the Dark Knight, they can be the thrilling but thin shadows of mythic substance as yet unattained. It's difficult to turn out mythic entertainment in multiple monthly titles, year after year, decade after decade, so when Christopher Nolan presents three epic films summing up the mythic essence of Batman's career, he is merely realizing the potential that has always dwelled within this creature of the night, pouring a decade of effort and expense into his Dark Knight apotheosis.

The strength of the fiction of C. S. Lewis, as well as that of J. R. R. Tolkien, is derived in part from the authors' drawing from the Western narrative tradition that included the mythologies of Europe and the values and doctrines of the Jewish and Christian religions. From these components the authors could weave rich mythopoeic narratives. If today's comics creators are to more fully realize the medium's potential for mythic evocation, a similar reliance on such a rich heritage would be necessary.

Neil Gaiman's Sandman stories, discussed in Chapter 4, have constructed a mythical cosmos borrowing liberally from Western literary and religious tradition, and perhaps no other example of comics art has succeeded so well at suggesting the greater reaches possible for exploring the mythopoeic. Yet, despite this remarkable achievement, the work strikes a reader more as an intriguing intertextual mythological potpourri than as a nourishing source of the mythopoeic that touches the human soul. One gets the sense that the author has appropriated mythological ingredients in order to play with them, creating a stimulating, well-pedigreed diversion, but one that lacks a sense of the author's investment and belief in the mythic forms he employs. This is perhaps typical of a post-modern reluctance among would-be contemporary myth-makers to believe in the tradition they exploit, and such reluctance will always limit the mythic potential of their stories. When the story is told in a distancing ironic mode, its transcendent potential is sapped. If the comics medium is to truly realize greater mythopoeic possibilities than such examples as Batman achieve, a deeper commitment to the Western narrative tradition or any long-established cultural tradition (as described above) will have to occur.

Comics is a medium just coming into its own as an art form. The comic strip is well past its hundredth anniversary and the modern comic book is over 75 years old. Sequential art in one form or another has a history many centuries old and is an essential and fundamental means of transmitting meaning. This book has shown that sequential art, in the comic book form, can evoke the mythic and that film can find cinematic equivalents for that mythic content.

In Batman's case, this is done through a character who encapsulates his audience's fear and anger and reflects their values. Batman's enduring potency as a complex symbol realized in the comics medium is only a small indication of that medium's potential for achieving mythic evocation in its deceptively static panels.

Appendix

Charting the Mythic in Mass Media

The character Batman is merely one example of how the mythic aspects of a figure may be evoked through the particular characteristics of sequential art. As such, Batman is an exemplar demonstrating the unique ability of the comics medium to evoke the mythic. In this appendix, the concepts and principles of Northrop Frye and Scott McCloud that formed the basis for much of the theorizing and analyses in this book will be used to form a chart exploring how diverse examples from comics, cinema, television, literature, and other media may be located in relation to their capacity to evoke the mythic.

McCloud's Scale of Iconic Abstraction

The horizontal axis of the chart is formed by what I have referred to as the Scale of Iconic Abstraction as described by Scott McCloud and featured in Chapter 4. The scale begins on the far left with realism, exemplified by photorealistic illustration and moves to the right toward increasingly abstract drawings characterized by decreased detail and by increased potential for reader-provided meaning. As iconic abstraction increases and any semblance of realism disappears, the scale crosses over into the area of pure abstraction, i.e., the realm of language or words. Whereas pictures of relative abstraction had represented an object or idea, now words represent them. Thus, in McCloud's scale, a face moves from photorealistic depiction increasingly toward the abstract until it becomes the word "face" and then is described rather than drawn: "two eyes, one nose, one mouth" and, finally, a literary rendering demonstrated by use of a quoted poem ("Thy youth's proud livery, so

175

Appendix, Figure 1: McCloud's Scale of Iconic Abstraction adapted from *Understanding Comics*.

gazed on now ..."). On McCloud's scale comics and cartoons begin where enough detail has been removed to begin the process of abstraction that allows for the involvement of the reader's imagination in a way not possible through photorealistic depiction. As abstraction increases, so does involvement in the realm of ideas.

The depiction of objects in the photorealistic medium of film is heavily weighted toward realism or toward what McCloud calls "the world without," whereas cartoons portray "the world within" (41). Film must use other techniques to mitigate its inherent realism such as the many formalistic techniques developed over the past century, which would include such devices as editing, lighting, music, and special effects.

Frye's Scale of Literary Design

The vertical axis of the chart adapts the "literary design" Frye describes in *Anatomy of Criticism,* a design that places myth at one end and realism or naturalism at the other, with the broad middle region occupied by romance (136). Myth is concerned with stories of gods and demons; realism is concerned with life as it is experienced; and romance borrows from both extremes to create stories that feature characters in "real-life" settings who display qualities derived from myth. This displacement of myth into romance provides forms and characteristics that distinguish such stories from prosaic realism. This idealization of character and events is necessarily distanced from "life as we know it" in order to create the appeal of the romance. As Frye explains:

> This affinity between the mythical and the abstractly literary illuminates many aspects of fiction, especially the more popular fiction which is realistic enough to be plausible in its incidents and yet romantic enough to be a "good story," which means a clearly designed one [*Anatomy* 139].

The romance is contrived to allow for a pleasing form that displaces aspects of myth, while at the same time borrowing a semblance of realism, to ensure

$$\longleftarrow \hspace{8cm} \longrightarrow$$

Realism   R O M A N C E   The Mythic **Myth**

Appendix, Figure 2: The Scale of Literary Design adapted from Northrop Frye's *Anatomy of Criticism.*

a level of plausibility. Abstracting from the concrete, i.e., the realistic, toward the mythic, the romance mixes elements of the two poles to become a story form broad and flexible enough to include an enormous range of narratives.

The chief purpose of Frye's scale here is to locate a given artifact in terms of its ability to render the mythic qualities of its content. Thus the chart would contain within it a region in which the mythic is to be found, as well as areas where it will not be found. The areas in Frye's scale are not neatly segmented into realism, romance, and myth but are understood to move in fine gradations as shown in Figure 2, Appendix.

For the purposes of this study, the above shows three principle areas in Frye's scale: realism at one end, myth on the other, and the broad area of romance in between. In the upper reaches of romance, toward the right of the scale, is where I place the mythic. Realism contains any story that features settings, plots, and characters that matches our experience of life. The stories can be documentary or semi-documentary in form, open-ended in narrative, with all the details that reflect everyday life. This area graduates into the area of the romance, where characters, plots, and settings are more idealized and can be said to contain elements displaced from myth. A character in a romance is not a mythological person but certain qualities about him or her may contain symbolic traits drawn from myth. For instance, to say a hero is "Adonis-like," is to impute certain qualities without making him a mythological character. A private detective's hunt for a missing heiress, set in a gritty urban locale, may resonate with tales of a myth of a great hero in search of a princess. Plots are clearly structured to fit a formula that indicates the shared values of the writer and reader.

Moving farther to the right on the scale, romance passes into an area in which the similarities to myth itself are more pronounced. Displacement still occurs from myth and there can be realistic ingredients, yet settings, plots, and characters are heightened and less based in realism than the rest of the area of the romance. The main character or characters are likely to exhibit extraordinary, even fantastic, abilities. Kings, queens, and other members of royalty (or characters of such stature) may be featured prominently. Here plots are even more concerned with the conflicting values of protagonist and antagonist. There is little or no room for shades of gray in this world of black and white.

The Scale of Mythic Design

By aligning McCloud's horizontal Scale of Iconic Abstraction at a right angle to Frye's vertical Literary Design Scale, a chart is constructed that enables the locating of various mass media artifacts according to their capacity to evoke the mythic.

Batman has been discussed as a character whose mythic qualities are evoked by the iconic abstraction of which the comics medium is capable. What is realistically impossible and ridiculous becomes plausible and effective in the abstracted iconic rendering of comics. Thus, as was demonstrated in Chapter 4, various versions of Batman comics depictions, being abstracted from a real-

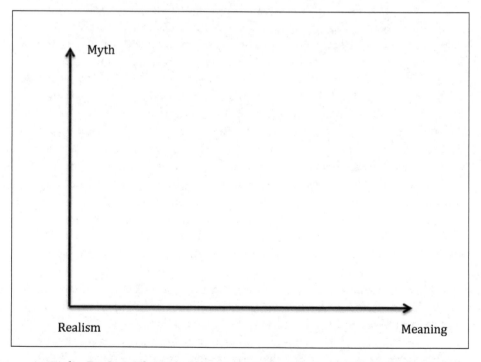

Appendix, Figure 3: The Scale of Mythic Design combining McCloud's Scale of Iconic Abstraction as the horizontal axis with Frye's Scale of Literary Design as the vertical axis.

Batman in comics

Realism   **R O M A N C E**   The Mythic **Myth**

Appendix, Figure 4: The Scale of Literary Design adapted from Northrop Frye's *Anatomy of Criticism* indicating Batman's mythic status on it.

istic rendering, fall to the right of the far left-hand end of the Scale of Iconic Abstraction. This abstraction correlates with Frye's description of the abstraction necessary in the form of the romance.

It has been established that the Batman stories fit into this mythic portion of what this study refers to as Frye's Literary Design Scale, containing elements derived from myth set in a more or less realistic urban locale. Set on a perpetual quest for justice and vengeance, Batman is more than an outraged vigilante, but less than a divine nemesis of evil. Partaking of qualities derived from earlier mythological sources and patterns, he symbolically fights against the chaos that frightens and angers us by adopting the fearsome visage of a night creature. Though apparently mortal, he transcends human limits in his keen ratiocination and athletic grace and power. Thus, as a mythic figure expressed in the comics medium, on the Literary Design Scale, he belongs at the upper levels of romance as an idealized, extraordinary heroic figure in a still-recognizable urban setting.

For purposes of illustration, I will discuss several different depictions of Batman in various media to demonstrate how they would fall on the Scale of Mythic Design. A Batman comic book such as *The Batman Adventures,* done in the animated style, would be located in the upper right of the center portion of the scale. On the Scale of Iconic Abstraction, the flat, simplified drawing style is far enough removed from realistic depiction to warrant this location. The characters, content, and setting, i.e., a costumed crime fighter with a dualistic mystique, fighting equally fantastic and colorful adversaries in a relatively realistic urban setting, would place it on the upper section of the Literary Design Scale, within the realm of the romance termed the mythic but deriving elements from realism. The animated series episodes, though drawn in the same style, would be located to the left and down slightly in both horizontal and vertical scales toward increased realism because of the addition of movement. The live-action feature *Batman Begins* would be located further down and leftward being photorealistic versions of the same story. To get a better overall perspective of the situations of diverse media, the next figure (Figure 5, Appendix) shows representative examples as they would be located

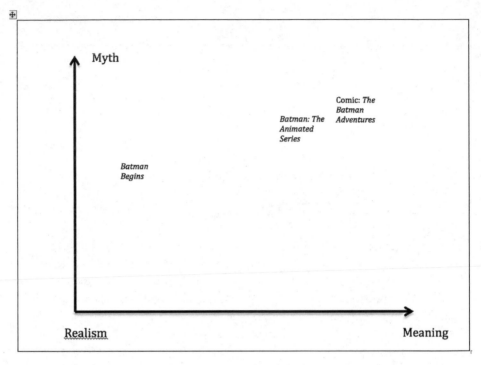

Appendix, Figure 5: The Scale of Mythic Design indicates the relative positions of three versions of Batman.

on the scale. A documentary film such as *Hoop Dreams* (1995), depicting the careers of two young, black, high-school basketball players, is a documentary account of two real individuals, featuring film and video footage shot over several years of their lives. Such a realistic record falls very close to but not quite in to the lower left-hand corner of the scale. Both in visual depiction and in verisimilitude to actual experience, *Hoop Dreams* is notable precisely for its realism, yet like all documentaries, it was shaped by film editors. The only type of recorded documentation that could be called completely realistic would be such that are recorded by surveillance cameras at a bank or retail store. Some artistic shaping of the material is done even in the rawest documentary record.

In contrast, a written biography such as David McCullough's *Truman,* recounting the life of a U.S. president would, lacking illustrations (except the accompanying photographic section), fall into the lower right-hand corner, because it uses words to convey meaning. Diametrically opposed to this example is the film adaptation of the Greek myth of *Jason and the Argonauts* (1963). Very near the far left of the iconic-abstraction axis, because of its photorealism,

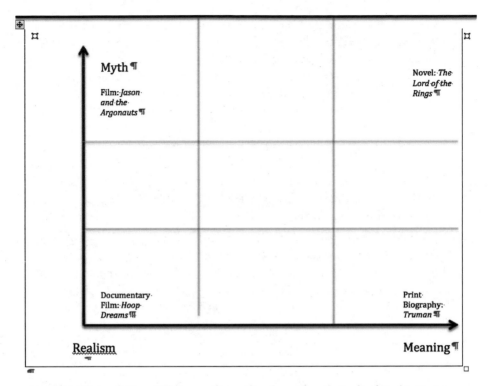

Appendix, Figure 6: Four different media artifacts located on the Scale of Mythic Design.

it seeks to convey the content of Greek myths featuring gods, goddesses, heroes, and great monsters. Its general lack of many recognizable film stars lends it a greater sense of the mythological: there are few if any well-known faces to remind the audience of those actors' associations with previous roles. The mythic figures in the film seem more themselves than if familiar faces had played them.

Finally in Figure 6, Appendix J. R. R. Tolkien's fantasy novel *The Lord of the Rings* is located in the fictional "Middle-earth," in a distant past (before recorded history), and it contains diverse races and fantastic creatures. It is difficult to imagine an upper right-hand area. With only maps for illustration, it is set in a story approaching much closer to myth on the vertical axis that is the Scale of Literary Design. Thoroughly engaging the imagination through the author's abundant and detailed descriptions of place, character, and incident, the written text creates another world in the reader's mind. These four examples offer a sort of lay of the land that the scale is able to encompass. Other examples in various media can, of course, be placed on the scale, and, in doing so, two basic questions must be asked:

1. Where do the qualities of the medium's images fall on the range between photographic realism (film, television, etc.) and iconic abstraction (comics, animation, prose, etc.) on the Scale of Iconic Abstraction?

2. Where does the story content of the example fall on the Scale of Literary Design? Is it generally realistic, romantic, or mythological? (Here various considerations such as a given example's setting, time period, and characterization will help locate where along the scale it falls.) This scale cannot, of course, place a given media example with mathematical precision, nor is it designed to. Rather, it indicates the relative positions of such artifacts vis-à-vis the two scale's juxtaposed relationships and, more importantly, it establishes a graduated context within which a medium's potential for mythic evocation can be better understood.

Viewed as such, this scale underlines and illustrates the propositions of this study, which maintains that it is a peculiar ability of comics or sequential art to evoke the mythic qualities of a character like Batman. Other media contain some potential for realizing the mythic, but those using photographic technology, such as film and television, suffer from the mitigating effect photorealism brings to the depiction of the mythic.

Chapter Notes

Chapter 1

1. Another way of viewing the relationship between superheroes and ancient mythologies is featured in Terrence R. Wandtke's *The Meaning of Superhero Comic Books* which posits that comics storytelling in certain ways resembles the oral tradition whereby there is no specific author of a epic poem nor of a superhero's story given the nature of ancient oral cultures and the collaborative processes of modern comic book storytelling.

Chapter 2

1. In a rare instance, in *Batman* #4, p. 43, interrupting an assault on a man by gangsters, Batman picks up a dropped automatic and fires it at a fleeing assailant who had been firing a machine gun from an automobile. "Just want to wing him," says Batman, which he does, causing the gunman to drop his weapon. At the bottom of the panel a caption states, "Editor's Note: The Batman never carries or kills with a gun!"

Chapter 3

1. The sense of liminality as used by Victor Turner refers to the rites of passage wherein a person is in transition from one state to another and is on the threshold between the two. In such a process, the state of liminality is temporary, ending as one emerges into the new state. This study uses the term liminality in the more limited sense of simply being in a state of possessing traits of two distinct states or qualities, such as in the case of a bat being a winged mammal.

2. Although he was referred to as the "gillman" in the films featuring him.

3. In another effort to provide consistent continuity in all the "DC Universe's" characters' histories, DC's "Zero Hour" stories saw the "restart" of the DC universe's history in order to save it from destruction. When the superheroes had finished the restart, certain details of characters' histories were changed; in Batman's case, he does not know who killed his parents.

4. Robert Sklar, in *Movie Made America,* asserts that audiences identified with gangsters as heroes struggling against the initial social pathos of the Depression (181).

5. It is true that undercover agents may testify in court wearing a mask, yet Batman differs in at least two ways. Being unaccountable to the higher authorities, he has no superiors who can validate his credibility by knowing who he is, and these true-life agents don't wear masks in their undercover work. Batman's anonymity gives him his mystery and makes him realistically unviable.

Chapter 4

1. At times, stories have mentioned that Batman's cowl contains night vision technol-

ogy, which motivates the usually white eye coverings. When, at the end of *The Dark Knight,* Batman's cowl contains a heads-up display of electronically delivered tactical information, the eyes are whitened, but with the oval shape of the mask's eye holes, they lack the eeriness of the comics version.

explanation for the relative success of this scene is that the long shot renders the Elves more emblematic. Distance from the camera eliminates the textured detail characteristic of photography, which in medium- and close-up shots betrays the demythologizing effect of the camera.

Chapter 5

1. To better illustrate the manner in which the concepts drawn from Frye's Scale of Literary Design and McCloud's Scale of Iconic Abstraction can work together to illustrate the occurrence of the mythic in various media, I have designed a scale that incorporates both of their concepts of meaning in the Appendix.

2. There is a scene in the Extended Version of *The Fellowship of the Ring* DVD in which Frodo and Sam see a party of Elves departing for the Grey Havens. The long shot of the procession is closer to the description of the Wood Elves quoted above than anything in the theatrical release. There is a special effects-rendered ethereal aura about the party that accords with the verbal text account. One

Chapter 6

1. The two-part second season episodes "A Piece of the Action" and "Batman's Satisfaction," aired on March 1–2, 1967.

2. But just like a Batman fan reading during the Golden Age, sharp eyes could distinguish the subtle differences between artists of both the Kane and Timm styles.

Chapter 7

1. I am indebted to Salvatore Ciano for the phrase "rationalized myth," which so aptly encapsulates my theory of Nolan's approach to adapting Batman to film.

2. I am indebted to Roberto Rivera for the concept of Batman as urban warlord.

Bibliography

Works Cited

In listing comic book information where the publication contains a single story, only the writer and artist are listed when known.

Abbott, Lawrence L. "Comic Art: Characteristics and Potentialities of a Narrative Medium." *The Journal of Popular Culture* 19.4 (1986): 155–176.

"All Time Worldwide Box Office Grosses." *Box Office Mojo* (Accessed March 12, 2013).

Andrew, Dudley. *Concepts in Film Theory.* New York: Oxford University Press, 1984.

Augustyn, Brian, and Michael Mignola. *Gotham by Gaslight: An Alternative History of the Batman.* New York: DC Comics, 1989.

Barr, Mike S., Alan Davis, and Todd McFarlane. *Batman: Year Two.* New York: Warner, 1990.

Batman Begins, directed by Christopher Nolan (2005; Burbank, CA: Warner Bros.), DVD.

"Batman Unmasked: The Psychology of the Dark Knight." In *The Dark Knight,* directed by Christopher Nolan (2008; Burbank, CA: Warner Bros.), Blu-ray; disc 2.

Bazin, André. "The Ontology of the Photographic Image." In *Film Theory and Criticism: Introductory Readings*, edited by Leo Braudy and Marshall Cohen. New York: Oxford University Press, 1999.

Beck, Jerry, ed. *The Greatest Cartoons: As Selected by 1,000 Animation Professionals.* Atlanta: Turner, 1994.

Berger, Arthur Asa. *The Comic-stripped American: What Dick Tracy, Blondie, Daddy Warbucks, and Charlie Brown Tell Us about Ourselves.* Baltimore: Penguin, 1974.

_____. *Popular Culture Genres.* Newbury Park, CA: Sage, 1992.

Bernardo, Susan M. "Recycling Victims and Villains in 'Batman Returns.'" *Literature/Film Quarterly* 22 (1994): 16–20.

Bernstein, Amy. "Where Have You Gone, Jughead?" *U.S. News and World Report* (1994): 56.

Bettelheim, Bruno. *The Uses of Enchantment: The Meaning and Importance of Fairy Tales.* New York: Alfred A. Knopf, 1977.

Biallas, Leonard J. *Myths: Gods, Heroes and Saviors.* Mystic, CT: Twenty-third, 1986.

Blackmore, Tim. "The Dark Knight of Democracy: Tocqueville and Miller Cast Some Light on the Subject." *Journal of American Culture* 14 (1991): 37–56.

Bluestone, George. *Novels Into Film.* Berkeley: University of California Press, 1971.

Blythe, Hal, and Charlie Sweet. "Superhero: The Six-Step Progression." In *The Hero in Transition*, edited by Ray B. Browne and Marshall Fishwick. Bowling Green, OH: Popular, 1992.

Booth, Wayne C. "The Company We Keep: Self-making in Imaginative Art, Old and New." In *Television: The Critical View*, edited by Horace Newcomb. New York: Oxford University Press, 1987.

Braudy, Leo. "Acting: Stage vs. Screen." In *Film Theory and Criticism*, edited by Gerald Mast, Marshall Cohen, and Leo Braudy. New York: Oxford University Press, 1992.

Bridwell, E. Nelson, and Bob Kane. *Batman: From the 30s to the 70s*. New York: Bonanza, 1971.

Brummett, Barry. "How to Propose a Discourse—a Reply to Rowland." *Communication Studies* 41 (1990): 128–135.

Busiek, Kurt, Brent Anderson, and Alex Ross. *Astro City: Life in the Big City*. New York: DC Comics, 1995. Print.

Busiek, Kurt, and Alex Ross. *Marvels, Book Three: Judgment Day*. New York: Marvel Comics, 1994.

Bukatman, Scott. *Matters of Gravity: Special Effects and Supermen in the 20th Century*. Durham: Duke University Press, 2003.

Campbell, Joseph. *The Hero with a Thousand Faces*. Princeton: Princeton University Press, 1973.

"Cape and Cowl." In *Batman Begins*, directed by Christopher Nolan (2005; Burbank, CA: Warner Bros.) DVD, disc 2.

Carroll, Noel. *The Philosophy of Horror or Paradoxes of the Heart*. New York: Routledge, 1990.

Carpenter, Humphrey. *The Inklings: C.S. Lewis, J.R.R. Tolkien, Charles Williams, and Their Friends*. Boston: Houghton Mifflin, 1979.

Chesterton, G. K. "A Defence of Penny Dreadfuls" (Accessed August 13, 2013).

_____. "What Novels Can Do that Films Can't (and Vice Versa)." In *Film Theory and Criticism*, edited by Gerald Mast, Marshall Cohen, and Leo Braudy. New York: Oxford University Press, 1992.

Cline, William C. *In the Nick of Time: Motion Picture Sound Serials*. Jefferson, NC: McFarland, 1984.

Coleman, Earle J. "The Funnies, the Movies and Aesthetics." *Journal of Popular Culture* 18 (1985): 89–100.

Coogan, Peter. *Superhero: The Secret Origin of a Genre*. Austin: Monkeybrain Books, 2006.

Cotta Vaz, Mark. *Tales of the Dark Knight*. New York: Ballantine, 1989. Print.

Crocker, Jonathan. "Tim Burton Puts the Goth into Gotham." *Total Film* (2012): 77.

Crutcher, Paul. "Complexity in the Comic and Graphic Novel Medium: Inquiry through Bestselling Batman Stories." *Journal of Popular Culture* 44.1 (2011): 53–72.

Daniels, Les, and Chip Kidd. *Batman: The Complete History*. San Francisco: Chronicle, 1999.

Daniels, Les. *DC Comics: 60 Years of the World's Favorite Comic Book Heroes*. Boston: Little, Brown, 1995.

Danna, Elizabeth. "Wonder Woman Mythology: Heroes from the Ancient World and Their Progeny." In *The Gospel According to Superheroes: Religion and Pop Culture*. New York: Peter Lang, 2005.

Dargis, Manohla. "Dark Was the Young Knight Battling His Inner Demons." *New York Times*, June 15, 2005.

_____. "Showdown in Gotham Town." *New York Times*, July 18, 2008.

The Dark Knight, directed by Christopher Nolan (2008; Burbank, CA: Warner Bros.), DVD.

The Dark Knight Rises, directed by Christopher Nolan (2012; Burbank, CA: Warner Bros.), DVD.

Darnell, Steve. "Working with a Legend: The Men Who Made the Batman Fly." *Hero Illustrated Special Edition: Batman: From Darknight to Knightfall* (1993): 32–37.

Desris, Joe. "The Batman Hall-of-Fame." *Hero Illustrated Special Edition: Batman: From Darknight to Knightfall* (1993): 39–59.

Dini, Paul, and Bruce Timm. Personal interview conducted by Thom Parham. July 29, 1995.

Dipaolo, Marc Edward. "Terrorist, Technocrat, and Feudal Lord: Batman in Comic Book and Film Adaptations." In *Heroes of*

Film, Comics and American Culture: Essays on Real and Fictional Defenders of Home, edited by Lisa M. Detora. Jefferson, NC: McFarland, 2009.

Dargis, Mahola. "Showdown in Gotham Town." Review of *The Dark Knight. New York Times,* July 18, 2008.

Duncan, Ralph Randolph. "Panel Analysis: A Critical Method for Analyzing the Rhetoric of Comic Book Form." Diss., Louisiana State University and Mechanical College, 1990.

_____, "Rolling the Boulder in Gotham." In *Riddle Me This, Batman! Essays on the Universe of the Dark Knight,* edited by Kevin K. Durand and Mary K. Leigh. Jefferson, NC: McFarland, 2011.

_____, Matthew J. Smith. *The Power of Comics: History, Form & Culture.* New York, London: Continuum, 2009.

Ebert, Roger. "Batman Begins." www.rogerebert. June 13, 2005 (Accessed June 3, 2013).

Eco, Umberto. "The Myth of Superman." Review of *The Amazing Adventures of Superman.* In *Diacritics* 2, number 1 (Spring 1972): 14–22, http://www.jstor.org/stable/46492 (Accessed May 23, 2012).

Eisenstein, Sergei. "Collision of Ideas." In *A Montage of Theories,* edited by Richard Dyer MacCann. New York: Dutton, 1966.

Eisner, Will. *Comics and Sequential Art.* Tamarac, FL: Poorhouse, 1985.

Eliade, Mircea. "Masks: Mythical and Ritual Origins." In *Symbolism, the Sacred & the Arts,* edited by Diane Apostolos-Cappadona. New York: Crossroad, 1988.

_____. *Myths, Dreams & Mysteries: The Encounter Between Contemporary Faiths and Archaic Reality.* London: Collins, 1968.

_____. *The Sacred & the Profane: The Nature of Religion.* New York: Harvest/HBJ, 1959.

_____. "Survivals and Camouflages of Myth." In *Symbolism, the Sacred & the Arts,* edited by Diane Apostolos-Cappadona. New York: Crossroad, 1988.

_____. "The Symbolism of Shadows in Archaic Religion." *Symbolism, the Sacred & the Arts,* edited by Diane Apostolos-Cappadona. New York: Crossroad, 1988.

Ellul, Jacques. *The Humiliation of the Word.* Grand Rapids: Eerdmans, 1985.

Engle, Gary. "What Makes Superman So Darned American?" *Superman at Fifty!: The Persistence of a Legend.* Edited by Dennis Dooley and Gary Engle. New York: Macmillan, 1988.

Feiffer, Jules. *The Great Comic Book Heroes.* New York: Bonanza, 1965.

Fell, John L. *Film and the Narrative Tradition.* Berkeley: University of California Press, 1974.

Friedman, Cary A. *Wisdom from the Batcave: How to Live a Super, Heroic Life.* Linden, NJ: Compass, 2006.

Frye, Northrop. *Anatomy of Criticism: Four Essays.* Princeton: Princeton University Press, 1957.

Fuchs, Wolfgang, and Reinhold Reitberger. *Comics: Anatomy of a Mass Medium.* Boston: Little, Brown, 1972.

Funk, Joe. "The Dark Knight Returns ... Again!!!" *Hero Illustrated Special Edition: Batman: From Darknight to Knightfall* (1993): 60–66.

Gaiman, Neil. *The Sandman: Season of Mists.* New York: DC Comics, 1991.

Garcia, Bob. "Batman: The Animated Adventures." *Cinefantastique* (1994): 68–111.

_____. "Batman: Playing the Caped Crusader Tongue-in-Cheek for the '60s." *Cinefantastique* (1994): 8–63.

Giannetti, Louis. *Understanding Movies,* 4th ed. Englewood Cliffs, NJ: Prentice Hall, 1987.

"Gotham." In *Macmillan Contemporary Dictionary.* New York: Macmillan, 1979.

Graser, Marc, and Cathy Dunkley. "The Bat and the Beautiful." *Variety,* February 8, 2004.

The Greatest Batman Stories Ever Told. New York: Warner, 1988.

Greenberg, Martin H., ed. *Tales of the Batman.* New York: Fine Communications, 1995.

Guirand, F. "Greek Mythology." In *Larousse Encyclopedia of Mythology.* London: Paul Hamlyn, 1959.

Halbfinger, David M. "Batman's Burden: A Director Confronts Darkness and Death." *New York Times,* March 9, 2008.

Hamilton, Edith. *Mythology*. Reprint. Boston: Little, Brown, 1942. Print.

Harvey, Robert C. "The Aesthetics of the Comic Strip." *The Journal of Popular Culture* 12.4 (1979): 640–652. Print.

Hawke, Simon. *Batman: To Stalk a Specter*. New York: Warner, 1991.

Hill, Geoffrey. *Illuminating Shadows: The Mythic Power of Film*. Boston: Shambhala, 1992.

Holleran, Scott. "Wing Kid." *Wing Kid. Box Office Mojo*, October 20, 2005. (Accessed May 21, 2014).

Holtsmark, Erling B. *Tarzan and Tradition: Classical Myth in Popular Literature*. Westport, CT: Greenwood, 1981.

Inchausti, Robert. "The Superhero's Two Worlds." In *The Hero in Transition*, edited by Ray B. Browne and Marshall Fishwick. Bowling Green, OH: Popular, 1992.

Inge, Thomas M. *Comics as Culture*. Jackson: University Press of Mississippi, 1990.

_____. "Introduction to the Comics as Culture." *Journal of Popular Culture* 12 (1979): 631–639.

Jacobs, Will, and Gerard Jones. *The Comic Book Heroes: From the Silver Age to the Present*. New York: Crown, 1985.

Jensen, Jeff. "Christopher Nolan: Behind the Camera." *Entertainment Weekly*, July 20, 2012.

Jolin, Dan. "It Begins with an Ending." *Empire*, July 2013.

"The Journey Begins," In *Batman Begins*, directed by Christopher Nolan (2005; Burbank, CA: Warner Bros.), DVD, disc 2.

Kane, Bob. *Batman Archives*, Vol. 1. New York: DC Comics, 1990.

_____, with Tom Andrae. *Batman & Me: An Autobiography*. Forestville, CA: Eclipse, 1989.

Kracauer, Siegfried. "Basic Concepts." In *Film Theory and Criticism*, edited by Gerald Mast, Marshall Cohen, and Leo Braudy, 9–20. New York: Oxford University Press, 1992.

Lang, Jeffrey S., and Patrick Trimble. "Whatever Happened to the Man of Tomorrow? An Examination of the American Monomyth and the Comic Book Superhero." *Journal of Popular Culture* 22 (1988): 157–173.

Larousse Encyclopedia of Mythology. London: Paul Hamlyn, 1959.

Last, Jonathan V. "A One-Man Department of Justice: Batman as the American Hero." *The Weekly Standard*, August 13, 2012. (Accessed May 20, 2014).

Lee, Stan. "Zap! Pow! Bam!" *American Film* (1987): 59–61.

_____, and John Buscema. *How to Draw Comics the Marvel Way*. New York: Simon & Schuster, 1978.

Lehr, Jeff. "'Me Tarzan. You, Odysseus': Classical Myth in Popular Culture." In *Media USA*, 2d ed., edited by Arthur Asa Berger. New York: Longman, 1991.

Leigh, Mary K., and Kevin K. Durand, eds. "Virtue in Gotham: Aristotle's Batman." In *Riddle Me This, Batman! Essays on the Universe of the Dark Knight*. Jefferson, NC: McFarland, 2011.

Leitch, Thomas. *Film Adaptation and Its Discontents*. Baltimore: Johns Hopkins University Press, 2007.

Lemanna, Dean. "Tale of the Cape." *Cinescape* (1995): 22–34.

Lewis, C.S. *An Experiment in Criticism*. New York: Cambridge University Press, 1969.

_____. "The Mythopoeic Gift of H. Rider Haggard." In *On Stories and Other Essays on Literature*, edited by Walter Hooper. New York: Harvest/HBJ, 1982.

_____, ed. *On Stories: Essays Presented to Charles Williams*. Grand Rapids: Eerdmans, 1978.

Lowentrout, Peter. "Batman: Winging Through the Ruins of the American Baroque." *Extrapolation* 33.1 (1992): 25–31.

MacIntyre, Alasdair. "Myth." In *Encyclopedia of Philosophy*, edited by Paul Edwards. New York: Macmillan, 1972.

Maltin, Leonard. *Of Mice and Magic: A History of American Animated Cartoons*. New York: New American Library, 1987.

Mangels, Andy. "Hollywood Heroes: Batman Special." *Hero Illustrated Special Edition: Batman: From Darknight to Knightfall* (1993): 80–85.

McAllistar, Matthew Paul. "Cultural Argument and Organizational Constraint in the Comic Book Industry." *Journal of Communication* 40.1 (1990): 55–71.

____, Ian Gordon, and Mark Jancovich. "Block Buster Art House: Meets Superhero Comic, or Meets Graphic Novel?: The Contradictory Relationship between Film and Comic Art." *Journal of Popular Film and Television* 34.3 (2006): 108–15. Web.

McCloud, Scott. *Understanding Comics: The Invisible Art.* Northampton, MA: Kitchen Sink, 1993.

McConnell, Frank. "Comic Relief: From Gilgamesh to 'Spiderman.'" *Commonweal* 28 (1992): 21–22.

McGhee, Richard D. "John Wayne: Hero with a Thousand Faces." *Literature/Film Quarterly* 16 (1988): 10–21.

McLuhan, Marshall. *Understanding Media: The Extensions of Man.* New York: Signet, 1964.

Miller, Cyndee. "Comic Book Publishers Battle for Market Share, Advertisers." *Marketing News* (1993): 1.

Miller, Frank, with Klaus Janson and Lynn Varley. *Batman: The Dark Knight Returns.* New York: Warner, 1986.

Miller, Frank, David Mazzuccelli, with Richmond Lewis. *Batman: Year One.* New York: Warner, 1988.

Moench, Doug, and Kelly Jones. *Batman & Dracula: Red Rain.* New York: DC Comics, 1991.

Morrow, James, and Murray Suid. *Moviemaking Illustrated: The Comicbook Filmbook.* Rochelle Park, NJ: Hayden, 1973.

Mottram, James. "Interview with Christopher Nolan." In *Batman Begins:* London: Faber and Faber, 2005.

Murray, Henry A., ed. *Myth and Mythmaking.* New York: George Braziller, 1960.

Murray, Rebecca. "Director Christopher Nolan Talks about 'Batman Begins.'" *About.com Hollywood Movies* (Accessed June 2013). http://movies.about.com/od/batman/a/batmancn060805.htm.

Nash, Jesse W. "Gotham's Dark Knight: The Postmodern Transformation of the Arthurian Mythos." In *Popular Arthurian Traditions,* edited by Jesse W. Nash. Bowling Green, OH: Popular, 1992.

Neff, William Albert. *The Pictorial and Linguistic Features of Comic Book Formulas.* Ann Arbor: University Microfilms, 1977.

Newman, Graeme. "Batman and Justice: The True Story." *Humanity & Society* 17, no. 3 (1993): 297–320.

Nolan, Christopher, David S. Goyer, and Bob Kane. *Batman Begins.* London: Faber and Faber, 2005.

Nolan, Christopher, and David S. Goyer. *The Dark Knight Trilogy: The Batman Screenplays.* New York: Opus, 2013.

"Nothing to Fear." Directed by Boyd Kirkland. *Batman: The Animated Series.* Fox Network (WTVZ, Norfolk, VA), September 15, 1992.

"On Mythic Criticism: The Conversation Continues." *Communication Studies* 41 (1990): 278–298.

O'Neil, Dennis. Personal interview conducted by Thom Parham. July 28, 1995.

Osborn, Michael. "In Defense of Broad Mythic Criticism: a Reply to Rowland." *Communication Studies* 41 (1990): 121–127.

Pearson, Roberta E., and William Uricchio, eds. "I'm Not Fooled by That Cheap Disguise." In *The Many Lives of the Batman: Critical Approaches to a Superhero and His Media.* New York: Routledge, 1991.

____. "Notes from the Batcave: An Interview with Dennis O'Neil." In *The Many Lives of the Batman: Critical Approaches to a Superhero and His Media.* New York: Routledge, 1991.

Perry, George, and Alan Aldridge. *The Penguin Book of Comics.* London: Penguin, 1971.

Pulver, Andrew. "He's Not a God, He's Human." *The Guardian* (UK), June 14, 2005.

Propp, V. *Morphology of the Folktale.* Austin: University of Texas Press, 1968.

Reynolds, Richard. *Super Heroes: A Modern Mythology.* Jackson: University Press of Mississippi, 1992.

Robbins, Frank, and Bob Brown. "Batman for a Night." *Detective Comics* 417 (1971).

Robertson, C. K. "The True Übermensch:

Batman as Humanistic Myth." In *The Gospel According to Superheroes: Religion and Pop Culture*, edited by B. J. Oropeza. New York: Peter Lang, 2005.

Rollin, Roger R. "The Lone Ranger and Lenny Skutnik: The Hero as Popular Culture." In *The Hero in Transition*, edited by Ray B. Browne and Marshall Fishwick. Bowling Green, OH: Popular, 1983.

Roth, Lane. "Death and Rebirth in 'Star Trek II: The Wrath of Khan.'" *Extrapolation* 28 (1987): 159–166.

Rowland, Robert C. "On a Limited Approach to Mythic Criticism-Rowland's Rejoinder." *Communication Studies* 41 (1990): 150–160.

_____. "On Mythic Criticism." *Communication Studies* 41 (1990): 101–116.

Rushing, Janice Hocker. "E.T. as Rhetorical Transcendence." In *Rhetorical Criticism: Exploration & Practice*, edited by Sonja K. Foss. Prospect Heights, IL: Waveland, 1989.

_____. "On Saving Mythic Criticism—a Reply to Rowland." *Communication Studies* 41 (1990): 136–149.

_____, and Thomas S. Frentz. "The Frankenstein Myth in Contemporary Cinema." *Critical Studies in Mass Communication* 6.1 (1989): 61–80. Web.

Salisbury, Mark, ed. *Burton on Burton*. London: Faber and Faber, 2006.

Sassienie, Paul. *The Comic Book*. Edited by Nison. Edison, NJ: Smithbooks, 1994.

Schatz, Thomas. *Hollywood Genres: Filmmaking and the Studio System*. Philadelphia: Temple University Press, 1981.

Schechter, Harold. "Comicons." In *Icons of America*, edited by Ray B. Browne and Marshall Fishwick. Bowling Green, OH: Popular, 1978.

Schrader, Paul. *Transcendental Style in Film: Ozu, Bresson, Dreyer*. Berkeley: University of California Press, 1972.

"The Screenplay." In *Batman Begins*, directed by Christopher Nolan (2005; Burbank, CA: Warner Bros.), DVD, disc 2.

Sharrett, Christopher. "Batman and the Twilight of the Idols: An Interview with Frank Miller." In *The Many Lives of the Batman: Critical Approaches to a Super-hero and His Media*. New York: Routledge, 1991.

Sklar, Robert, ed. *Movie-Made America: A Cultural History of American Movies*. New York: Random House, 1994. Print.

Smith, Henry Nash. *Virgin Land*. New York: Vintage, 1950.

Smith, Jonathan Z., and Richard G.A. Buxton. "Myth and Mythology." *Encyclopædia Britannica* (1994).

Solman, Gregory. "Fancy Math." *Film Comment* (July/August 2002): 22, 25–26.

Soloman, Martha. "Responding to Rowland's Myth or In Defense of Pluralism—a Reply to Rowland." *Communication Studies* 41 (1990): 117–120.

Spanakos, Tony. "Governing Gotham." In *Batman and Philosophy*. Hoboken, NJ: John Wiley & Sons, 2008.

Stamp, Jimmy. "Batman, Gotham City, and an Overzealous Architecture Historian with a Working Knowledge of Explosives." *Life Without Buildings* (June 2009): n.p.

Steranko, James. *The Steranko History of Comics*, Vol. 1. Reading, PA: Supergraphics, 1970.

Terrill, Robert E. "Put On a Happy Face: Batman as Schizophrenic Savior." *The Quarterly Journal of Speech* 79 (1993): 319–335.

Tiefenbacher, Mike. *Hero Illustrated Special Edition: Batman: From Darknight to Knightfall* (October 1993): 12–31.

Tolkien, J.R.R. *The Fellowship of the Ring*. Boston: Houghton Mifflin, 1954.

_____. "On Fairy Stories." In *Essays Presented to Charles Williams*, edited by C.S. Lewis. Grand Rapids: Eerdmans, 1978.

Turner, Victor. *Dramas, Fields, and Metaphors*. Ithaca: Cornell University Press, 1974.

Tyler, Parker. *Magic and Myth of the Movies*. New York: Simon & Schuster, 1970.

Tyrell, William Blake. "*Star Trek* as Myth and Television as Mythmaker." *Journal of Popular Culture* 10 (1977): 711–719.

Uslan, Michael. *The Boy Who Loved Batman: A Memoir*. San Francisco: Chronicle Books, 2011.

Vachss, Andrew. *Batman: The Ultimate Evil*. New York: Warner, 1995.

Walinsky, Adam. "The Crisis of Public Order." *The Atlantic* (Accessed May 15, 2013).

Wandtke, Terrence R. *The Meaning of Superhero Comic Books*. Jefferson, NC: McFarland, 2012.

Werness, Hope B. "Bat." *The Continuum Encyclopedia of Animal Symbolism in World Art*. 2006 (Accessed May 16, 2013).

White, Taylor. "Comic Book Vision." *Cinefantastique* (February 1994): 67.

Wiater, Stanley, and Stephen R. Bissette, eds. *Comic Book Rebels: Conversations with the Creators of the New Comics*. New York: Donald E. Fine, 1993.

Williams, Owen. "The Theme." *Empire*. (July 2012): n.p. (Accessed June 1, 2013).

Zakia, Richard D. *Perception and Photography*. Rochester, NY: Light Impressions, 1979.

Index

Numbers in *bold italics* indicate pages with photographs.